W9-AYD-429

Perspectives on Race, Ethnicity,
and Religion

Perspectives on Race, Ethnicity, and Religion

Identity Politics in America

Valerie Martinez-Ebers
UNIVERSITY OF NORTH TEXAS
Manochehr Dorraj
TEXAS CHRISTIAN UNIVERSITY

New York   Oxford
OXFORD UNIVERSITY PRESS
2010

Oxford University Press, Inc., publishes works that further
Oxford University's objective of excellence
in research, scholarship, and education.

Oxford   New York
Auckland   Cape Town   Dar es Salaam   Hong Kong   Karachi
Kuala Lumpur   Madrid   Melbourne   Mexico City   Nairobi
New Delhi   Shanghai   Taipei   Toronto

With offices in
Argentina   Austria   Brazil   Chile   Czech Republic   France   Greece
Guatemala   Hungary   Italy   Japan   Poland   Portugal   Singapore
South Korea   Switzerland   Thailand   Turkey   Ukraine   Vietnam

Copyright © 2010 by Oxford University Press, Inc.

Published by Oxford University Press, Inc.
198 Madison Avenue, New York, New York 10016

http://www.oup.com

Oxford is a registered trademark of Oxford University Press

All rights reserved. No part of this publication may be reproduced,
stored in a retrieval system, or transmitted, in any form or by any means,
electronic, mechanical, photocopying, recording, or otherwise,
without the prior permission of Oxford University Press.

Library of Congress Cataloging-in-Publication Data
Perspectives on race, ethnicity, and religion : identity politics in America / [edited by]
Valerie Martinez-Ebers [and] Manochehr Dorraj.
       p. cm.
    Includes bibliographical references and index.
    ISBN 978-0-19-538170-2 (pbk. : alk. paper)   1. United States—Race relations—Political
aspects.   2. United States—Ethnic relations—Political aspects.   3. Christianity and politics—
United States.   4. Group identity—Political aspects—United States.   5. Political culture—
United States.   I. Martinez-Ebers, Valerie.   II. Dorraj, Manochehr.
    E184.A1p47 2009
    305.800973—dc22   2008052704

9 8 7 6 5 4 3 2 1
Printed in the United States of America
on acid-free paper

To the memory of my beloved mother,
Eshrat, my best mentor in life.

M. Dorraj

To my beloved father, Charles Martinez,
who left this world much too soon.

V. Martinez-Ebers

Contents

Preface

I have been teaching classes on race, ethnicity, and politics for ten years. It is *by far* my favorite class to teach, but it is also one of the most challenging because of both the sensitivity and complexity of the subject. Other challenges are that many students (most Americans, in fact) have very limited knowledge of and/or hold misperceptions about various racial, ethnic, or religious groups in the United States; and a significant portion of young people (not just my undergraduate students) also do not feel any personal connection with the discriminatory treatment/experiences of minority groups. To help me successfully address these challenges, I was always in search of a textbook or a combination of readings that struck the right balance between description, explanation, and critical assessment of minority group politics, but I never seemed to find one. Consequently, almost four years ago I approached the former editor and owner of Roxbury Press, Claude Teweles, with the general idea of writing my own textbook. My thanks to him for helping me to distill my general idea into a concrete proposal for an undergraduate introductory reader that would have a balanced presentation of history and an assessment of the current political status of America's minorities told from the perspective of minority individuals who were also credentialed experts in their respective topics. The next thing I had to do was to identify and persuade the best people to write the chapters. One year later I was still struggling with this task and, fortunately for me, my friend and colleague, Manochehr Dorraj, agreed to step in and help me with the editorial task. He also wisely persuaded me to expand the content of the book to include more emphasis on the development of group identity and the influence of globalization. Shortly after that time, Claude made the decision to get out of the book publishing business and he sold his catalogue of contracted books to Oxford University Press and our book became the responsibility of Jennifer Carpenter, Executive Editor for politics.

Manochehr and I are especially grateful to Jennifer for her great patience and sage advice as we first struggled to get the substantive chapters finished and assembled, and then to complete all the other components of the book. We also are grateful for the able assistance of Tom Pold, Editorial Assistant for politics, and Lisa Grzan, Senior Production Editor. Our sincere thanks also are extended to each of our contributing authors for their excellent chapters and for their wonderful cooperation and responsiveness to our editorial suggestions. Finally, I would like acknowledge and thank my husband Scott and son Nate for their cooperation and support, especially for the many times they cooked dinner or brought in "take-out" so Mom could keep writing when she was on a roll.

Valerie Martinez-Ebers

I always felt that there was a void in the current pervasive literature on race and ethnicity in so far as it did not address the broader issues of globalization and its impact in reframing and redefining identity in general, and race and ethnicity in particular. Equally important, in my opinion, is the significance of how migration is changing the face of America. While there is a growing scholarship on second-generation migrants and their socialization experience, values, dilemmas, and impact, conspicuously absent is much work on the first generation of migrants, those who live in the world between. I thought as well that a discussion of the increasingly significant issue of religious identity was lacking in much of the literature on identity politics. I also came to the realization that lacking in the scholarly books on minority politics is a discussion of the role and experiences of Jewish and Muslim Americans. Since I believe that race, ethnicity, and identity are dynamic social constructs rather than immutable biological fixtures, I concluded that there was a need to introduce a book that would study theses issues in a broader context. When my friend and colleague, Valerie Martinez-Ebers, approached me to coedit the book with her, I pounced on the opportunity to produce such a unique volume.

Valerie and I believe the multidisciplinary scope and the breadth of issues covered in this volume will broaden the discussion of race, ethnicity, and identity politics and also fill an important gap in the currently available literature written for the classroom. We endeavored to produce an edited book that was theoretically informed and analytically erudite, yet accessible to undergraduate students and the public at large. While our contributors have attempted to instill critical thinking in their readers, they have done so without the cumbersome use of social science jargon. We leave it to the judgment of our readers and colleagues if we have been successful in achieving our goals and ambitions for this book.

Compiling, editing, and producing this book would not have been possible without the contributions and help of our colleagues. We are grateful to our contributors for producing their chapters according to our instructions and heeding the calls for revisions. Without their commitment and endeavor this volume would not have been possible. We extend our thanks to each of our anonymous reviewers for their helpful comments and insights. We would also like to express our gratitude to Jennifer Carpenter, Executive Editor for political science at Oxford University Press, and her colleagues for their stewardship and successful completion of this project. Last but not least, I would like to thank my wife and daughters for their love and support.

Manochehr Dorraj

I n addition, we would like to thank the following reviewers for their comments, which helped us to create a stronger and more compelling text: David Bills, University of Iowa; Stefanie Chambers, Trinity College; Joseph Foy, University of Wisconsin; Terri R. Jett, Butler University; Angela K. Lewis, University of Alabama at Birmingham; Pei-te Lien, University of California, Santa Barbara; Benjamin Marquez, University of Wisconsin, Madison; Brian McKenzie, Texas A&M University; John E. McNulty, Binghamton University; Mark Sawyer, University of California, Los Angeles; James D. Slack, University of Alabama at Birmingham; Sherri Wallace, University of Louisville; David E. Wilkins, University of Minnesota, Twin Cities Campus

Editors and Contributors

Edwina Barvosa is an associate professor of social and political theory in the Department of Chicana and Chicano Studies at the University of California in Santa Barbara. She received her PhD in political science from Harvard University, her MA in social and political science from Cambridge University, and her BA in government from Pomona College. Her areas of specialization are political philosophy, intellectual history, and Latina/Latino and gender politics, with current research interests in identity and extremism, race and multicultural democracy, and Latina/Latino immigration politics. Her first book, *Wealth of Selves: Multiple Identities and the Subject of Politics*, is forthcoming from Texas A&M University Press. She has also published articles in the *Georgetown Journal of International Affairs*, *Journal of Political Philosophy*, *Contemporary Justice Review*, and *International Journal of Sexuality* and *Gender Studies*. Her current book project is on the relationship between identity and political extremism.

Lisa García Bedolla is associate professor of political science and Chicano/Latino studies at the University of California, Irvine. She earned her PhD from Yale University in 1999. She is author of *Fluid Borders: Latino Power, Identity, and Politics in Los Angeles* (2005), the winner of the American Political Science Association (APSA) Ralph Bunche Award and a Best Book award from the APSA Race, Ethnicity, and Politics Section. Her articles have appeared in *The Journal of Politics*, *Politics and Gender*, *Social Science Quarterly*, and *Latino Studies* and in numerous edited volumes. She has received grants from the James Irvine Foundation, the Russell Sage Foundation, and the Haynes

Foundation. Her work focuses on U.S. political incorporation, with a particular emphasis on the intersection of race, class, and gender. Her forthcoming book is titled *Introduction to Latino Politics*.

Sheila Croucher is the Paul Rejai Professor of Political Science at Miami University of Ohio and jointly appointed in the American Studies program. She earned her doctorate at the University of Florida in 1993. Her research and teaching interests are the areas of globalization, immigration, and the politics of belonging. She is the author of *Globalization and Belonging: The Politics of Identity in a Changing World* (2003), *Imagining Miami: Ethnic Politics in a Postmodern World* (1998), and *On the Other Side of the Fence: American Migrants in Mexico* (forthcoming).

Manochehr Dorraj is a professor of political science at Texas Christian University. He earned his doctorate from the University of Texas at Austin in 1984. He has published extensively on the politics and culture of the Middle East and the Muslim world. Among his publications that deal with issues surrounding Islamic identity politics and their impact on international affairs are *From Zarathustra to Khomeini: Populism and Dissent in Iran* (1990), *Middle East at a Crossroads* (1999), *Iran Today: An Encyclopedia of Life in the Islamic Republic* (coeditor with M. Kamrava, two volumes, 2008), "The Intellectual Dilemmas of a Muslim Modernist: Politics and Poetics of Iqbal" in *The Muslim World* (1995), "Symbolic and Utilitarian Political Value of a Tradition: Martyrdom in the Iranian Political Culture," in *The Review of Politics* (1997), "The Crisis of Modernity and Religious Revivalism: A Comparative Study of Islamic Fundamentalism, Jewish Fundamentalism, and Liberation Theology" in *The Social Compass* (1999), and "The Secular Mirage: Modernity, the Post-Modern Turn and Religious Revivalism" in *The Journal of Globalization for the Common Good* (2007).

Gloria J. Hampton is a doctoral candidate and instructor of political science at Ohio State University. Her research and teaching interests include American politics, civil rights and liberties, and black politics. She has contributed a chapter to *Legacies of the 1964 Civil Rights Act* (2000).

Valerie Martinez-Ebers is professor of political science at the University of North Texas. Her teaching and research interests include race, ethnicity, and politics; Latino politics; public policy; political tolerance, and the politics of music. Many of her publications are on the consequences of education policy for minority students, but she also has publications on Latino politics, women in politics, methods of survey research, and aging policy. Some of her recent publications include "Should They Dance with the One Who Brung 'Em? Latinos and the 2008 Presidential Election" in PS: *Political Science and Politics* (2008), *Politicas: Latina Public Officials in Texas* (2007), "Gender and Ethnicity: Patterns of Representation and Advocacy Among Latina and Latino Legislators" in *Journal of Women, Politics & Policy* (2007), and "Su Casa Es Nuestra Casa: Latino Politics Research and the Development of American Political Science" in *American Political Science Review* (2006). Martinez-Ebers is a coprincipal investigator of the Latino National Survey (LNS) funded by the Ford, Carnegie, Russell Sage, Hewlett, Joyce, and National Science Foundations. She received her doctorate in political science in 1990 from Ohio State University.

Paul Mendes-Flohr, Professor Emeritus, earned his doctorate in 1972 from Brandeis University. He taught modern Jewish thought at the Hebrew University of Jerusalem from 1973 until his recent retirement. He currently teaches at the Divinity School, The University of Chicago. Among his more recent publications are *German Jews: A Dual Identity* (1999), *Love, Accusative and Dative: Reflections on Leviticus 19:18* (2007), and *Jewish Intellectuals on the Anvil of Modernity* (2008). Together with Peter Schäfer, he is the chief editor of a 22-volume critical edition of Martin Buber's writings (in German). He is presently preparing the third edition of *The Jew in the Modern World: A Documentary History*, coauthored with Jehuda Reinharz, originally published by Oxford University Press in 1995.

Jessica Lavariega Monforti is an assistant professor of political science and senior faculty research associate at the Center for Survey Research at the University of Texas, Pan American. She specializes in public policy analysis, race and politics, and survey research. While much of her research focuses on the differential impact of public policy according to race, gender, and ethnicity, she is specifically interested in the political incorporation and representation of Latinos, immigrants, and women. Her latest research project is a survey of the political attitudes and behaviors of Latinos and other minority groups in Florida. Recent publications include articles in PS: *Political Science*, the *Latino/a Research Review*, and the *Journal of Women, Politics & Policy*. She also edited a book with William E. Nelson, Jr., entitled *Black and Latino/a Politics: Issues in Political Development in the United States* (2006).

Melanye T. Price is assistant professor of government at Wesleyan University. Her research and teaching interests include American politics, public opinion, black politics, social movements, and political psychology. Her forthcoming manuscript, *Dreaming Blackness...: Understanding Black Nationalism in Post-Civil Rights America*, will be published by New York

University Press. Professor Price received her PhD from Ohio State University in 2003.

Jocelyn Sage Weiner received a BA in both political science and Middle Eastern studies at Brown University and is currently a PhD candidate (ABD) in the Department of Government at Georgetown University. Her primary research interests include regime transitions, Islamist politics, and political institutions; and her dissertation will focus on political pluralization, regime-opposition strategies, and the distribution of oil wealth in the Gulf states. She has also written on topics such as religious institutions as political mobilizers and the link between presidential candidacy rhetoric and electoral success.

Clyde Wilcox is professor of government at Georgetown University. He is the author or editor of more than 20 books and numerous chapters and articles on religion and politics, gender politics, interest groups, public opinion, and science fiction and politics. His publications on religion and politics include *God's Warriors: The Christian Right in 20th Century America* (1992), *Onward Christian Soldiers: The Christian Right in American Politics* (1996), *God at the Grassroots: The Christian Right in the 1994 Election* (1995), *Religion and Politics in Comparative Perspective: The One, the Few, and the Many* (coedited with Ted J. Jelen, 2001), *Marching to the Millennium: The Christian Right in the States: 1980–2000* (coedited with John C. Green and Mark Rozell, 2001).

David E. Wilkins is a professor of American Indian studies, political science, law, and American studies at the University of Minnesota. He teaches and writes in the areas of comparative politics, American political theory, federal Indian policy, tribal government, and history of colonialism and native peoples. A member of the American Indian Professoriate, Professor Wilkins has published numerous articles on federal Indian policy and native peoples. He is the author of *American Indian Sovereignty and the U.S. Supreme Court: The Masking of Justice* (1997) and *American Indian Politics and the American Political System*, 2nd ed. (2002). Professor Wilkins received his PhD from the University of North Carolina–Chapel Hill in 1990.

Morrison G. Wong is professor of sociology at Texas Christian University. His fields of specializations are race and ethnic relations in general with subspecialties in the Asian American experience (with a special emphasis on the Chinese American experience) and Asian immigration and adaptation. Publications focusing on the Asian American educational and socioeconomic adjustment or on the immigration experience have appeared in such journals as the *American Journal of Sociology, Social Forces, Sociological Quarterly, Sociological*

Perspectives, and Sociology of Education. He has also contributed numerous chapters in books focusing on a myriad of topics that include an overview of the Chinese experience in the United States, the Chinese elderly and the issues they face in receiving adequate care, the ever-changing Chinese American family, the rise in anti-Asian activities in the United States, the Chinese sweatshops in the United States, and Asian immigration and immigrants to the United States.

Chapter 1

Introduction

Change and Continuity in the Experiences of Racial, Ethnic, and Religious Minorities in America

Valerie Martinez-Ebers
Manochehr Dorraj

"Primary Voting Eclipses All Records."[1] This headline from our local Texas newspaper captures the excitement and political mobilization in the 2008 U.S. presidential primaries. In Texas, as in other states across the country, people voted and caucused in record-smashing numbers. One important change from past elections, especially on the Democratic Party side, is the increased diversity of those who participated. Compared to 2004, Democratic primary participants in 2008 included significantly higher percentages of younger people, women, and racial/ethnic minorities.[2] While some of this increased diversity could simply be the result of demographic change in the U.S. population, in large part it is more likely due to the historic contest between Senators Hillary Clinton and Barack Obama. Senator Obama, of course, eventually won the Democratic Party's nomination; and he would ultimately become the United States' first black president.[3] Preceding this historic milestone, for the first time in history the nominee of one of the two major political parties in the United States (Democrats and Republicans) was a member of a *minority* group, meaning a group with a history of unequal or discriminatory treatment and other distinguishing characteristics that identify them as subordinate or marginalized in the dominant society. Thus, Obama's electoral success exemplifies the positive change that has occurred in the social and political status of blacks and other minority groups in the United States.

Indeed, we've come a long way since the struggles of the civil rights movement in the 1960s. In his essay entitled "Race and Democracy," political scientist Joel Lieske notes some of the positive change that has occurred for all minority groups in the United States over the past fifty years: Supreme Court decisions and civil rights legislation have ended most *de jure* (created by law) barriers to equality. Increasing numbers of minority individuals are running competitive political campaigns and being elected or appointed to positions in local, state, and national government. Opinion polls also reflect greater sensitivity to racial and social injustice and increased tolerance of marriage outside of one's racial, ethnic, and religious group.[4]

At the same time, however, inequalities and negative experiences continue for minority groups in this country and, in some instances, they have gotten worse. For example, the level of *de facto* (by fact or social custom) segregation today is as high as it was in the 1960s in many cities and metropolitan areas, especially within urban school districts.[5] Moreover, the increasing gap in wealth (or net worth) is at the core of many long-standing socioeconomic differences between whites and many racial/ethnic minority groups.[6] Finally, the persistence of prejudice and stereotypes contributes to continuing serious problems with individual acts of intolerance, such as hate crimes, and institutionalized forms of discrimination, like redlining.[7]

Although considerable progress has been made in rectifying inequalities and improving relations between minority and majority groups, there is considerably more progress that must occur if America is to successfully address the challenges and accommodate the needs of its increasingly diverse, multicultural population.

Growing Diversity in a Global Context

The demographics of this country are changing rapidly. According to a May 2007 report from the U.S. Census Bureau, the racial ethnic minority population in the United States had grown from 98.3 million in 2005 to 100.7 million in 2006, an increase of 2.4 million people in only one year![8] The minority population as identified by the Census Bureau included African Americans (blacks), American Indians or Alaskan Natives (AIANs), Asians, Native Hawaiians or Pacific Islanders (NHPIs), and Hispanics. Today, approximately one in three U.S. residents is a racial/ethnic minority and the U.S. minority population is larger than the total population of all but eleven countries.[9]

The overall U.S. population increased from 296.5 million in 2005 to 299.3 million in 2006. The majority racial/ethnic group, non-Hispanic whites, represented 66% of the total population but accounted for less than one-fifth (18%) of the nation's total population growth. Hispanics, also referred to as "Latinos," are the largest minority group (14.8% of the total population) and the fastest-growing, accounting for approximately 50% of the increase in the U.S. population between 2005 and 2006. Asians were the second fastest-growing population, but they represented only 5% of U.S. residents. African Americans are the second largest minority group (13.44% of the total population). The growth rate for African Americans was modest, as was the increase in AIANs and NHPIs.[10] However, all minority groups increased at a faster rate than non-Hispanic whites. Population projections by the Census Bureau and the Pew Research Center suggest that the majority of the U.S. population could be made up of minorities as early as 2050.[11]

There is also growing religious diversity in the United States. Although more than three-quarters of the adults in this country identify as "Christian," there are dramatic differences in their professed practices and some of their beliefs across the three major types of Christians (Protestant, Catholic, and Orthodox) and among the hundreds of various Christian denominations and independent churches.[12] Membership in Evangelical Christian churches is on the upswing, while membership in mainline Protestant churches has declined. Roughly 16% of the U.S. population self-identifies as "unaffiliated" and that includes atheists, agnostics, and simply nonreligious people. Only about 5% of the population says they belong to non-Christian religions, but the recent growth in their numbers (primarily due to immigration) and their distinct visibility within the general population has led to increased attention from the media and the general public—probably much higher than is warranted. An extensive 2007 national study by the Pew Research Center's Forum on Religion and Public Life concludes that the United States is on the verge of becoming a minority Protestant country as the number of residents who report that they are members of Protestant denominations now stands at barely 51%.[13]

This growing diversity in the population is occurring at the same time the United States is also becoming increasingly more integrated in the global economy and more entangled in political and cultural world affairs. Globalization, along with the impact of technological advancements and satellite communication, has effectively caused the world to shrink (metaphorically speaking). One hallmark of the new global context in America may be the surging population of immigrants and their enhanced ability to maintain transnational ties and identities. Approximately 1.1 million immigrants arrive in the United States each year, and the number of immigrants nationwide reached an all-time high of 35.7 million in 2006.[14]

The Basic Concepts Used in This Book

Before proceeding, it is important to briefly discuss the basic concepts that are used throughout our book. *Identity* may be simply understood as a sense of attachment or belonging to a *group*, which is defined as a collection of people with something in common. How individuals identify themselves, the strength of their identity, and how they are identified by others is serious business! Identity determined who could be sold as slaves in the United States before President Lincoln issued the General Emancipation Proclamation and the basis for who lived or died in Nazi Germany. In 1942, identity was the rationalization for dispossessing and imprisoning 110,000 Japanese Americans in "temporary relocation centers."[15] More recently, identity was behind the "voluntary call-in" of 8,000 Arab and Muslim American citizens and immigrants to detention centers across the United States following the 9/11/2001 terrorist attacks.[16] Finally, identity played a primary role in the decisions of more than 702,589 immigrants in 2006 to complete the expensive and difficult process necessary to become U.S. citizens.[17]

We already introduced the concept of "minority" in our previous discussion. This term is commonly used to explain a smaller segment or subgroup of a population. However, the designation of a minority group is not as easily understood as it may seem from the reporting of the U.S. Census Bureau. Minority status is not necessarily the result of being outnumbered. For our purposes, "minority" is a political concept. It specifies a power relationship. As sociologist Michael LeMay explains, "Relationships between dominant and minority groups are not determined by numbers but rather by the distribution of power. The minority's presence in society implies the existence of a corresponding dominant group with higher social status and greater privileges."[18]

Members of the dominant, or "majority," group hold most positions of authority and have significantly greater access to resources (e.g., education, wealth). They have sufficient power to decide the values and norms of the society and to set public policy.[19] As a result, a minority group is a subordinate or oppressed group whose members have considerably less power over their lives than members of the majority group have over theirs.

Minorities are generally perceived as "different" and are more subject to prejudice, negative stereotypes, and discriminatory treatment by members of the dominant group. They are frequently excluded from full participation in politics and mainstream society. Studies show minorities also may hold prejudiced and stereotypical views of the dominant group and of other minority groups, but they are considerably less likely to have the power to act on those prejudicial beliefs.[20]

A variety of factors determine minority (as well as majority) status. Race and ethnicity are the most prevalent bases for minority status in American society, but religion, gender, age, disabilities, sexual orientation, citizenship status, and social class are other factors associated with subordinated groups. Racial, ethnic, and religious minority group experiences are the primary focus of this book, although minority experiences based on gender, citizenship status, and social class are also considered. *Racial* classifications are based on inborn physical characteristics, such as hair texture, facial features, and especially skin color.[21] *Ethnic* classifications are based on learned cultural traits often associated with countries of origin; some of these include language, style of dress, food habits, marriage, and parenting practices, and distinctive attitudes regarding commerce, law, and government. Some scholars view religion as a cultural trait of an ethnic group.[22] However, because religious practices and organizations receive extra legal considerations under federal law and in recognition of the fundamental role that religion plays in national and world politics, *religious* allegiance is viewed separately from ethnicity in our conceptual framework. The differing reasons or bases for minority status are important because they affect the way a minority views itself and the manner in which the group deals with resulting problems. The basis for minority status also influences majority attitudes toward the group and the manner in which the majority structures the options available to the minority group.[23]

A Cautionary Note

Minority groups have five things in common, with a few exceptions depending on the type of group: (1) their group membership is involuntary, that is, they are usually born into it; (2) they have distinguishing physical and/or cultural traits; (3) they receive unequal treatment; (4) they are aware of their lower status and have a consequent sense of group solidarity; and (5) they frequently marry within their group by choice or by necessity.[24] Aside from these commonalities associated with subordinate status, minority groups are usually quite different from one another. Within a particular group, there is also likely to be variation. For example, Latinos are members of an ethnic minority group with national origins in 22 different countries. Aside from their common language of Spanish and the high number who are Catholics—both characteristics are the result of their origin countries' shared experience of Spanish conquest—the Hispanic national origin groups have different social, political, and migratory histories and different levels of human capital or resources (i.e., education, income, social networks, and citizenship status). It is important, and strongly advised, to recognize and respect the differences in histories, experiences, resources, orientations, and behaviors among and within the various groups when studying minority group politics.

The Rationale for This Reader

The presence of so many and such diverse minority groups in the United States continues to have a profound impact on American politics. The increasing diversity of America will be the source of important challenges and opportunities facing the nation in the twenty-first century. Our belief is that everyone needs to be better informed about the current situation of minority groups and to think about the broader context that influences minority–majority relations.

Our intended primary audience is college undergraduates and interested lay readers. This reader is an introduction to the relevant history, current issues, and dynamics of select minority groups in the United States. While previously written books on these topics usually confine their group coverage to blacks/African Americans, Hispanics/Latinos, Asian Americans, and American Indians, this volume expands the number of groups examined to include those previously noted, plus Jewish and Muslim Americans. As we review their historical, legal, and political experiences as well as their attitudes and behaviors, you can evaluate the importance of race, ethnicity, and religion in understanding the outcomes of American politics. You also will see how the structure and operation of American society as well as our political system sometimes obstruct the efforts of these groups to gain the full benefits of freedom and equal treatment promised under the U.S. Constitution.

It is also important to consider the impact of globalization on individual, group, and national identity and the social impact of immigration and immigrants in particular. The discussion of these issues, overlooked in much of the literature on minority politics, is particularly pertinent to understanding the larger context in which the issues of race, ethnicity, and religious identity evolve and are constantly redefined. For these reasons, we included chapters on globalization and its impact on identity politics and on immigration and immigrant incorporation to introduce these important topics and provide a larger panorama to study the issues of race, ethnicity, religion, and equality in multicultural America.

A unique and, we think, valuable feature of this reader is that the contributing authors belong to the minority groups about which they write. They also are all credentialed experts in their fields of expertise, with advanced degrees in political science, sociology, history, or religion. Thus, they are able to draw upon the unique experiences of a group of people they are intimately familiar with, while at the same time using the rational systematic approach of social scientists. Each chapter begins with an individual narrative or "story" that ties the following analyses to the reality of what it is like for the minority individuals or groups who are studied.

The Structure of This Reader

Our volume is organized around our two general themes, change and continuity, in minority group politics. The first part of the reader focuses on the changing character of American identity, which is influenced by such factors as globalization, immigration, and birth trends. The common predicaments and dilemmas of first-generation immigrants as well as the increasing significance of religious diversity to American politics and culture are also highlighted. In the second part, we focus on the factors that contribute to continuing issues and challenges for specific minority groups as they attempt to improve their subordinate status by political means. The topics covered in each of the chapters are summarized as follows:

In Chapter 2, "Globalization and the American Nation," Sheila Croucher lays out the changing character of national and individual identity in a globalized world, including an extended discussion of the meanings of, and relationships between, globalization, nationhood, and transnational ties. She explains why individuals may hold multiple identities or a hybrid identity and why globalization could lead to the transcendence of the American nation-state and to the transformation of American identity. Toward the end of her chapter, she reviews historical and contemporary efforts to "defend the nation" and reinvigorate American nationalism in response to real and perceived threats of global intrusion.

In Chapter 3, "A World Between: Multiple Identities and the Challenges Faced by First-Generation Immigrants," Edwina Barvosa identifies and describes the specific challenges faced by immigrants and sometimes, in a modified form, their U.S.-born children. Using the analogy of what it is like to be a first-year college student, Barvosa conveys the parallel feelings and experiences of first-generation immigrants. In her discussion of the complexities associated with assimilation, she explains why immigrants frequently retain multiple ethnic identities even as they commit themselves to living permanently in America. Finally, she considers how misperceptions and racial attitudes held by Americans may complicate the efforts of immigrants to acculturate and balance their ethnic identities.

In Chapter 4, "Immigration: Trends, Demographics, and Patterns of Political Incorporation," Jessica Lavariega Monforti begins by discussing the concepts of citizenship, immigration, and political incorporation and explains the basic "nuts and bolts" for immigrating and naturalizing. In subsequent sections she reviews contemporary immigration patterns and trends, clarifies popular misconceptions about immigration and immigrants, and chronicles recent legal changes in immigration policy and proposed reforms. In her review of current immigration, she answers these simple but central questions: Who are immigrants today? Where do they come from? Where do they settle? Her discussion of proposed immigration reform also includes a review of public opinion on the topic.

In Chapter 5, "Bridging the Cultural Divide: Accommodating Religious Diversity," Jocelyn Sage-Weiner and Clyde Wilcox discuss the new religious diversity of the United States, including its historical, social, and political implications. They focus on the intersection of religious diversity and public opinion, public policy, social interaction, and personal responses. First, they examine how Americans feel about minority religions and how these attitudes relate to their policy preferences. Next, they examine how religion affects electoral politics and policy making and specifically how politicians combine religious appeals with other salient issues in an effort to win the votes of particular communities. Last, they speculate on the future of religious diversity in the United States, on the ways in which political parties, government, and social communities will seek to address the changing religious landscape.

In Chapter 6, "'Measured Sovereignty': the Political Experiences of Indigenous Peoples as Nations and Individuals," David E. Wilkins clarifies the unique status of American Indians, individually and collectively, relative to other minority populations in the United States. He begins by summarizing the history that explains the distinctive legal, governmental, cultural, and landowning status of nationally recognized Native tribes/nations and the lack of status for unrecognized tribes. Then, Wilkins describes the background, significance, and complexity of treble citizenship status for individuals who are members of a recognized tribe. The remainder of his essay examines ways in which Native nations and individuals have and are engaged in U.S. politics, especially via voting and campaign contributions.

In Chapter 7, "Linked Fates, Disconnected Realities: The Post–Civil Rights African American Politics," Melanye T. Price and Gloria J. Hampton consider whether the solidarity and sense of "linked fate" that mobilized African American political efforts during the civil rights era continue to have the same relevance and influence on contemporary black political behavior. Price and Hampton describe the social and economic differences within the African American population as they discuss new challenges for black leadership and the current black political agenda. The last part of their essay examines whether black voting behavior, specifically their taken-for-granted support of Democratic candidates and other electoral strategies, has yielded the results intended in terms of a greater black presence in political and policy-making positions.

In Chapter 8, "The Influence of Context and History on the Policy Positions and Partisanship of Hispanics in the United States," Jessica Lavariega Monforti and Lisa García Bedolla begin with an overview of the historical and migratory experiences among Hispanic populations in the United States. They emphasize the diversity of opinion, priorities, and behavioral patterns that mark the political experiences of the various Hispanic country-of-origin groups. Using recent survey data, the authors demonstrate how prior explanations of partisan attachment and policy preferences among whites and African Americans are not as useful for explaining partisanship and policy views within Latino communities, specifically Cuban Americans and Puerto Ricans.

In Chapter 9, "Model Minority or Perpetual Foreigner? The Political Experience of Asian Americans," Morrison G. Wong describes the socioeconomic status and other demographic trends of the many national origin groups that are collectively known as "Asian Americans." He provides both qualified support and refutation for the stereotypes that are commonly associated with persons of Asian origin in the United States. Wong specifically examines the bases of the somewhat contradictory popular images of Asians as "model minorities" and "perpetual foreigners." He also demonstrates the significance and implications of these two stereotypes for understanding the complexities associated with their partisan identification, voting behavior, and electoral success. Wong ends his chapter with a discussion of the barriers that hinder the full participation of Asian Americans in the American political process.

In Chapter 10, "Anti-Semitism and the Jewish American Political Experience," Paul Mendes-Flohr explains the history and long-term effects of anti-Semitism and the organizational efforts of Jewish Americans to defeat it. He begins with an overview of the ideological claims and origins of anti-Semitism in Europe, and then considers the American Founding Fathers' commitment to religious pluralism and other factors that explain the failure of anti-Semitism to fully take root in the United States, in spite of the presence of some anti-Jewish sentiment among the protestant majority. The primary focus of his chapter is on the efforts of Jewish organizations to successfully combat prejudice and discrimination, but he also considers the ongoing challenges to Jews and Judaism presented by the policies of the state of Israel.

In Chapter 11, "Islamophobia, the Muslim Stereotype, and the Muslim American Political Experience," Manochehr Dorraj explains the paradox of Muslim Americans, being a well-assimilated group that is currently perceived as being very "different" from other minority groups and consequently the target of more serious discrimination. Dorraj provides the historical background and political causes that contribute to the recent development of "Islamophobia" as well as other longer-standing Muslim stereotypes. He chronicles the influence of critical events and explains how the bias in media coverage, the presentation of negative Muslim images, and the agendas of some politicians work together to amplify negative attitudes and behaviors toward Muslim Americans and Muslim immigrants, especially during times of war or conflict with Muslim nations. Dorraj concludes by listing the factors that he identifies as contributing to the continued resiliency of Islamophobia and Muslim stereotypes and his recommendations for what it would take to overcome it.

In the final chapter, "Concluding Thoughts on a Changing America," we (the book editors) return to the subject of Barack Obama's presidential candidacy to more closely consider the meaning and significance of his success for the politics of identity, race, ethnicity, and religion in the future. In light of the factual information and normative discussions provided in the chapters of our contributing authors, we also expand on our general themes of change and continuity in the status of minority groups.

DISCUSSION QUESTIONS

1. Why is "identity" so important? What group do you most identity with and for what reasons? How does your "identity" influence your relationships?
2. How do the authors describe the relationship between minorities and the majority group in the United States? Do you agree with this characterization? Why or why not?
3. Assuming that the population trends described in the chapter continue, what will the U.S. population be like by 2050?
4. What positive changes have occurred for minorities in the United States, and what are some of the serious problems that they continue to face?
5. What are the ramifications of growing diversity in a global context?

Chapter 2

Globalization and the American Nation

Sheila Croucher

Adeed Dawisha, professor of political science at Miami University, first arrived in the United States in the fall of 1983. Born in Baghdad, Iraq, on November 2, 1944, Professor Dawisha attended graduate school at the London School of Economics, where he met and married his American wife, Karen. During a study leave from England, both Adeed and Karen secured tenured professorships in the Washington, D.C., area, and his residency in the United States, then became permanent. Professor Dawisha explains:

> *Being married to an American citizen made naturalization easy. I became an American citizen on July 17, 1990 (to this very day, one of the most memorable days of my life).*
>
> *I have always believed that you can certainly hold multiple identities, a strong attachment, and a sense of "belonging" to more than one entity. But I also believe that intellectually and emotionally one builds a hierarchy of sorts for these identities; that is, they are not equal, but they are subconsciously and consciously aggregated. So as long as these identities are not in conflict with each other, then the hierarchy is not relevant. It becomes meaningful if at some point, for whatever reason, it becomes intellectually or emotionally difficult to reconcile two or more of these identities or make them coexist. Then the hierarchy becomes pivotal in constructing preferences.*
>
> *In the case of Iraq [which according to its new constitution does not restrict citizenship only to Iraq], I undoubtedly have a strong sense of belonging to that*

country, even to the extent of actually doing something (if asked) to contribute to the well-being and prosperity of the country. For example, I would consider seriously, say, a stint in some political position in Iraq (even in a governmental agency) if I felt that I would be of help to the political development of the country, without in any way feeling that I am jeopardizing my sense of belonging to America. However, the important point here is that I would only do this if I were sure that I would be cementing and routinizing the values that are essentially embedded in American culture (e.g., rule of law, civil liberties, representative institutions, free market economy, etc.).

That sets me thinking that my love for American values (which anchors my strong sense of belonging to America) is paramount in my own hierarchy of identities. So if Iraq were to take a turn away from these very values that I cherish, then there is absolutely no doubt that any sense of belonging to Iraq would be considerably diminished. I suppose you can say, therefore, that I am both American and Iraqi but, when push comes to shove, I am more American than Iraqi.

Introduction

The battle for the U.S. presidency in the year 2000 will be remembered as one of the most contentious and protracted elections in American history. After a long evening of the media declaring a winner and then retracting the claim, a tense month of court challenges and vote recounts, and a controversial five-to-four U.S. Supreme Court decision allowing Florida to certify its vote, George W. Bush was declared the victor by a margin of 537 votes. But the Bush/Gore race was not the only presidential contest playing out in the United States during that year. In early July 2000, thousands of Syrian Americans at 25 polling locations across the United States cast ballots for the candidate who would replace the late Syrian president Hafez Assad.[1] Later that same month, Venezuelans throughout the United States cast their votes in a presidential election that brought to power the current Venezuelan president Hugo Chavez.[2] Mexico also held an important presidential election in 2000. Preceding the final vote in July, Vicente Fox, the ultimate victor, campaigned heavily throughout Mexico and in Chicago, Los Angeles, and Dallas, recognizing that millions of potential Mexican voters reside outside Mexico and proclaiming his intention to be president of "all Mexicans"—at home and abroad.[3] As it turned out, potential candidates (as well as voters) for Mexican political office also resided in the United States. In 2000, Los Angeles businessperson Eddie Varon Levy won a seat in the Mexican Congress, becoming the first person living abroad to hold that office, and California millionaire Andres Bermudez, living and campaigning in the United States, won the mayoral race in his hometown of Jerez, Zacarecas, becoming the first U.S. resident to serve as a Mexican mayor.[4]

The 2000 U.S. presidential election was a notable one in American history, but every year thousands of voters in the United States participate in foreign elections; and both their numbers and opportunities to influence politics in other countries are expanding. The same is true of the growing number of Americans who reside permanently outside of the United States, in countries that range from Mexico and Canada to the Philippines and Greece, but retain their right to participate in U.S. politics. The population of Americans living overseas is estimated to be more than 6 million. These U.S. citizens maintain active chapters of the Democrats and Republicans Abroad and raise money to support their favored candidates, and in elections as close as those in 2000 and 2004, their absentee ballots have the capacity to tip the electoral balance.[5] The specter of U.S. citizens and residents voting to select leaders of countries sometimes continents away, of politicians from other countries campaigning in the United States to garner the support of their countrypeople who have migrated, and of a constituency of American voters extending far beyond the borders of the United States illustrates some of the ways globalization is reconfiguring the way people identify and belong in the world.

The notion that individuals are born into one specific nation-state, that they will remain in their nation-state of birth, and that that one nation-state will persist as a primary source of their identity over a lifetime is becoming less viable. Goods, services, people, and ideas are crossing borders at unprecedented rates. The result is a set of transnational networks that are not only political in nature, as illustrated above, but economic, social, and cultural as well. These networks are one indicator of how globalization has led to a compression of space and time and lessened the significance of political and geographic borders. Emerging transnational networks among immigrants, their homelands, and their new lands are also an important reminder that any contemporary discussion of identity and identity politics in the United States must be situated within the contemporary context of globalization.

As the title of this book infers, identity in America is changing; and, as this chapter will emphasize, globalization constitutes a primary backdrop to the changing face and politics of American identity and identities. Globalization is increasing the numbers of immigrants arriving in the United States and altering the landscape in which both newcomers and established residents negotiate their sense of political and cultural belonging. Central to this renegotiation is the role of the nation as a mechanism for creating unity and solidarity among an ethnically, racially, and religiously diverse population. For students of American identity, two key questions come to mind: Will globalization, through its penetration of geographic and cultural borders, undermine the relevance of nationhood as a form of identity; and, if not, will nation-states like the United States respond to the global challenges of immigration, cultural diversity, and economic and political uncertainty in a manner that upholds their commitment to democratic principles of equality and inclusion or seek refuge in a nationalism of exclusion? This chapter begins with a clarification of the concepts of "globalization" and "nation" and a discussion of the analytical linkages between them. The remainder of the chapter applies this framework to the United States, looking first at how globalization is leading to a transcendence of the American nation-state as it has long been imagined and next at how those same global forces result in a politics focused on defending and fortifying the American nation.

Clarifying the Concepts

WHAT IS GLOBALIZATION?

"Globalization" and "nation" (including related terms such as "nationalism," "nationhood," and "nation-state") are among the most widely used and slippery concepts in our contemporary lexicon. Both terms aim to describe powerful and pervasive phenomena, but these phenomena are so complex and multifaceted as to defy social scientific precision. Definitions of "globalization" range from the very basic to the very complex. Roland Robertson defines *globalization* very simply as "the crystallization of the entire world as a single place."[6] James Mittelman, on the other hand, offers a more complex definition:

> [G]lobalization...include[s] the spatial reorganization of production, the interpenetration of industries across borders, the spread of financial markets, the diffusion of identical consumer goods to distant countries, massive transfers of population within the South as well as from the South and East to the West, resultant conflicts between immigrant and established communities in formerly tight-knit neighborhoods, and emerging world-wide preference for democracy.[7]

Definitions of "globalization" also vary in their emphases, spanning from the economic and political to the cultural and technological. Economics is widely perceived as the engine of globalization, specifically in terms of the increasingly free and rapid flow of money, goods, and services. Over the past thirty years, world trade, for example, has skyrocketed. In 1982, the world's foreign direct investment inflows and outflows were $58 billion and $37 billion, respectively. By 2000, those figures had increased more than eightfold to $1.271 trillion and $1.150 trillion.[8] No one discounts the central role of capitalism in integrating the globe, but globalization has political dimensions as well. The world is now home to thousands of different international governmental and nongovernmental organization. The World Trade Organization and the United Nations are prime examples of the former. Amnesty International, Greenpeace, and the International Committee of the Red Cross are but a few examples of the latter. In 1909, international nongovernmental organizations numbered a mere 176; by 1993, the number had soared to 28,900 and by the year 2000, to 37,000.[9]

Neither the economic nor political interconnectedness that characterizes globalization would be possible without sophisticated advances in communication and information technology. In fact, some scholars contend that the technological revolution in communication is "the leading influence in the globalization of society over the past 20 or 30 years."[10] Consider the impact of satellite technology on telephone communication. In 1930, the price of a three-minute call from New York to London was $244.65. In 1970, the same call cost $31.58. By 1990, the price dropped to $3.32 and by 1999, to 35 cents.[11] Similarly, the number of television receivers in the world went from 192 million in 1965 to 1.361 billion in 1996. Perhaps the most obvious example of technology's role in globalization is the Internet—a vehicle through which users around the world can mobilize social movements, lobby politicians, chat, date, and shop. In 2005, the number of Internet users worldwide surpassed 1 billion, up from only 45 million in 1995 and 420 million in 2000. By 2011, the world's Internet users are expected to reach 2 billion.[12] For the technologically savvy users with voice-over-Internet software, the three-minute phone call between London and New York is now free.

These technological advances allow messages, ideas, and symbols to travel vast distances more rapidly and inexpensively than ever before, facilitating a high degree of global cultural and political and economic interconnectedness; but this growing interconnectedness is also the product of the unprecedented movement of human beings. According to the United Nations, at least 190 million people worldwide currently live outside their country of birth, up from 80 million three decades ago.[13] For many immigrant-receiving societies such as the United States, Canada, Australia, and France, the foreign-born now comprise between 13% and 22% of the country's total population. This human migration is a key dimension of globalization but is simultaneously influenced by other dimensions. Many of the factors that push migrants to leave their home country or pull them to a new one relate to economic, political, and cultural changes in the global system. Economic and political instability, for example, motivates many migrants to leave home; and for those who are destined for the United States, the global prominence of American culture and the promise of economic wealth or political freedom may act as powerful pull factors.

Globalization is clearly a complex and multifaceted phenomenon. For the purposes of this chapter, it will be defined as follows: a cluster of related changes that are increasing the interconnectedness of the world. These changes are occurring in, but not limited to, economic, technological, cultural, and political realms. Furthermore, globalization is not restricted to merely enhancing the interdependence of already existing entities, such as states, or the intensification of established networks or flows; it also facilitates the creation of new ones.[14] Among the many changes wrought by globalization are shifts in identity and forms of cultural and political belonging—including challenges to national identity and belonging. Before examining more closely how globalization affects national, and specifically American, identity and identities, we need to explore briefly the meaning of the term "nation."

What Is a Nation?

As contested as the definition of "globalization" is, the meaning of "nation" is even more so. Writing in 1977, renowned historian Hugh Seton-Watson proclaimed, "I am driven to the conclusion that no 'scientific definition' of the nation can be devised."[15] And almost thirty years later, Valery Tishkov concluded that, "All attempts to develop terminological consensus around *nation* [have] resulted in grand failure."[16] What we do know from many scholars of nationhood is that the concept of "nation," while related to "state," is not synonymous with the state. A state, as Walker Connor reminds us, is readily identifiable through quantitative measures. "Peru," he writes, "can be defined in an easily conceptualized manner as the territorial–political unit consisting of the sixteen million inhabitants of the 514,060 square miles located on the west coast of South America between 69° and 80°, and 2° and 18° 21 South."[17] A nation, however, has a much more intangible essence and is repeatedly defined through subjective and psychological criteria. Sociologist Max Weber defined nations in terms of a "sentiment of solidarity;"[18] and Rupert Emerson stated that a nation is "a body of people who feel that they are a nation."[19] Although distinct, the nation and the state are certainly not unrelated. Many, if not most, nations either have or want their own state; and states typically justify their existence by reference to representing the will of a nation. The latter is what Appadurai refers to when he describes the nation as the "ideological alibi" of the state.[20]

In addition to the analytical distinction between nation and state, recent scholarship teaches us that nations are made, not born. Rather than conceptualize nations as static entities with pristine origins that can be traced far back in history, nations are now widely recognized as social and political constructions with birth dates in the modern era. Benedict Anderson famously coined the phrase "imagined communities," arguing that nations are imagined, in part, because the members of any given nation will never know most of their fellow members, yet their shared sense of attachment to and identification with that national community may be quite strong. Perspectives vary on how precisely nations are imagined, by whom, and with what content; but scholars generally point to the prominent role of political elites and the media who manipulate powerful symbols and historical memories in order to fortify sentiments of shared national belonging.[21]

Also important to this discussion of nationhood is whether the communities are imagined on the basis of civic or ethnic criteria. Civic nations define their membership in political terms. Belonging is not a function of race, ethnicity, or religion, for example, but is based on an individual's willingness to embrace the nation's political principles. The United States is often considered a quintessential example of a civic nation. Anyone can become an American, the rhetoric promises, if he or she is willing to pledge allegiance to the U.S. Constitution — or to "shed the European skin never to resume it," as John Quincy Adams proclaimed to prospective immigrants in 1818.[21a] Ethnic nations, on the other hand, define membership in ethnic terms. Hence, until the late 1990s, German citizenship, for example, was based on German ancestry. This led one commentator to observe that, "In Germany, it can be easier for a child whose family lived in Russia for 200 years to become a German citizen than it is for the German-born child of a Turkish 'guest worker,' even if that child speaks no Turkish and has been educated in German schools."[22] Today, few nation-states publicly define themselves in purely ethnic terms, though, as will be clear even in the case of the United States, notions of ethnicity as a foundation for national belonging persist.

What, then, is the relationship between these two phenomena, globalization and nationhood? How does increased global interconnectedness affect the formation and maintenance of nations and the significance of national belonging? Several scholars have pondered this question. Their responses vary and reflect their views of what the nation is. For example, if "nation" refers to a community of people who identify with and share membership in a given state, then globalization's weakening of states has immediate implications for the nation. This assumption seems to underlie Eric Hobsbawm's prediction that "Nation-states and nations will be seen as retreating before, resisting, adapting to, being absorbed or dislocated by, the new supranational restructuring of the globe."[23] Similar assumptions underpin the widespread characterization of the contemporary era as "postnational." Arjun Appadurai writes, "We are looking at the birth of a variety of complex, postnational social formations. . . . The new organizational forms are simply less implicated in the comparative advantages of the nation-state."[24] But two important caveats are in order. First, if the state is not, in fact, dead (and evidence exists that it is not), then neither is the nation as its alibi. In fact, the struggle of states to maintain their legitimacy and autonomy in the face of globalization may be reflected in the state-sponsored invigoration of nations and national alibis. Such has been the case in the United States, as will be discussed later. Second, if, however, nations are entities that exist outside of or distinct from states, then globalization's impact on nationhood is more complicated. Globalization can, for example, create opportunities for national belonging that transcend, challenge, or reject the boundaries of states but still use the language of nationhood. Such is the case with the growing prevalence of *transnationalism*, which is in part the stretching of national belonging across established geographic and political borders. The following section will illustrate these divergent implications of globalization for the American nation. We look, first, at the ways in which globalization seems to mark a transcendence of the conventional model of the nation-state and, second, at contemporary efforts to invigorate American nationhood in response to global trends.

Transcending the American Nation

> I really live in El Salvador, not in LA. When we have the regular fiestas to collect funds for La Esperanza, I am the leader and am treated with respect. When I go back home to inspect the works paid with our contributions, I am as important as the mayor. In LA, I just earn money, but my thoughts are really back home. It's only three hours away.[25]

Mr. González, quoted above, is a Salvadoran, living in Los Angeles and serving as president of a local civic committee devoted to improving conditions back in the small town of La Esperanza in El Salvador. He is also what many scholars have come to refer to as a "transmigrant," whose daily life illustrates an emergent social field characterized as "transnationalism." *Transnationalism* is defined as "the processes by which immigrants build social fields that link together their country of origin and their country of settlement."[26] Immigrants who build such social fields are designated "transmigrants."

> Transmigrants develop and maintain multiple relations—familial, economic, social, organizational, religious, and political that span borders. Transmigrants take actions, make decisions, and feel concerns, and develop identities within social networks that connect them to two or more societies simultaneously.[27]

Immigration to the United States is certainly not new, nor is the phenomenon of immigrants maintaining ties to their homeland. What is changing, however, is that the numbers of migrants and their proportion of the overall population are increasing. Between 1995 and 2000, the United States experienced a net increase of 6,195,000 immigrants—almost double the net increase of 3,775,000 a decade earlier between 1985 and 1990.[28] Of the 190 million people the United Nations reported living outside their countries of birth in 2005, 38 million lived in the United States, creating a foreign-born population that comprised over 13% of the total U.S. population.[29] What is also new is the enhanced ability and tendency of some immigrants to maintain close ties to their homeland. Whether in the increased intensity of exchanges, improved methods of transacting, or multiplication of activities that rely on sustained cross-border contacts, the result is, as Portes explains, a "growing number of persons who live dual lives: speaking two languages, having homes in two countries, and making a living through continuous regular contact across national borders."[30]

The phenomenon of transnational political ties was illustrated in the introduction to this chapter, but it is worth clarifying that the trend of immigrants in the United States voting in foreign elections reflects, in part, the growing willingness of many states in the world to recognize dual citizenship. In fact, close to one hundred countries now allow expatriates to retain their home country citizenship while also pursuing citizenship in the host country to which they have migrated. Many of the countries on this list are among the top sending states of migrants to the United States: Argentina, Brazil, Canada, Colombia, Costa Rica, the Dominican Republic, Ecuador, El Salvador, Israel, Panama, and the United Kingdom. Officials estimate that over 40 million Americans could be dual citizens.[31] For its part, the United States does not officially recognize dual citizenship. In fact, the citizenship oath in the United States requires prospective citizens to "renounce and abjure absolutely and entirely all allegiance and fidelity to any foreign prince, potentate, state, or sovereignty of whom or which the applicant was before a subject or citizen." In practice, however, U.S. law and policy are ambiguous with regard to dual citizenship and akin to what one analyst describes as "don't ask, don't tell."[32] For opponents of dual citizenship, the result is that the once sacred union between a citizen and his or her state (sometimes likened to the marriage of one woman and one man) has become dangerously tenuous.[33] Supporters of dual citizenship offer a different analogy. Francisco Duran, a U.S. citizen since 1999 who retained his Mexican nationality, explains that "Asking me to choose between two countries is like asking a child whose parents are divorcing to pick which parent he wants to live with." Jan Jaben-Eilon, a U.S. citizen who also took Israeli citizenship in 1996, echoes this sentiment: "America is the country who made me who I am, but that doesn't mean that I don't have very deep feelings for Israel as well."[34]

The linkages that are currently multiplying among immigrants, their countries of origin, and their countries of settlement are not only political in nature but also social and economic. The flow of migrants and the close ties they maintain to their homelands (owing to advances in communications and transportation technology) have eliminated socially the physical space that divides distant places. In communities throughout the United States, immigrants stay increasingly connected to families and villages through phone calls, faxes, and videotapes that travel back and forth, allowing absent loved ones to share in special celebrations. In fact, the rhythms of life across borders have become so synchronized that some scholars speak of the emergence of entirely new social spaces or transnational locales. In a fascinating ethnography of an emergent transnational locale, Alison Mountz and Richard Wright focus on the large population of immigrants from the village of San Agustín, Oaxaca, who live and work in Poughkeepsie, New York:

> ...the Mexicans do not view their existence in Poughkeepsie as disconnected from San Agustín.... Through *paisanaje*, the shared connection of being from the same community, Oaxacans in New York help each other and watch each other, sharing news of San Agustín in Poughkeepsie and vice versa.[35]

Some transnational spaces emerge and persist informally; others, however, are more coordinated. Throughout the United States, immigrants have formed organizations and associations that facilitate both their adaptation to the United States and their continued relationships with the life of the homeland. Take, for example, the growing number of *Casas Guanajuatos* throughout the United States. The Mexican state of Guanajuato is one of the top three sending states of migrants to the United States. As the numbers of *Guanajuatenses* in the United States grows, many immigrants, with the active support and encouragement of the Mexican government, have begun to form civic and cultural organizations in the United States to assist them and their fellow nationals from Guanajuato in adapting to a new home and way of life in the United States. At least fifty *Casas Guanajuatos* now exist throughout the United States, in places ranging from Idaho to Wisconsin to North Carolina. Their functions include promoting the national culture; increasing brotherhood among immigrants from Guanajuato living in the United States; maintaining a channel of communication with the government in Mexico; protecting human, labor, and civil rights; and promoting leadership.

Casas Guanajuatos, and other similar immigrant organizations in the United States, have an additional goal, which is promoting development in the homeland. Transnational ties, in this way, are also economic. As immigration from many less developed countries to the United States boomed in the late 1960s, scholars and policy makers began to speak of a "brain drain" that was luring the brightest minds out of the developing world. Beginning in the late 1960s, India, for example, saw more than 25,000 of its top graduates move to the United States. More recently, however, globalization—in its technological, economic, cultural, and political dimensions—has transformed the pattern of a linear one-way brain drain into a "paradigm of brains that circulate between native and adopted countries."[36] Airplanes, telephones, e-mail, and fax machines; the increasingly open Indian economy; and the efforts of the current Indian government to embrace its expatriates have motivated some of India's biggest American success stories to renew ties with their homeland and establish dual lives across continents.

The surge in remittances that migrants send to their homeland is further evidence of transnationalism in the economic realm. Recorded remittances received by developing countries exceeded $93 billion in 2003; and in thirty-six of 153 developing countries, remittances are larger than all capital flows, both public and private. In Mexico, for example, money sent home by Mexican emigrants is second only to oil as an important source of the country's income. Nearly one Mexican in five regularly receives money from relatives in the United States. This income, exceeding $15 billion a year, helps feed, house, and educate more than a quarter of Mexico's 100 million people.[37] In the small town of Indaparapeo in Michoacán, Mexico, forty students are completing university studies thanks to the sponsorship of immigrants from Indaparapeo who are living in the United States. The Indaparapeo Project is sustained by the fund-raising activities of an estimated 1,000 immigrants from the town who live in Napa Valley, California, and hundreds more who live in Chicago.[38]

As growing numbers of people maintain close political, social, and economic ties across nations and states and secure plural memberships in different political and cultural units, American identity is being transformed. But the transformation is a result of the porosity of not merely geographic borders but cultural ones as well. As more immigrants arrive in the United States and from a broader range of places, the notion of America as a culturally homogenous unit based largely on an Anglo-Saxon, Protestant heritage is difficult to sustain. In reality, the United States never was as culturally, ethnically, linguistically, or religiously homogenous as some history books and politicians would have us believe; nonetheless, the multiplicity of cultures now coexisting within the United States challenges notions of, and attempts to forge, national unity rooted in cultural sameness. Many of these challenges are typically discussed under the heading "multiculturalism." The growing prevalence of Spanish in the United States is one example, whether uttered haltingly from the mouths of presidential candidates courting the Latino vote or lyrically from the mouths of Latinos themselves singing the U.S. national anthem in their mother tongue. Immigrants bring with them not only different languages but sometimes different religious and cultural practices as well.

Some of these cultural changes and persistent transnational ties exist without controversy. Few eyebrows were raised when salsa officially surpassed ketchup as the most popular condiment in the United States or when large numbers of Italian Americans across the United States gathered to cheer on Italy in the finals of the 2006 World Cup. These Americans donned the colors of the Italian flag, sang the Italian national hymn, ate Italian sausage, and placed soccer balls in the arms of statues of Saint Peter for good luck.[39] In other cases, however, the maintenance of cultural ties to the homeland or to a set of beliefs that are not widespread in the new land poses greater problems. In 2003, for example, a Florida judge ruled that Sultaana Freeman, a Muslim, was prohibited from wearing a veil in her driver's license photograph. For the state, a photo that obscured the driver's face posed a potential security threat. For Freeman, she was being denied her right to the free exercise of religion.[40] Another example relates to the growing numbers of immigrants to the United States arriving from communities in Africa and the Middle East that practice female genital cutting. Some immigrants from these regions desire to preserve their cultural heritage by having their daughters circumcised in the United States. Doctors, politicians, human rights organizations, and immigrant groups in the United States have struggled to balance their respect for cultural differences with their need to safeguard the physical and emotional well-being of the more than 150,000 young girls and women that the Centers for Disease Control and Prevention estimates are at risk of the procedure.[41] The practice was officially outlawed in the United States in 1996, but as recently as November 2006, an immigrant father from Ethiopia, living in Georgia, was sentenced to 10 years in prison for performing genital mutilation on his daughter.[42]

These examples highlight the ways that globalization can contribute to the transcendence of nation-states and to the transformation of national identities. Globalization spurs a freer and faster flow of people, ideas, goods, and money. In the United States, large numbers of immigrants not only are arriving from other places but also have an enhanced capacity to maintain closer connections to their homeland, while simultaneously forming new attachments and identities. As a result, growing numbers of people in the United States and around the world identify with and maintain close attachments to more than one nation and state. Meanwhile, nation-states, like the United States, face the challenge of forging unity and commonality among a constituency that has access to and exhibits multiple identities and attachments. It is too soon to know with certainty how globalization and its related transformation will affect identity in the United States. Significant reconfigurations are evident, but so is a backlash in the form of efforts to clarify and fortify the nation's identity and the political and cultural boundaries of who does and does not belong.

Fortifying the American Nation

Now this nation that I love
Has fallen under attack
A mighty sucker punch came flying in

From somewhere in the back
Soon as we could see clearly
Through our big black eye
Man, we lit up your world
Like the 4th of July
Justice will be served
And the battle will rage
This big dog will fight
When you rattle his cage
And you'll be sorry that you messed with
The U.S. of A.
cause we will put a boot in your ass
It's the American way

Toby Keith, "Courtesy of the Red,
White and Blue," 2002

Within the United States, responses to the 9/11 attacks varied, but love and loyalty to the nation were widespread. Written a few days after 9/11, Toby Keith's hit "Courtesy of the Red, White, and Blue" struck a chord with many Americans. The "nation" had been attacked, and "we" would mobilize our superior military strength to fight back quickly and violently. Other Americans pondered the question "Why do 'they' hate 'us'?" Thousands of Americans rushed to buy and display—on their bodies, cars, houses, and barns—the American flag. Many enlisted in the armed services or joined the FBI. Some saw 9/11 as a call to reach out to their fellow Americans by volunteering. In his first state-of-the-union address after 9/11, President Bush asked Americans to contribute 4,000 hours over their lifetime to serving their country. In 2005, 65.4 million people said they donated time to a charitable cause, 5.6 million more than in 2002. This and various other measures of civic involvement led some to speculate that 9/11 was producing a generation of volunteers.[43] For other Americans, however, 9/11 was a motivation (or excuse) for engaging in hate speech and violent crime against ethnic or religious "others." Mosques were vandalized, individuals of Arab descent and practicing Muslims were harassed, and one Sikh gas station attendant in Arizona, mistaken for a Muslim, was murdered. The responses to 9/11 were varied, but taken together, all reveal, for better or worse, the persistent power and appeal of the nation as a source of identity and a refuge of belonging.

While the events surrounding 9/11 highlighted a state of national insecurity in the United States, perceptions of threat to the American nation and calls for its protection predate (in some cases by centuries) the terrorist attacks of 2001. Even prior to the American Revolution, many of the country's Founding Fathers worried about an influx of non-English immigrants. Benjamin Franklin denounced the "swarthy complexion" of the "Spaniards, Italians, French, Russians, Swedes" and the Germans, whom he labeled as "ignorant a set of people as the Indians." Franklin's opposition to immigration, widely shared at the time, was based on his belief that these Europeans "will never adopt our Language or Customs, any more than they can acquire our Complexion."[44] Perceived as especially threatening were the Irish, who Ralph Waldo Emerson described as "deteriorated in size and shape, the nose sunk, the gum exposed...a diminished brain."[45] By the 1850s, anti-immigrant and anti-Catholic sentiment gave rise to the nativist Know-Nothing Party, which was instrumental in electing eight governors and over one hundred members of the U.S. Congress.

The anti-immigrant sentiment was fueled by the fact that between 1815 and 1860 5 million Europeans arrived on eastern U.S. shores, followed by a huge influx of Chinese immigrants to the West Coast. This influx and the hysteria it provoked resulted in a series of legislative acts designed to restrict immigration. The Chinese Exclusion Act of 1882 barred Chinese laborers from entering the country and denied them naturalization, and National Origins Quotas Acts in 1921 and 1924 served to severely restrict immigration from southern and eastern Europe. In the decades that followed, various historical factors worked to lessen anti-immigrant hysteria, at least temporarily. The Great Depression during the 1930s reduced the influx of immigrants. World War II and its aftermath changed the mood in the country with regard to democratic inclusion, as did the civil rights movement. The latter helped to prompt the final removal of national origins quotas in the 1960s.

By the 1980s, any semblance of national tolerance toward newcomers was shattered again by a rising U.S. nativism, evidenced in part by the mobilization of and widespread support for groups like Official English and U.S. English. By 1988, all but two of the fifty states had at least considered legislation to declare English their official language, and 28 states eventually enacted such legislation. In 1985, former governor of Colorado Richard Lamm published *The Immigration Time Bomb: The Fragmenting of America*, foreshadowing a series of books by politicians and public figures decrying the dangers of immigration and ethnic group identification to the American nation. Arthur Schlesinger, Jr., former special adviser to President Kennedy, wrote *The Disuniting of America* in 1991; and in 2002, Patrick Buchanan published *The Death of the West: How Dying Populations and Immigrant Invasions Imperil Our Country and Civilization*. Buchanan's book was built on years of anti-immigrant political rhetoric honed since his first presidential run in 1996 when he began calling for a security fence and deployment of U.S. troops along the southern U.S. border. Beyond a worry over the numbers of immigrants to the United States, Buchanan is concerned with their countries of origin. Echoing sentiments similar to those heard at the turn of the century that led to the passage of the

National Origins Quotas, Buchanan proclaimed in 2002 that "The immigrant tsunami rolling over America is not coming from all the races of Europe. The largest population transfer in history is coming from all the races of Asia, Africa, and Latin America, and they are not melting and reforming."[46]

This brief overview of past decades makes clear that perceived threats of global intrusions into the American nation have a long history in the United States. Nonetheless, the events of 9/11 served to invigorate powerfully those fears and the surrounding debate. For his part, Buchanan quickly turned attention, post-9/11, to a connection between immigration and terrorism: "How many others among our 11 million undocumented immigrants are ready to carry out truck bombings, assassinations, sabotage, skyjackings?"[47] A large percentage of Americans seemed to share his concerns as public opinion polls post-9/11 showed widespread support for restricting immigration; increasing surveillance of minority ethnic, racial, and religious groups; and limiting the rights of noncitizens. Eighty-five percent of Americans surveyed in December 2001 believed that immigration laws were too lax.[48] Seventy-nine percent were willing to restrict the immigration of certain ethnic or religious groups.[49] Thirty-one percent favored allowing the federal government "to hold Arabs who are U.S. citizens in camps until it can be determined whether they have links to terrorist organizations"; and 32% agreed that the United States "should put Arabs and Arab Americans in this country under special surveillance."[50] And as noted previously, a small but dangerous minority of Americans translated their negative attitudes toward "foreigners" or those perceived as "foreign" into harmful actions. In November 2002, Human Rights Watch released a report, "We Are Not the Enemy," documenting that anti-Muslim hate crimes in the United States rose by 1,700% during 2001.[51]

Anti-immigrant sentiment has continued to surge in the United States in the years since 9/11. By 2006, Buchanan's dreams of a security fence and a militarized border came true when President Bush ordered National Guard troops to be deployed along the southern border and signed legislation authorizing the construction of a 700-mile fence and the U.S. Senate voted 63 to 34 in support of an amendment declaring English the official language of the United States. Across the country at least thirty states passed more than fifty different laws addressing undocumented immigration, and countless locales did the same. Many of these laws declared English the official language, some empowered state or local law enforcement officials to detain undocumented immigrants, and others levied fines on businesses that hired or rented homes to undocumented workers.[52] One city in Nevada passed a law prohibiting the flying of a foreign flag unless flown with, and beneath, the American flag. Gwinnette County, Georgia, outlawed street corner taco stands; and one sheriff in southwest Ohio hung a yellow sign and arrow pointing to the jail that read "Illegal

Aliens Here."[53] In addition to familiar complaints about immigrants taking jobs or lowering wages, the contemporary rhetoric of politicians and their constituencies portrays immigrants as a threat to "our" culture and "our" way of life.

The exclusionary attitudes toward and treatment of Arab Americans, Muslims, and immigrants after 9/11 contradict America's long-standing claim to democratic inclusion. In fact, the events that surrounded 9/11, and those since, are another reminder of the historic tension between the rhetoric of civic belonging in America and the reality of ethnic, racial, and religious exclusion. Benjamin Barber captures the essence of the civic claim when he writes

> The success of the American experiment [is] in grafting the sentiments of patriotism onto a constitutional frame.... Our "tribal" sources from which we derive our sense of national identity are the Declaration of Independence, the Constitution, and the Bill of Rights.[54]

In a statement made just after 9/11, former New York mayor Rudolph Giuliani also invoked the rhetoric of America's civic nationhood:

> All that matters is that you embrace America and understand its ideals and what it's all about. Abraham Lincoln used to say that the test of your Americanism was how much you believed in America. Because we're like a religion really. A secular religion.[55]

These ideals are lofty ones, and adherence to them has contributed immeasurably to the success of the American political experiment. The rhetoric, however, and in many cases the reality of civic inclusion have always belied an ugly and persistent politics of exclusion, whether on the basis of race, gender, national origin, religion, or, most recently, sexual orientation. After 9/11, Bush attempted to clarify to Muslims in the United States and around the world that "our war is not with Islam." Yet, his description of the war on terror as a "crusade," his citations of or subtle allusions to the Bible, and his invocations of the Christian God suggest a "tribalism," to use Barber's phrase, that is not merely, or even primarily, derived from the Constitution. President Bush is certainly not alone in either displaying or fortifying these tribal ties; and his rhetoric is certainly much more measured than that of politicians like Republican member of Congress John Cooksey, who referred to Muslims as wearing diapers on their head.[55a] Finally, the anti-immigration rhetoric that has surged since 9/11 is not simply focused on the rule of law or orderly borders (potentially legitimate concerns of a civic nation-state) but, rather, repeatedly invokes perceived threats to "our" or "American" culture. These fearful invocations rarely clarify who is properly included in the category "our," what exactly constitutes "American" culture, or how immigrants pose a legitimate cultural threat. These fears are also contradicted by studies of the United States and other immigrant-receiving societies that show that "there is no evidence that assimilation is not occurring."[56] Instead, these studies show that, in terms of intermarriage, educational attainment, and political behavior, immigrants and their children are assimilating.[57]

Conclusions: Globalization's Implications for the American Nation

To return to the guiding focus of this chapter, globalization's influence on American identity, the evidence suggests that the growing interconnectedness of the world has multiple and varied implications for the American nation. The United States is often characterized as a, if not the, primary agent of globalization; but even the country known as the sole superpower is not immune to the global forces (political, economic, technological, and cultural) that are weakening borders, challenging the power of states, and changing the way many people identify with and belong in the world. Economic, political, and cultural uncertainties abound; and so do new and different opportunities for cultural and political identification and attachment. The events surrounding 9/11 illustrated this new reality in poignant ways. Although the terrorists are often portrayed as resisting globalization, they made effective use of it (technology in particular) in executing their attack. The relative ease with which the attackers penetrated U.S. security awakened Americans to the vulnerabilities associated with global interconnectedness and to the shifting terrain of a postmodern, post–cold war, and perhaps postnational world. The enemy was no longer another state but a vast network of combatants who came from twenty different countries and supported an organization that had spread across as many as sixty different states.[58] Unlike during World War II, with a more self-sufficient U.S. economy based on manufacturing, when Americans were told to support the nation by conserving resources, after 9/11 Americans, now living in a high-tech, global service economy, were encouraged to shop. The fluidity of identity was also evident in the fact that although thousands of U.S. citizens stepped up to support the country, militarily and otherwise, so did noncitizens. Immigrants with green cards now make up more than 7% of America's active fighting force;[59] and in the days after 9/11 many countries with long-standing quarrels with the United States responded to the attacks with headlines like those in France: "We Are All Americans Now."[60]

What does all of this mean for nations, and specifically the American nation? Are the forces of globalization transcending the nation-state such that this form of belonging has lost its significance in a postmodern world? The material presented in this chapter reveals ways in which the nation-state as a source and site of belonging is being both transcended and reinvigorated. Since the country's birth, immigration has connected the United States to the rest of the world. But globalization, in its contemporary manifestations, has intensified the flow of migrants and, more notably, has altered the circumstances in which they adapt to their new land and remain connected to their country and culture of origin. This is the case whether immigrants in the United States are actively voting for candidates and running for office in their homeland or sponsoring social events among their ethnic counterparts in the United States in order to raise money for civic works projects in their homelands that they will help to oversee. These examples suggest a declining significance of geographic and political borders and seem to support the claims of postnational scholars that the nation-state is being reconfigured in response to the forces of globalization. However, the recent politics of identity and belonging in the United States also attest to the persistent power and appeal of nationhood and to the potential of exclusionary rhetoric and actions that flow from it.

It is not imperative to answer definitively that globalization is leading to one particular outcome or the other—to the transcendence of national belonging or to its invigoration. It is leading to both. The same fluidity and uncertainty that create opportunities for new forms of attachment across or outside of established nations and states lead some people to cling more tightly to the privileges and protections that come with formal membership in a state and to reinscribe, through reference to membership in an imagined national community, who is and who is not properly entitled to the privileges and protections of nation-state belonging. Perhaps a more pertinent question for students of and participants in American identity is not the empirical one—How is globalization affecting American identity?—but, rather, a normative one—How *should* America, the people and the government, respond to the changes wrought by globalization? These changes include the growing numbers of residents who maintain multiple attachments, sometimes to more than one nation and state; the increased diversity of cultures that coexist within the United States; and the heightened sense of insecurity among Americans regarding global terrorism, the vagaries of the global economy, and the perceived threat to the "American" way of life.

We might ask, for example, whether the current and unprecedented level of global interconnectedness suggests that we heed the call of cosmopolitan thinkers to move beyond the narrowness of patriotism as devoted attachment to our own nation-state and think instead as citizens of the world. In the aftermath of 9/11, for example, a cosmopolitan would likely join the patriot in mourning the tragic loss of American lives in the World Trade Center; but she or he would also mourn with equal intensity the colossal loss of human life (Afghan, Iraqi, and American) in the incessant warfare that has followed. On the other hand, does the current uncertainty in the world demand that we hunker down as a nation-state, build fences—real and imagined—and communicate to newcomers or "outsiders" that you cannot truly belong to America unless you share "our" ancestry (Anglo), worship "our" god (Christian), have attachments to no other national community beyond "ours," and speak no language other than "ours" (English)?

As many respected thinkers have noted, cosmopolitanism and patriotism can be reconciled. Philosopher Charles Taylor writes, "We have no choice but to be cosmopolitans and patriots, which means to fight for the kind of patriotism that is open to universal solidarities against other, more closed kinds."[61] Philosopher Hilary Putnam also contends that "We do not have to choose between patriotism and universal reason: critical intelligence and loyalty to what is best in our traditions…are interdependent."[62] It is possible, in other words, to have love and respect for your nation and your state while simultaneously having love and respect for humankind, the commonalities that unite us and the differences that do not have to divide us. But if attachment to a particular nation-state is to remain benign, it must avoid the all too common slip from civic belonging, which embraces all members on the basis of their allegiance to a set of shared political principles, to ethnic belonging, which privileges the cultural backgrounds and beliefs of some members over others.

These are complicated debates, and the prescription for solving them is far more complicated than the previous sentence implies. Fortunately, America has a long history of dealing with identity and difference and has successes to build upon as well as failures to learn from. There are a few important lessons to keep in mind. The very same concerns now being expressed about immigrants and their unwillingness to melt were expressed decades earlier about the Germans, the Irish, the Italians, and others. They melted. With regard to the exercise of dual citizenship, in whatever ways it challenges conventional notions of state membership, it would behoove us to remember the prognostication of political theorists like John Stuart Mill, who emphasized the importance of social and political inclusion so that all members of society would have a stake in their common welfare. Globalization has created a very mobile planet. It seems reasonable (although perhaps not to a country with voter turnout rates as low as they are in the United States) that individuals today could have a stake and desire to actively participate in more than one political community. It might even be considered encouraging!

Finally, the questions that surround the issue of multiculturalism and the persistence of transnational ties are particularly complex. One of the most gripping questions that culturally diverse countries like the United States now confront is how to recognize and respect diversity while still maintaining a basis for unity and commonality. A recent and positive example of the United States' ability to do just that appears in an October 23, 2006, headline in the *Christian Science Monitor*: "Radical Islam Finds U.S. to Be 'Sterile Ground'." The article discusses how, in contrast to Europe, homegrown terror cells have not emerged in the United States and attributes their absence to "America's melting pot mentality": "In a nation where mosques have sprung up alongside churches and synagogues, where Muslim women are free to wear the hijab (or not)... the resentments that can breed extremism do not seem very evident in the Muslim community." One New York–born Muslim commented, "In America, it's a lot easier to practice our religion without complications." Another concurred, "We weren't isolated growing up. We were part of the culture." Notably, the article also discusses fears on the part of Muslims in America that many U.S. foreign and domestic policies since 9/11 (including racial profiling) have caused angst and resentment in the Muslim community.[63] Studies of assimilation and citizenship in immigrant-receiving societies like the United States have concluded that the treatment extended to newcomers in the form of citizenship practices and policies will shape the degree to which immigrants integrate into their adopted homeland or not. Restrictive practices tend to impede immigrant incorporation, while tolerance of transnational ties, promotion of political rights, and inclusion in the economic and social life of the receiving society can encourage immigrant adaptation to and embrace of the host society.[64] The *Christian Science Monitor*'s account of young Muslim Americans reveals both the promises and the potential pitfalls of negotiating identity and belonging in a changing America and a changing world.

DISCUSSION QUESTIONS

1. Is the increase in dual citizenship—membership in more than one state—a threatening trend or a promising one? Why?
2. Is globalization likely to lead to the demise of the nation-state as we know it? Why or why not? What would be the implications of such a demise?
3. Identify specific ways that globalization (and be clear as to how you are defining the term) is affecting the American nation.
4. Is it possible for a nation to be imagined solely on the basis of civic criteria, or does some form of ethnocultural content always come into play in an effort to unify a population? In what ways has American nation-shaping post-9/11 invoked civic or ethnic criteria?
5. Should the United States respond to the influences of globalization, and specifically the influx of immigrants and their maintenance of transnational ties, by encouraging and facilitating assimilation or respecting and celebrating multiculturalism? What types of policies should guide either approach?

Chapter 3

A World Between

Multiple Identities and the Challenges Faced by First-Generation Immigrants

Edwina Barvosa

Mr. Núñez arrived in the United States when he was fourteen years old from Mexico's southern state of Guerrero—his father had died seven years before. Years later, in 1970, his wife came to the United States after receiving her green card on Thanksgiving Day. As a couple, they spent nearly the next 30 years living in the American Southwest working for a lettuce company as migrant farmworkers. She wrapped and packed lettuce, and he worked as field supervisor and foreman. Together they followed the annual lettuce harvest from Salinas, California, to Hatch, New Mexico, a distance of over 1,000 miles across three American states. When farmwork was not available, they would often travel to Guerrero to visit family who still lived in their ancestral homeland. Eventually, in the late 1990s, the Núñez family settled in Calexico, where they continued to work as seasonal farmworkers but no longer traveled to follow the harvest. Their travel then consisted only of visits to family in Guerrero several times per year.

During their years as migrant farmworkers, Mr. and Mrs. Núñez raised five children—Guillermina (Gina), Betty, Thomas, Juanita, and Franco. All of the Núñez children were born in the United States between 1972 and 1980 in different cities along the migrant route—Salinas and Camarillo, California, and Phoenix, Arizona. At various times, the Núñez family experienced hostility directed at them both as Mexican immigrants and as migrant farmworkers. In various locations public schools were unwilling to take the Núñez children into existing classes despite laws requiring them to do so. Eventually, Mr. and Mrs. Núñez themselves learned the laws governing public education and became skilled advocates for their children in the U.S. school system. Once they settled in Calexico, Mr. and Mrs. Núñez took up studies themselves, including English and computer classes, and became activists and leaders, helping other migrant parents to learn their rights and become better advocates for their children in the U.S. schools. Mrs. Núñez became a talented fund-raiser for migrant causes and served as the president of the local Migrant Parent Association in Calexico in 1997. Since then, all five of the Núñez children have earned graduate degrees and are working today as educators.[1]

Introduction

Everyone in America who is not of Native American origin comes from immigrant stock. Immigrant experiences vary widely both among different immigrant groups and within those groups. Yet, while immigrant experiences are diverse, there are also challenges that all first-generation immigrants new to a society and its culture(s) must face. This chapter will explore six basic kinds of challenges that first-generation immigrants encounter as they live in a nation that is new to them. These six existential challenges—i.e., challenges associated with being a migrant—are specific to *first-generation immigrants*, defined as those who have themselves relocated to a new land after the age of thirteen. However, a modified version of these challenges is also often experienced by *second-generation immigrants*, who are born and raised in a land that is new to their immigrant parents. The first three of these six challenges involve how immigrants form identities within a new society. The second three challenges arise from the political and social conflicts from which new immigrants frequently gain and live multiple identities in their new homelands. Together all six of these challenges represent the complexities of what it means to be an immigrant in America—that is, they describe what it means to be a "border crosser" who knows what it is to live a life in and in between two or more social worlds.

New American Lives and New American Identities

Almost every American college student who moves away from home to attend college leaves behind a place—sometimes the only place—that he or she has known as home. As first-year college students, they leave behind the streets, towns, schools, and parks that have shaped them and been their world perhaps since childhood. In most cases, college students also leave behind their families, including parents, siblings, grandparents, cousins, aunts, and uncles, all of whom continue populating a place that has now suddenly become both familiar and far away. Exactly what lies ahead for new college students is unknown.

But this uncertainty is often balanced by hope and belief in the promise that whatever hard work lies ahead will bring a future far brighter than what they would have if they remained at home. For some students, remaining at home is not an option. To have any hope, they must leave. For a few others, they will arrive at college not having had a secure home.

In leaving home to follow hope in an unknown place, first-year college students all over America have a kind of immigrant experience. Once they arrive on a new campus as first-year students, they stick out to others as newcomers in a place where many others already belong. They struggle to learn and navigate new streets, new buildings, new food, new words, and new practices. On some campuses, their lack of familiarity with new surroundings makes them the butt of jokes or the object of sneers or annoyance from upperclass students who have little patience for the "invading newbies." In classrooms, new college students struggle to learn and meet new expectations. Some professors seem harsh, others are helpful, and still others seem not to notice first-years whatever they contribute to campus life. Unsure of themselves in this new setting, first-year students often stick together in groups, hoping to find security among those like themselves as they try to learn this new campus world—a world that is at once exciting and intimidating, beckoning and yet sometimes closed.

First-generation immigrants in America face circumstances that are in many ways similar to those faced by first-year college students. Like new students to campus, virtually everything in American life is novel to a new immigrant: streets, workplaces, living spaces, words, phrases, and many practices. Immigrants also often have encounters with established residents, who may or may not welcome their presence in a place where they already feel at home. Like first-year students who stick together in freshman dorms seeking security, immigrants also often find comfort in *immigrant enclaves*—communities of coethnic immigrants. In those immigrant enclaves, immigrants can find others with similar experiences who can support and encourage them in their transition to a new life. In those enclaves, they can also find familiar things from their heritage lands that reassure them as they slowly grow accustomed to their new environment.

In all of this, an immigrant in America and a first-year college student face the same *first challenge*: to acculturate to their new realm by learning and becoming able to participate in the meanings, values, and practices associated with their new social world and to add that knowledge to their existing repertoire of other knowledge. This means that both immigrants and students must come to have a new *identity* associated with their new social arena: the campus culture or mainstream American culture. An identity can be defined as an *identity scheme* that is comprised of socially constructed sets of cognitive, affective, and motivational elements—that is, meanings, values, and practices—that are learned and internalized in association with a particular way of life.[2] To have a gender identity as a woman, for example, is to say that one knows and practices a variety of the meanings, values, and practices associated with femininity. Moreover, to actively identify oneself as a woman is to implicitly claim membership in the broad social category of women and to imply a wish to be recognized and treated as a woman. This structure of internalized identity schemes combined with practicing and claiming of group identities also gives form to all other types of group identities, including, but not limited to, ethnic, national, and religious identities.[3]

In this way of thinking about identity, identity schemes themselves can be further divided into two categories: personal identities and social identities. *Personal identities* are identity schemes associated with the unique relationships that we have with specific individuals. For example, Gina Núñez is sister to Betty Núñez and together Gina and Betty have memories and ways of being together that are specific and unique to their relationship and personal identities as sisters. *Social identities*, in contrast, are identities we have as members of particular social groups. These may include ethnic groups, national groups, or religious groups. They may include social categories based on gender (male, female, transgendered); sexuality (straight, gay, lesbian, bisexual, or queer); physical ability (hearing-impaired); generational identities (baby boomer); subcultural or regional identities (biker, Southerner); urban, rural, or suburban identities (New Yorker, country girl); or social role or professional identities (doctor, farmworker, or "soccer mom"). Virtually everyone born and raised in a complex society has internalized multiple identity schemes. Such individuals know and live through a variety of identities associated with multiple social groups and their ways of life. In this definition of identity, both immigrants and first-year college students inevitably face the same challenge of acculturation that involves gaining knowledge of a culture that is new to them and forming a new identity with that culture.

Common Hardships of Immigrant Life

While there are many similarities between the first-year experience of a college student and the experience of first-generation immigrants to America, there are also important differences in the lives of immigrants—differences that involve challenging hardships. Thus, in addition to learning and gaining an identity with a new culture, immigrants typically face a *second challenge* of coping with the hardships commonly associated with immigrant life. The specifics of those hardships vary in their effects on individuals, on different immigrant groups, and on different waves of immigrants. Yet, on the whole, those immigrant hardships are typically associated with (1) poor labor and living conditions, (2) lack of formal support systems for incorporation, (3) uncertainties associated with legal status, and (4) language barriers to recognition and inclusion.

With the exception of those who immigrate to the United States specifically to work in technical and highly specialized positions in high demand, many immigrants to the United States work in difficult manual labor positions that pay poverty-level wages.[4] In turn, for those immigrants who work for sub-living wages, low wages condemn them to poor living conditions. Gina Núñez, for example, remembers what it was like to travel in an old pickup truck that her family used to follow the lettuce harvest. She writes, "we called the [truck] *cotorra* (parrot) for its bright green color. We lined the flatbed of the *cotorra* with blankets and small mattresses for us to sleep on. For suitcases we used *cajas de lechuga*, cardboard boxes used to pack lettuce. As a family of seven...we only owned what we could carry."[5] In this, as in so many cases, working poor immigrant families must get by in conditions that nonimmigrants would find unbearable.

As hardworking migrants, the Núñez family rented places to live for a few months at a time, often having difficulty finding people willing to rent to them seasonally. Their living spaces consisted of rented motel rooms, trailers, apartments, or homes that sometimes were poorly suited to children's needs. Gina Núñez recalls, for example, that in 1980, "my family rented a cramped mobile home. My parents and baby brother slept in the small bedroom, while three of my other siblings and I slept on a sofa-bed."[6] Gina's cousin Dominga had immigrated from Guerrero to serve as babysitter for the five children, and Dominga slept on an army surplus cot next to them. However, the nights in the Hatch, New Mexico, desert were extremely cold and the rented trailer was unheated. Núñez writes, "I recall the nights when my anguished mother covered us with layers upon layers of blankets while we cried ourselves to sleep, shivering in the unforgiving frosty nights. I looked forward to the days when my sisters and I would play house under the sun's warm blanket."[7] The anguish of Mrs. Núñez at the suffering of her children is the kind of immigrant hardship that results from the low wages and poor living conditions endured by many first-generation immigrants. Mrs. Núñez's suffering as a working poor immigrant mother comes on top of the fact that she, her husband, and other working poor Latina/Latino immigrants have long performed some of the most dirty, dangerous, and physically grueling work in America in areas such as meatpacking, janitorial service, and agricultural labor.[8]

The experience of poverty-level wages is not uncommon among immigrants, particularly those with low levels of educational attainment such as many Latina/Latino immigrants. For example, U.S. census data show that in 1990 and 2000 roughly 23% of immigrant Latino males lived below the official U.S.

poverty line.[9] Moreover, despite stereotypes to the contrary and as the Núñez family exemplifies, working poor Latina/Latino immigrants have among the highest rates of employment, high rates of intact families, and low rates of use of public assistance. In California, for instance, in the sixty years between 1940 and 2000 Latina/Latino immigrants had the highest labor participation rate of any demographic group including whites, blacks, Asian/Pacific Islanders, and U.S.-born Latinas/Latinos.[10] While many immigrant Latina/Latino families live in poverty and are eligible for public assistance, demographic research shows that only 18.5% of poor Latinas/Latinos claimed the assistance for which they were eligible in the period leading up to 1990. According to the 2000 U.S. Census, the rate of welfare usage among immigrant Latinas/Latinos had fallen to 12.7%, a rate less than half that of U.S.-born Latinas/Latinos. Moreover, while immigrant Latinas/Latinos claim little public assistance, they nonetheless often maintain stable families. Immigrant Latinas/Latinos are nearly twice as likely as U.S.-born Latinas/Latinos to have intact families.[11] Despite hard work, however, immigrants in America often face hardships of laborious work and living conditions associated with the sub-living wages that are common in the segments of the American economy in which immigrants are likely to find work. As I will discuss below, as a consequence of their unauthorized immigrant status, unauthorized immigrants are particularly vulnerable to sub-living wages in U.S. labor markets.

At the same time that immigrants to the United States often face hardships associated with poor labor and living conditions, they will often find few support systems to aid them in their incorporation to the United States. In contrast, first-year college students have access to various established systems of support in residence hall advisors, friendly faculty, teaching assistants, counselors, and other university staff who are employed to help students become accustomed to their new environment. Yet, with some exceptions, immigrants in America are "on their own" and must get by without many established systems of support to help their incorporation. Consequently, successful immigrants tend to be self-reliant and likely to turn to family members and informal networks of other immigrants for help when necessary. For example, when faced with difficulty locating temporary housing, the Núñez family as legal residents and migrant workers did not turn to public assistance for help. Rather, they turned to family members—such as their niece Dominga for child care—and to informal networks for assistance with low-income housing. As Gina Núñez recalls, "[m]y parents relied on friends and coworkers to help us find a rental or a family with whom we could stay. I remember one particular cold winter when we were unable to find an apartment to rent. My father's friend and *paisano* let us live out of his garage in Salinas." Gina remembers that "[o]n bitter-cold nights, the *paisano* or his wife would open the doors to their house, allowing us to sleep on their living room floor—a gesture that is often remembered and much appreciated."[12] The lack of U.S. governmental support for immigrants makes the incorporation of immigrants much more challenging and dependent on assistance from family, friends, strangers, and coethnics within immigrant enclaves or broader immigrant communities.

Although a lack of formal support systems shapes the experience of many first-generation immigrants in the United States, this is not always the case. In some cases, particular immigrant groups have received extended assistance, often for reasons associated with political conflicts. Cuban exiles, refugees, and immigrants who fled the Fidel Castro regime during the cold war, for example, were welcomed to the United States with extensive settlement programs, including educational assistance and other benefits. The practice of extending government aid to those who fled Cuba continued until 1994, when then president Bill Clinton ended support programs for the fifth major wave of Cuban immigrants. Each major wave had different class, educational, and racial profiles—from the largely well-educated, affluent, and predominantly white Cuban immigrants of the 1960s and 1970s to the generally dark-skinned and poorer Cubans who came in 1980 as part of the Mariel boat wave.[13] Recent research in immigrant incorporation shows that many of the hardships common among immigrants can be significantly alleviated through institutional structures that offer support to a society's newcomers.[14]

In addition to immigrant hardships associated with lack of formal support systems, many immigrants often face hardships associated with having an uncertain legal status for an extended period of time. Among the most urgent needs of first-generation immigrants is a sense of stability and legitimate inclusion in their new homeland. Yet, the American immigration process is long and complicated and sometimes exposes new immigrants to suspicious or belittling treatment. Those immigrants who seek legal authorization for U.S. residency embark on a difficult process that places them in the vulnerable position of having their life trajectory potentially rerouted virtually overnight. As long as one's immigration status is uncertain, however, you might never feel right in your own shoes. By analogy, a first-year college student could experience this kind of extended uncertainty if the college admissions process took several years, such that a college student could complete years of coursework before knowing whether or not he or she was admitted to the university. The uncertainty of that period would be a challenge in itself, independent of the other challenges of new student life.

The existential hardship of extended uncertainty is intensified for those immigrants who are unauthorized residents in America. The number of unauthorized residents of the United States has grown considerably in recent decades, partly as a consequence of labor demands in the United States, harsher border regulations that prevent return migration, and the length and difficulty of the U.S. immigration process. Unauthorized residents can be found among all major immigrant groups. Although the number of unauthorized residents in the United States is uncertain, it is estimated to be roughly 10.3 million including 600,000 from Canada and Europe, 400,000 from Africa, 1 million from Asia, 5.9 million from Mexico, and 2.5 million from elsewhere in Latin America, principally Central America.[15] While recent American efforts to detect and deport unauthorized immigrants are relatively modest compared to America's history of mass deportations, unauthorized immigrants nonetheless live under the constant strain of being detected and potentially deported to a nation where they have not lived for years, in some cases for decades.[16] Unauthorized immigrants are thus more vulnerable to crime or labor exploitation in that they are often less likely to seek help from law enforcement officials. A person who has American citizenship by birth can only imagine what it would be like to be engaged in everyday living with the continual worry of being excluded from the place in which one lives, works, and has built a life. As Gina Núñez notes, as a native-born "English-speaking U.S. citizen," her "reality as a border resident and border crosser" is very different from that of "other migrants who could not legally cross and move freely along the border without fearing the threat of detention and deportation."[17]

Finally, as Gina Núñez's reference to herself as an English speaker points out, there are privileges of being a native American English speaker that many first-generation immigrations are for the most part denied. All immigrants to America for whom English is not a first language will likely face hardships associated with learning a new language and suffer the hierarchies and social challenges associated with speaking accented English. In comparison, students who go away to college in America overwhelmingly attend English-speaking colleges and universities. Although some words will be new to them, first-year students will soon gain the vocabulary specific to their college life. Imagine how it would be, however, to arrive on a campus on which everyone spoke French, Spanish, or Farsi. In addition to everything that would be otherwise new, a freshman would need to learn a new language in order to function effectively. That is the situation of immigrants to America, who must learn American English in order to become incorporated into American life. Given the importance of speech in everyday commercial and social interactions, failure to learn English quickly often places new immigrants at a disadvantage.

Yet, even for the most determined immigrant language-learner, English is an especially difficult language to acquire because it has many irregular and idiosyncratic structures compared with more regularized languages. Learning English well is thus a demanding process that takes a major investment of time and resources that many immigrants who are working to support themselves and their families do not readily have available. It is no coincidence that after nearly three decades of living and working in the United States, among the first things that Mr. and Mrs. Núñez did after settling in Calexico was to take night courses in English. One can easily see, from their labor and housing situations, how that was likely to be their first chance they had to do so.

However, the hardships of language acquisition for first-generation immigrants go deeper, for if an adult language-learner has not learned, or at least often heard, English pronunciation in early childhood before the ages of six or seven, he or she most likely will *not* be physically able to pronounce sounds that are unique to English no matter how hard he or she studies and practices the language. Research indicates that this pattern of the significance of early childhood training holds for many world languages.[18] For example, a native English speaker who begins to learn Mandarin Chinese as an adult but who did not learn or often hear Mandarin by the age of six or seven will most likely *never* be able to properly pronounce the diphthongs and other sounds that are unique to Mandarin. Thus, however proficient a native English speaker becomes in Mandarin, he or she will typically always speak Mandarin with an English-language accent.

Similarly, first-generation immigrants to America who successfully learn American English as a second language—a difficult task in itself—but who did not learn English as children are likely to *always* speak English with an accent associated with their first, or "mother," tongue. Thus, when accented American English pronunciation is used by native-born Americans as a marker of "foreignness," indicative of not being American, English-speaking immigrants face the frustration of having their American identities questioned based on their accented patterns of speech. Thus, regardless of how hard immigrants study and practice or how grammatically sound their English speech has become, immigrants are often not regarded as Americans based on their accented speech. The hardship of learning English as a second language and the disadvantages of persistent immigrant accents are common experiences among first-generation immigrants.

Negotiating Multiple Ethnic Identities: Acculturation, Border Crossing, and Hybridity

In addition to the hardships that often face first-generation immigrants, immigrants eventually face a *third challenge* of learning to balance their multiple ethnic identities. For immigrants this means deciding how to balance their new American identities with the ethnic identifications they already have with their ancestral homelands and connections with family members far away.

Immigrants such as Mr. and Mrs. Núñez who come as adults to the United States bring with them their memories of and identifications with the place where they were born and raised. They also bring their love for and personal identities with the family members who remain behind. This is much like a first-year college student who arrives at college with an identity associated with his or her hometown and the family that he or she has left behind. Up until the 1960s scholarly studies on American immigration concluded that immigrants must *assimilate* to American life. To assimilate meant to abandon all identification with and care for the homeland of one's ancestors and to adopt instead the culture of mainstream America. As conceived by early proponents, American assimilationist models rejected the idea that diverse peoples could incorporate into American society on any basis other than being white, Anglo-Saxon, and Protestant in their identities. This assimilationist approach saw no value in immigrant ethnic identities, did not see value in ethnic enclaves, and did not recognize how ethnic subeconomies can often aid immigrant incorporation into the broader society. Moreover, assimilation failed to explain how some immigrant communities seemed to retain immigrant ethnic identities even as they incorporated into American life.[19]

As a result of these failings, scholars since the 1960s have increasingly rejected the view that immigrants must assimilate by relinquishing their inherited ethnic identities. Instead, scholars of American immigration have largely adopted the view that immigrants can, do, and should *acculturate* to American culture by becoming functionally versed and identified with the American mainstream culture, while also retaining identification with their ethnic cultures of origin. More recently, neoassimilationist scholars have argued that assimilation almost unavoidably takes place over multiple generations; the best mode of immigrant incorporation involves slow acculturation. That slow acculturation allows first-generation immigrants and their children to preserve and reap the benefits of their inherited cultures and identities while also gaining identification with American mainstream culture(s). Ultimately, acculturated immigrants will be in a position to choose to live by what they consider to be the best of both worlds.[20]

For immigrants this means that among the most definitive experiences of immigrant life is to not only acquire an American identity (first challenge) but also determine how they wish to balance that American identity with other identities they have internalized over time (third challenge). For immigrants, or anyone else who knows and lives in multiple cultural spheres, multiple ethnic identity schemes contain the knowledge of how to live and function effectively in more than one culture. Immigrants and others with multiple cultural identities are able to use multiple vocabularies and/or languages and to participate in the varied norms and practices of different cultural worlds. With that knowledge they may shift back and forth among those worlds, living as what we may call metaphorically "border crossers." Border crossers may not only shift back and forth across the social divides between different cultural spheres but also draw together different aspects of their multiple worlds in their daily lives as hybrid combinations of different cultural elements. Mr. and Mrs. Núñez, for example, were able to go back and forth between Guerrero and the American Southwest, living with their children in America as their adopted homeland and at times living in Mexico within the heritage culture of their families.

Living multiple ethnic identities is a complex process that has many advantages as well as some challenges. Decades ago scholarship in cross-cultural psychology, like scholarship in immigration, held that it is impossible for immigrants to live through multiple cultures. This view, however, like the insistence on rapid assimilation, has been rejected by scholars based on research which demonstrates that having multiple cultural identities can enhance self-esteem and personal security by giving immigrants access to multiple social networks and, thus, to greater sources of friendship and other social support. Studies also show that being bilingual or multilingual as part of having multiple cultural identities hones intellectual skills and can enhance academic performance.[21] In other academic disciplines, such as ethnic and racial studies, concepts such as "mestiza consciousness," "double consciousness," "métissage," and "mestizaje" have emerged in recent decades to represent the idea that individuals who are socialized in diverse or highly different settings will come to have multiple identities.[22]

Thus, as stated above, for first-generation immigrants who have multiple ethnic identities, their daily experience commonly involves both shifting among their multiple identities in different settings—as the Núñez family did between the American Southwest and Guerrero, Mexico—and the hybridization of ethnic ways of life in their daily thoughts and actions. For example, anthropologist Jayne Ifekwunigwe was born in Nigeria, lived during her early childhood in England, and then immigrated for her late childhood and teenage years with her family to southern California, where she lived in an upper middle-class Jewish suburb of West Los Angeles. Ifekwunigwe is the daughter of an Irish/English/Guyanese mother and an ethnically Igbo, Nigerian father (Igbo is one of three major ethnic groups of Nigeria) who had been born and raised in a part of Africa that had been colonized by the British and Anglican Christian missionaries.

As a Nigerian English immigrant in America, Ifekwunigwe describes herself as both a border crosser, who can shift easily among very different cultural settings, and a hybrid self—formed by different cultural and religious traditions. As a border crosser, Ifekwunigwe describes shifting back and forth among British and American English speech and mannerisms as a way of navigating the different cultural expectations at home and at school that she faced. She writes,

> I had learned that the only way I was going to survive on the playgrounds of West Los Angeles was by mutating my vowels and consonants to more approximate an American accent. I learned that my brothers and my sister had taken the linguistic plunge as well. It became our secret, we would speak "American" at school and resort to the "Queen's English" at home under the watchful eye of our quasi-ex-colonial Nigerian father...who revered *The Oxford English Dictionary* as much if not more than the Bible. Mum was a bit more relaxed. In fact, I noticed her speech patterns slowly shifting under the weight of American assimilation.[23]

In addition to easily shifting back and forth between American and British cultural contexts, Ifekwunigwe states that as a consequence of her complex family heritage and her various immigrations her "upbringing was an interesting *mélange* of Victorian English, South Shields Geordie, Onitsha Igbo, Le Guan Guyanese, Anglican Christian, and assimilating Southern California (upper middle-class Jewish West Los Angeles) cultural traditions."[24] The mélange or mixture that Ifekwunigwe writes of is a kind of familial hybridization of cultures in which elements of different cultures are brought together by the family into something that represents a distinct, although derivative, way of being—a cultural amalgam that leaves its source cultures in place. Just as the Ifekwunigwe family created a domestic cultural hybridization among themselves, individuals can also create cultural hybridity as they attempt to bring together how they think and act on an everyday basis. In so doing, they blend for themselves elements of the multiple cultural worlds with which they identify. This personal-level cultural hybridization can take place consciously or unconsciously.[25] For example, Ifekwunigwe describes how her immigrant hybridity is manifest in unconscious and uncommon combinations within her own speech patterns. She describes, for example, a conversation in which she meets a well-known British sociologist:

> While I was talking with him, I noticed that there was a rather puzzled expression on his face. I suddenly realized that, like so many other transatlantic linguistic monitors, he was trying "to place my accent"—by now among other influences an odd mixture of Bristolian English and Berkeley Californian. Eventually he exclaimed, "I cannot figure out if you are American or English!" "Well," I replied, "to be precise I am Americanized Nigerian-Irish-English-Guyanese." At which point he said, "Today, that means English."

As this example demonstrates, immigrants are not entirely in control of the way that others perceive them or how others recognize their identities or group membership. Ifekwunigwe may have grown up in America and may be a graduate student at the University of California at Berkeley, but for the purposes of her professional interaction with a British scholar, she is in his mind English. The role of others in determining and constraining how immigrants may successfully identify themselves in specific settings demonstrates the fluidity of multiple identities. All identities are ultimately a relational orientation. That is to say, while social identities give us a sense of self, they also place us in positions in relation to others. Thus, first-generation immigrants, and other individuals with multiple identities, may shift among their multiple ethnic identities based on their own desires, needs, and interests, thus balancing their multiple identities and group memberships as they see fit. But in doing so, first-generation immigrants will also always encounter challenges in the form of how others wish to place and identify them regardless of their own identity claims in specific contexts. This involuntary aspect of identity increases the challenge that immigrants face as they negotiate their multiple and hybrid identities in everyday life.

Grappling with Stereotyping, Racial Exclusion, and the Denial of Immigrant Identity Claims

Given the role that others around them play in whether or not immigrants can successfully claim their various identities in every day life, a *fourth challenge* that first-generation immigrants face is that of coping with the exclusions, stereotyping, and hostility toward immigrants still present today in the United States. That anti-immigrant hostility and exclusion is often racialized. In the encounter described above between Ifekwunigwe and another scholar, Ifekwunigwe's colleague means her no harm and is in fact quite welcoming, by claiming her as a fellow English person. Yet, other American immigrants experience harsh discrimination, in part through the routine denial of their American identities.

As migrant farmworkers, for example, the Núñez family often experienced discriminatory and harsh treatment from various people who stood in different relations to them. Residents of local areas would treat them resentfully on the assumption that they were taking local jobs—not considering perhaps that few locals tend to do the labor-intensive and time-consuming agricultural work that migrants complete. School officials would be unwelcoming and often unwilling to help the Núñez children get into classes. Once in classrooms, other schoolchildren would treat the Núñez children "as outsiders and as cultural 'others'," sometimes calling them "food tramps" or "wetbacks" and teasing them for "being poorly dressed, not speaking mainstream English, and for not fitting in with the already-established social cliques."[26]

The harshness of anti-immigrant hostility and hatred can inflict emotional scars on immigrants, including both first-generation immigrants and their second-generation children. Gina Núñez describes the emotional toll that racialized discrimination took on her and her family as immigrants. Her comments bear quoting at length.

> Outside of the classroom, my most painful childhood memory is when Anglo [white] children in New Mexico threw rocks at my siblings and me while we stood in line at a bus stop. As they bombarded us with stones, the boys shouted racial epithets and suggested that we go back to where we came from. At the time, I did not fully comprehend these racialized attitudes and hatred-filled behaviors; after all, my siblings and I were "Americans," born in the states of Arizona and California. My shameful memory of this event was not so much my inability to defend myself and my siblings (at the time we were outnumbered) but it was facing my parents with welts on my face and body, and profound scars on my wounded heart.... I did not have an explanation for showing up at home with bruises and a heart full of sadness. I felt I had dishonored my family by not being strong enough to defend my siblings and myself. [My father] expressed pain, anger, and disappointment at such maltreatment. I got my first lesson from my father about our position as Mexican farmworkers in the United States: "There is no shame in doing what we do for a living; we are the ones who work hard to put food on people's tables all over the world," he said. For proof, my father pulled out a check stub with his wages, tax contributions, and Social Security deductions. He asked me to take his check stub to school to help me prove his case. My father, who was a green card holder like my mother, took pride in his work. I took his paycheck stub to school but never showed it to anyone; I doubted that school-age bullies with rocks at a bus stop would understand this point or would care to see a piece of paper.[27]

The pain in these lines expresses the emotional challenges, and at times physical harm, that both first- and sometimes second-generation immigrants in America face at the hands of those who hold ethnocentric and/or racist beliefs. Aside from its raw hatred, the hostility of these children displays a variety of stereotypes and distorted visions likely learned at home, from the media, or from other children at school.[28] The racial epithets conflate and confuse race and ethnicity. To be Mexican American is to have an ethnicity and an ethnic heritage. Despite common assumptions to the contrary, ethnicity is at times related but is *not* equivalent to race. Those of Mexican cultural origin in the United States, like other Latinas/Latinos, are of mixed racial origin that includes in various combinations white European, indigenous, and (whether Latinas/Latinos commonly acknowledge it or not) black racial heritage. One challenge immigrants face in balancing their multiple ethnic identities is coping with how others tend to read ethnic identification either as racial identity and/or as national identity that is mutually exclusive with American identity.

This second error can also be seen in the assault on Gina Núñez and her family in which ethnicity and nationality are conflated in the assumption that she and her siblings do not belong in the United States. In a diverse society such as the United States, "ethnicity" refers to cultural group identity. "Nationality" or "national group membership," in contrast, refers to membership in and identification with a political regime and its laws and governing structures. In the case of Jayne Ifekwunigwe's father, his ethnicity is Igbo and his nationality is Nigerian to the extent that he had been a citizen of the political state of Nigeria. To have a national identity is to have a political identity that involves commitment to and identification with the political system of a given nation state. Voluntary immigrants to America are likely to gain a national identity with the United States as a liberal constitutional democracy, an identity that is arguably most often reflected in their commitment to living in a new nation-state.

Consequently, because ethnicity and nationality are distinct, there are significant numbers of immigrants from El Salvador, Guatemala, the Dominican Republic, Mexico, and other nation-states who continue to have ethnic identities with their heritage cultures but who do not have significant ongoing commitments to the political systems of the nation-states they have left behind. In some cases, first-generation immigrants are harshly critical of the political systems of their sending states, even if they maintain significant transnational practices.[29] For them, their immigrant ethnic identities are about local and familial heritage and are distinct from national or political identities and commitments. Consequently, the periodic visits of the Núñez family to Guerrero and their continued use of the Spanish language, for example, are confused by others as ongoing political commitments to Mexico, when they are in fact reflections of emotional bonds to a hometown where they no longer live and a lasting love and commitment to their relationships with Spanish-speaking family members who still live in that town of origin. In this sense Mr. and Mrs. Núñez are not much different from many other adult Americans who move away from their hometowns for work and never move back but continue to make return visits and to have emotional bonds to their place of origin and ongoing relationships with people who remain there. In balancing their multiple ethnic identities, however, many immigrants find that nonimmigrants regard their ethnic identities and relationship to their family and birthplace abroad as a betrayal of their American national identity.

The frustrations that immigrants feel at this assumption are understandable, for by confusing ethnic and national identities—partly on the basis of outdated assimilationist assumptions—Americans often label emotional ties that are important to immigrants as negative despite the fact that similar ties are something that other Americans often have themselves and equally value. If ethnic and national identities are distinct, then it should be no surprise that lasting commitments to heritage cultures and languages are common among first-generation immigrants who acculturate in and commit themselves to living in America. The expectation that immigrants will quickly shed their familial ties, languages, and memories is similar to expecting first-year college students new to campus to quickly forget where they have come from and to ignore and disregard the loved ones that they have left behind as a requirement for gaining a college degree.

If it is not reasonable to expect this conduct in first-year college students, it is likewise unreasonable to expect it of immigrants. Yet, this is exactly the kind of expectation that many immigrants face as they attempt to balance their multiple ethnic identities. Those who expect immigrants to forget their heritage lands and families either seem to desire immigrants to be like themselves or fail to understand that immigrants, like everyone else, have multiple identities that reflect the specific socialization that they have received in the course of their lives. On this understanding of others and ourselves, it is easy to see why immigrant life is often a complex intersection of multiple cultures, religions, and other social groupings.

A similar set of misunderstandings surrounds participation in immigrant enclaves. As indicated briefly above, immigrant enclaves can play a positive role in immigrant incorporation by providing spaces of coethnic support and familiarity and a shelter from anti-immigrant hostility that may be encountered in the broader American society. Such enclaves can support economic mobility among immigrants. Moreover, as studies indicate, the presence of immigrant enclaves in America does not prevent full bilingual and bicultural accultura-tion among the vast majority of second-generation immigrants, nor do enclaves necessarily prevent the drift toward English monolingualism and monocultural assimilation among most second- and third-generation immigrants.[30] Yet, immi-grants who participate in immigrant enclaves are often charged with sequester-ing themselves from the broader society. This is so despite there being much evidence to suggest that immigrant enclaves are, on the whole, positive systems of social and economic support for incorporation. Moreover, just as we would not blame first-year college students for venturing little beyond first-year circles where they may suffer undue hostility beyond those circles, there is little reason to blame those who rely on immigrant enclaves for safe spaces in which they are less likely to be subject to discrimination or racism.

The fact is, however, that immigrants who attempt to balance or integrate their multiple ethnic identifications in America often face hatred, hostility, and misunderstanding from others who wish to oversimplify a complex world. In America—the land of the free—Gina Núñez, like so many other children of immigrants, can be shouted at and told to "go back where she came from" when she was in fact born in California. Can Gina Núñez's place of belonging and that of her immigrant parents be read on her body by strangers on the street? The answer, of course, is no. But ironically, the fact that such indefensible assumptions are often directed at immigrants in America should also not be surprising given America's history. To a large extent, the type of hateful binary simplifications that were shouted at Gina Núñez and her family are readably recognizable as products of the ongoing historical legacy of racial hierarchies and conflict in America. In that legacy, all people in America are divided into two groups along what is known as "the color line." The color line is a sharp binary division between black and white, and children of all races in America learn this legacy as they grow up in mainstream society.

The ongoing construction of the American color line complicates the efforts of immigrants to acculturate and balance their ethnic identities because immigrants who arrive in America will inevitably find themselves positioned by others along the color line. Those who consider American national identity to necessarily be associated with the "white" side of the color line will tend to question the "Americanness" of immigrants who they perceive to be on the "black" side of the color line, such as the darker-skinned members of the Núñez family. On the assumption that Americanness is akin to whiteness, any immigrant who appears nonwhite may be assumed to be not American. In practice, such questioning is often based on stereotyping by phenotype alone without inquiry into an immigrant's place of birth or cultural or national identities. Thus, as Mia Tuan has argued in her book *Forever Foreigners or Honorary Whites?*, many first-generation Asian immigrants, as well as second- and third-generation Asian immigrants, are still treated as foreigners in America despite having lived in the United States for many years or being native-born U.S. citizens.[30a] The racialization of immigrants along the American color line thus adds a complicating factor to the challenges that immigrants face as they attempt to balance their multiple ethnic identities.

The complications that face first-generation immigrants as they balance and negotiate their multiple identities can take a somewhat different form for second-generation immigrants and may vary among members of the second generation. For some second-generation immigrants, such as Gina Núñez who grew up in a country that is new to her parents but commonplace to her, the claim that she does not belong in the nation of her birth on the basis of her physical appearance can be baffling and deeply unsettling to one's sense of self. One can imagine, however, that Gina's sister Betty—who is blond, fair-skinned, and named after Gerald Ford's wife—would not experience the same kind of treatment as Gina were Betty alone at the bus stop. Thus, given binary patterns of racialization in America, the immigrant experience of balancing multiple ethnic identities as second-generation Americans could vary significantly between Gina and Betty on no other grounds than that the sisters vary in their hair and skin color.

Jayne Ifekwunigwe also refers to the influence of racial constructions on immigrant experience and orientation when she describes family conversations in which she and her elder brother are noted to have dark skin tone with their mother's features and her other two siblings are said to have light skin tone with their father's African features. Ifekwunigwe describes this family self-portrait as an example of the "archaic yet still omnipresent constructions of 'race' and color which are socially reproduced as Black African (self-) hatred and White European (self-) Supremacy."[31] Looking back, Ifekwunigwe recognizes how as a child these racial constructions shaped her choices of self-presentation and her disinterest in her heritage cultures. She writes that, growing up in a white suburb of Los Angeles, it was easy for "me (and my siblings) to celebrate my (our) 'White English bits' at the expense of my (our) Brown Guyanese and Black Nigerian identities."[32] When children of immigrants seek to negotiate the American color line and racism by having no interest in their heritage cultures and languages, the lives and interests of first-generation immigrants and their children can diverge significantly. Rapid and deep cultural divergence, in turn, can make intergenerational communication difficult and potentially negatively affect first-generation efforts to successfully offer guidance to their children.

Immigration and the Challenges of Parent–Child Relationships

This factor of racialization of new immigrants relates to the *fifth challenge* that first-generation immigrants face, which is the challenge of having their own cumulative cultural experiences and knowledge potentially differ widely from those of their children. In some cases, such as Jayne Ifekwunigwe's father, first-generation immigrants seek to curb the rapid assimilation of their children, yet the weight of mainstream American socialization overwhelms their efforts. Other parents seek to promote balanced biculturalism and bilingualism in their second-generation children through slow-paced acculturation. Researchers consider this method of slow acculturation toward bilingualism and biculturalism to be the best for preserving intergenerational harmony and cooperation in immigrant families.[33] When this is possible, as it was in the Núñez family, cooperation and dialogue among immigrant parents and their children can exist even when the experiences of parents and children differ significantly. In the Núñez family, for example, as a child it was Gina's job to help her mother navigate southern California highways and to help ensure that they did not lose their way on the busy freeway system. This job was perhaps given to Gina on the basis of her bilingual skills. It would have been difficult for her to perform the task if she and her mother did not share a common level of fluency in at least one language. This example suggests the value of bilingualism among second-generation immigrant children for the purposes of both quality parenting and intergenerational cooperation and understanding.

As a consequence of the fact that their children are likely to have different cultural groundings from their own, first-generation immigrants often face challenges in cultivating a relationship with their own children. Ultimately, those parent–child relationships are also likely to be shaped by the varying degrees of acceptance that different generations experience in America or elsewhere. One first-generation immigrant from Nigeria to England interviewed by Jayne Ifekwunigwe contrasted her own immigrant experience with that of her biracial children. As an immigrant from Africa in England, she felt that in England "you're never completely invisible or at home, you are always a bit of a stranger.... My children are all English, and I still call myself a stranger."[34] In these words this immigrant mother articulates how she and her children have quite different immigrant experiences even within the same culture. This factor will shape many aspects of balancing multiple identities. In contrast to first-generation immigrants, for example, second-generation children will not need to gain a new national identity. As second-generation immigrants, they will only have firsthand knowledge of the political system into which they were born and raised.

Border Crossing and Coping with Multiple Marginalization

This last quotation also points to the *sixth challenge* that faces first-generation immigrants, which is to learn to cope with an ongoing sense of marginalization not only in their adopted homelands but also in the other cultures with which they identify. Many first-generation immigrants never feel a sense of belonging in their adopted homelands because others typically respond to them as if they are foreigners, even if they have been settled in the society for a long while. As indicated above, for many first-generation immigrants this treatment as being "forever foreigners" becomes an ongoing part of what it means to live between two or more worlds. Yet, many first- and even racialized second-generation immigrants long for a sense of belonging in which they will not be treated by others as strangers in lands that they consider their home.

This longing for belonging can be an intense and influential experience for some immigrants. As the immigrant mother quoted above puts it, "oh, I used to think maybe one could go to South America and just be able to walk down the street and not be a stranger—because of my appearance."[35] At the same time, she expresses moving beyond such longing through recognition of how the attitudes of those in England are changing such that first-generation immigrants have a greater potential to feel at home. She states, "[i]t's not so bad actually, there are places one could walk and not look out of place.... In many ways, it's getting better in that sense over here. I think Black people are more visible and more vocal. [And] you don't have to conform to any idea of a Black person any more, which is very nice."[36] In coping with this sixth challenge it is possible for immigrants to find hope in the possibility that prevailing attitudes toward racialized immigrants can always change.

Perhaps for first-generation immigrants in America similar changes will also come. In the meantime, many first-generation immigrants may not find it possible to experience America as a place of belonging. Rather, they may only find, in Ifekwunigwe's phrase, "scattered belongings" that are at times undercut by moments of marginality imposed on them by others who either do not understand immigrant experience or do not wish to accept it. From that perspective, an immigrant's own sense of commitment and belonging may be full and complete for various purposes and / or in specific contexts but also blended with other senses of belonging in ways that do not fit neatly together. This disjuncture between an immigrant's various identities and partial senses of belonging can create an inner critical distance from which to assess one's self and what others are saying. This sense of distance can be a resource for immigrants—a buffer between themselves and the judgments of others—as they cope with the marginalization produced by those who reject them and what they bring to the United States as a homeland.

Grappling with ongoing marginalization imposed on them by others is not easy for immigrants and varies in difficulty from day to day and context to context. As Jayne Ifekwunigwe remarks,

> [o]n an empowered day, I describe myself as a diaspora(s) daughter with multiple migratory and ancestral reference points in Nigeria, Ireland, England, Guyana and the United States. On a disempowered day, I am a nationless nomad who wanders from destination to destination in search of a singular site to name as home.[37]

Reflecting on her life and on the process of grappling with ongoing marginality, Gina Núñez holds out hope that first-generation immigrants and their children may find ways to reconcile a sense of belonging with their lives as border crossers. She writes,

> [t]hroughout my journey, I have grown to live, breathe, study, and represent the complexity of a life crossing borders.... I hold on to many places that for brief periods of time, held and shaped me along the way. I have reconciled living a life in between two nations, speaking two languages, belonging here and there, somewhere or perhaps nowhere.[37a]

In this description the experience of marginality itself becomes a mode of immigrant being—the only place left to immigrants when those around them do not consistently allow them to claim their homeland(s) as home.

Conclusion

Of the six existential challenges that first-generation immigrants in America face, three are produced by the reluctance in American society to accept immigrants and their children as belonging in America on the basis of obsolete notions of rapid assimilation. Thus, the question that determines much of immigrant experience today and for the future is "Will Americans in general allow immigrants to claim American identity along with the other multiple dimensions of themselves that make them who they are?" Immigrants to America hope for such acceptance. As Gina Núñez states, " I yearn to one day rejoice in the feeling of being rooted, as much as I yearn for the day in which other people in search of a homeland can one day move freely across borders."[38] Ultimately, it is that yearning that is perhaps the most common experience of immigrants in America—the yearning to be rooted in America as one's home and yet to be able to cross again freely in everyday life the multiple cultural borders that make up one's family heritage and oneself.

DISCUSSION QUESTIONS

1. What is assimilation and how does it differ from acculturation?
2. How does the color line affect first-generation immigrants in America?
3. What is a "border crosser"?
4. What are the six major challenges that first-generation immigrants face, with examples of each?
5. How would you compare and contrast the experiences of first- and second-generation immigrants?

Chapter 4

Immigration

Trends, Demographics, and Patterns of Political Incorporation

Jessica Lavariega Monforti

A young man, Miguel,[1] decides to leave his town in rural Mexico because the money he earns farming is no longer sufficient to provide for his family. He talks to friends about where he could go to find good, steady work opportunities and moves to the city to work for a manufacturing company that produces cable wiring for General Motors cars. He works twelve-hour shifts six days a week and is barely able to pay for his rent and food; he is unable to send much money to his parents to help support his younger siblings. He talks with friends who have been to el otro lado, the other side, to work in the United States. They claim that they earn enough in wages to live well in the United States and send money home to help their families. They encourage Miguel to go to the United States with them when they return. He borrows money from extended family members — enough money to pay for a bus ride to the northern border of Mexico, food, and a "coyote," or smuggler, to help him enter the United States without documents or inspection.

After a three-day bus ride to the northern Mexico border, he is nearly robbed and assaulted by Mexican authorities as he prepares to cross the Rio Grande and decides to attempt the crossing another day. He and two others decide to swim across the river. They strip down to their underclothes, put all of their belongings in a plastic bag, and begin to swim. One of the other men nearly drowns as he is struck by a tree branch that is moving along the river's current — the two others swim to save him and pull him to safety. Upon reaching the other side of the river, the three men quickly put on their shoes and run—jumping over and crouching underneath barbed-wire fences, sprinting across roads, keeping away from snakes, and escaping border control and immigration authorities—for almost four hours until they arrive at their destination in south Texas.

One of the men, the smuggler, leads them to what appears to be an abandoned shack. They are told to wait quietly for transportation to get them to la colonia, the neighborhood where they will live. They wait, but no transportation arrives. An elderly man enters the shack and tells them that la migra (immigration) is coming to search the premises and that they have to run. They run for about an hour; the sun has set and it is getting cold and dark. The two men jump into a garbage dumpster to hide and get out of the cold; they wait there for one full day before the smuggler finds them and transports them to the trailer park where they will live. They are greeted by the landlord of the trailer park, asked to pay one month's rent ($250 U.S.) in advance, and taken to their home—a 20-year-old trailer still on wheels with a single mattress and no running water. They ask their new neighbors about where they can find work and are told that there is a van that comes to la colonia every morning at about 5:00 a.m. to take workers to the fields to pick watermelons, cabbage, onions, cilantro, and so on. But the ride is not free; each worker pays for this transportation.

When there is enough work, Miguel works from 6:00 a.m. to 6:00 p.m. Monday through Saturday. When he is working full-time, he earns $100 to $200 weekly and is sometimes able to send money to his parents in Mexico. Miguel admits that he is depressed and lonely and wants to go home to be with his family, but he doesn't think he can do that until he earns enough money to repay the loans ($1,500 U.S.) that were given to him for his trip north and to travel back to Mexico ($1,000 U.S.). So when he talks to his family on the telephone, he tells them not to worry and that he is okay. He will send money when he can and he misses them. "Cuidense" he says. "No se preocupan."—"Take care of yourselves. Don't worry."

Introduction

Miguel's narrative is not uncommon. While the specific details of when, where, and how the migration occurred differ, many undocumented immigrants share similar experiences. Many come from rural or poverty-stricken areas in their home country. Many have attempted to migrate within their country, from a rural to an urban area or from one rural area to another, before deciding to migrate to the United States. Many believe that they will come to work and live in the United States temporarily, be able to improve their situation and that of their family at home, and return to their country-of-origin. Many see their migration as a tool of economic survival for themselves and their families, not economic advancement. However, complications arise—it is not that simple.

This chapter discusses some of those complications. It begins with a discussion of the concepts of citizenship, immigration, and political incorporation. Subsequent sections review contemporary immigration patterns and trends, clarify popular misconceptions about immigration and immigrants, and introduce recent congressional activity on immigration legislation.

Nuts and Bolts of Immigration and Citizenship

Citizenship has been a fluid, contested, and politically constructed concept throughout the history of the United States. Understanding this concept is important because it allows us to talk about who or what is defined as "legitimate" in the United States—it defines who is a full member of society and who is excluded from it. It was not until 1790 that Congress established the first naturalization law, which authorized free white persons who had lived in the United States for two years to become citizens; entry into the United States was virtually unlimited before that. Since then, immigration policy has vacillated between relatively open and nativist periods.

The U.S. Constitution does not define citizenship. However, there now exist three conceptions of citizenship in the United States which have been accepted through congressional legislation and federal codes. The first is *jus soli*, where a person is a citizen because he or she was born on U.S. soil.[2] The second is *jus sanguinis*—literally translated, "citizenship by blood." In this case, a person is a citizen because at least one of her or his parents is a U.S. citizen. Finally, a person who does not qualify within the given parameters of jus soli or jus sanguinis can go through the process of naturalization to become a U.S. citizen. *Naturalization* is the act whereby a person voluntarily and actively acquires a nationality which is not his or her nationality at birth.

In order to naturalize, a person must be admitted to the United States with a valid entry visa; have continuously resided in the United States for at least five years; be of good moral character; be able to speak, read, and write English; and have a working knowledge of civics. Naturalization applicants must also be fingerprinted and cleared by both a criminal background check and medical examination. Applicants must also take an oath of renunciation of their homeland and an oath of allegiance to the United States. A person who migrates to the United States without inspection or without a valid visa may not apply for naturalization while he or she resides within the borders of the United States.[3] Depending on the caseload of the U.S. Citizenship and Immigration Services (USCIS, formerly the Immigration and Naturalization Service [INS]) and the specific issues in each particular application, once all requirements have been met, the naturalization process can be completed in a minimum of two years for those who qualify. However, few cases are settled within this minimum time-line. The average naturalization case for a legal immigrant, from application filing to the granting of citizenship, is eight to nine years.[4]

Once citizenship is granted, immigrants receive the following rights: (1) the ability to vote, hold elected office (except president of the United States), and serve on a jury; (2) the ability to apply for and hold certain positions that require citizenship; (3) the ability to bring a spouse, unmarried children, and parents into the United States; (4) the ability to travel abroad for unrestricted periods of time; and (5) access to restricted federal programs such as financial aid for higher education.

It is important to note that not all immigrants who enter the United States are equal under the law. There are six categories of migrants: a refugee, an asylum-seeker, a nonimmigrant, an immigrant, a migrant with Temporary Protected Status, and an undocumented immigrant. A *refugee* is a person who is outside the United States and who seeks protection and entrance into the United States on the grounds that she or he fears persecution in the country of origin. Historically, the USCIS has defined acceptable forms of persecution to include the following areas: racial persecution, religious persecution, and persecution because of membership in a political or social group. According to the USCIS, 53,814 people were admitted to the United States as refugees in 2005 and the largest numbers of refugees came from Somalia, Laos, and Cuba.[5] An *asylum-seeker* is similar to a refugee, but the individual is already in the United States at the time of application for protection. This individual must prove to authorities that she or he is in danger if she or he were to return home. Refugee and asylum cases are difficult and often denied. For example, during the 2006 fiscal year, only 3.7% of all 27,492 asylum cases filed were approved (almost 70,000 are pending).[6] A *nonimmigrant* is an individual who temporarily enters the United States for a specific purpose such as business, study, temporary employment, or pleasure. Examples include international students and researchers. About half of all nonimmigrant visas are granted to applicants from four countries—the United Kingdom (4.5 million), Mexico (4.3 million), Japan (3.6 million), and Germany (1.4 million). Between 1985 and 2002, over 17 million nonimmigrant visas were granted by U.S. authorities; however, there has been a 15% decline in this area in the post-9/11 era.[7] Alternatively, *Temporary Protected Status* (TPS) is a different kind of conditional admission. In this case temporary immigration status is granted to eligible nationals of designated countries, or parts thereof, usually because of some crisis in the home country such as war or genocide. The authority to designate a country (or part thereof) for TPS and to extend and terminate TPS designations is held by the secretary of homeland security. Currently, only Burundi, El Salvador, Honduras, Liberia, Nicaragua, Somalia, and Sudan, or parts thereof, have been granted TPS.

In 2004 it was reported that there were nearly 300,000 Salvadorans, 82,000 Hondurans, and 4,300 Nicaraguans in the United States who had been granted TPS.[8] An *undocumented immigrant* is an individual who entered the United States without a visa or, more likely, a person who overstayed a valid visa. It is estimated that there are 11–12 million undocumented immigrants residing in the United States, of whom 60%-75% had a valid visa at one time. Finally, an *immigrant* is a foreign-born individual who is admitted to the United States with a visa and applies for and is given permission to reside in the United States as a lawful permanent resident.[9]

There are several types of categories through which an immigrant can request a visa. The most used category is *family-sponsored immigration*, where an individual who wants to migrate to the United States can have an immediate family member who is a legal permanent resident or U.S. citizen sponsor her or his petition for a visa. There is no ceiling on the number of visas allotted for immediate family members. The U.S. immigration system divides the family members eligible for sponsorship into two tiers. *Immediate relatives* of U.S. citizens—that is, spouses, unmarried minor children, and parents but not brothers and sisters or unmarried and married adult children—are admitted as their applications are processed. In recent years, more than 350,000 have immigrated per year. All other immigrants who come here through family sponsorship fall into the family preference system, which has been capped at 226,000 visas per year. Another category of visas is through *employment-based immigration*, which occurs in cases where U.S. employers sponsor individuals for specific positions due to a shortage in the labor market or because of the need for special skills. Currently, immigration laws allow a maximum of 140,000 employment-based visas to be granted annually.

Immigration based on the visa lottery is another option. A potential immigrant can win one of a number of visas offered to certain nations. The visa lottery, called the Diversity Visa Lottery Program, was created by the Immigration and Nationality Act of 1952. In its current form, the program allows for 50,000 immigrant visas, which are made available annually through a lottery to people who come from countries with low rates of immigration to the United States. These visas are not available for people who come from countries that have sent more than 50,000 immigrants to the United States in the past five years. The State Department's National Visa Center holds the lottery every year and chooses winners randomly from all qualified entries. Anyone who is selected under this lottery is given the opportunity to apply for permanent residence. If permanent residence is granted, then the individual is authorized to live and work permanently in the United States. He or she is also allowed to bring a spouse and any unmarried children under the age of 21 to the United States.

Contemporary Trends in Immigration

The arrival of newcomers to the United States touches every aspect of our society—its politics, economics, culture, and social relations. Therefore, this is an issue that should be thought about in a context that goes beyond the simple dichotomies of liberals and conservatives, Democrats and Republicans, citizens and noncitizens. We need to ask several questions: Who are immigrants today? Where do they come from? Where do they settle?

Today, more than 34 million of the 300 million people in the United States were born in another country—about 6 million immigrants have arrived since 2000. Of these, 59% came from Latin America, 23% from Asia, and 12% from Europe.[10] The most obvious difference between immigrants at the beginning and at the end of the twentieth century is their origins. Most immigrants around 1900 came from Italy, Austria-Hungary, Russia, Canada, and England. In fact, so many nineteenth-century immigrants came from Europe by ship that the U.S. government did not tabulate those who crossed into the United States from Mexico or Canada until 1908.[11] However, Mexico emerged as a significant contributor to U.S. immigration during the 1920s and today accounts for the greatest flow of immigrants entering the country. In terms of sending countries, the largest numbers of immigrants entering the U.S. today come from Mexico, followed by the Philippines, China, and India. As a result, the Latino and Asian populations of the United States are seeing relatively rapid growth.

Overall, slightly more than 1.1 million immigrants arrive in the United States each year. About 700,000 are legal permanent residents, with family-based admissions accounting for almost three-quarters of this flow. Refugees and other humanitarian admissions add another 100,000–150,000 each year, while undocumented immigration contributes about 200,000–300,000 net additions annually (less than 30% of the immigrant flow).[12] Thus, we see a change in the number of immigrants coming to the United States as well as changes in the demography of the newly arrived.

Historically, immigrants have been concentrated in just a few areas across the United States, such as New York, California, Florida, and Texas. The 1990s, however, marked the beginning of a new immigration trend in which the fastest growth in the foreign-born population began taking place in new regions—the Southeast, the Midwest, and Appalachia. To illustrate, between 1990 and 1999 the foreign-born populations of New York, California, New Jersey, Illinois, Texas, and Florida—the six largest immigrant-receiving states since 1980—grew on average by 30%. In contrast, states such as Minnesota, Iowa, Nebraska, Kansas, North Carolina, South Carolina, Kentucky, and Arkansas have seen their foreign-born populations grow at an average rate of 126% over the same ten-year period.[13] While the traditional immigrant-receiving states still have the largest absolute number of immigrants, small towns across the country are confronting the challenge of dealing justly and creatively with new immigrant populations. Some scholars hypothesize that this is the reason immigration became one of the hot-button issues in recent political discourse and campaigns.

Popular Misconceptions About Immigration and Immigrants

Immigration is an emotional issue, and many have reacted to immigration and immigrants with unsubstantiated charges about the negative effects they have on the U.S. economy and culture. Therefore, this section will identify and address popular misconceptions about immigration and immigrants, including issues concerning undocumented immigrants, the economic impacts of increased immigration, the children of immigrants, the laws and procedures involved with immigration, and the ability of immigrants to become part of the melting pot in the United States.

One of the most discussed concerns about immigration revolves around the status of immigrants. It is sometimes assumed that most immigrants, particularly those from Latin America, are undocumented. However, according to the Department of Homeland Security, around 75% of today's immigrants have legal permanent (immigrant) visas while 25% are undocumented.[14] Another related popular misconception is that **all** Mexican immigrants cross the U.S.–Mexican border illegally. The fact, however, is that more than a majority are in the United States legally. Among the undocumented immigrants from Mexico, approximately 60%–75% enter illegally while the remaining 25%–40% enter legally but subsequently overstay their visas or otherwise violate the terms of their admission.[15] The final misconception along this theme is that weak U.S. border enforcement has led to high rates of undocumented immigration. However, from 1986 to 1998 the Border Patrol's budget increased sixfold and the number of agents stationed on the southern border doubled to 8,500. In addition, the Border Patrol toughened its enforcement strategy, heavily fortifying typical urban entry points, such as San Diego, and pushing migrants into dangerous desert areas in hopes of deterring crossings. That the immigrant population doubled in that same period is not a sign of a weak border. Insufficient legal avenues for immigrants to enter the United States or regularize their visa status, compared with the number of jobs in need of workers, have significantly contributed to this current conundrum.[16] In other words, our laws and enforcement thereof, including the laws and practice surrounding immigrant employment, send contradictory messages to would-be migrants. We want the workers, but we don't want to let them into the country legally; so they come however they can. One illustration of this is a case from California. In September 2006, a severe labor shortage resulted in about 10,000 tons of pears being overripe and dumped because the crop could not be picked in time.[17] California farmers who have been hit hard by labor shortages said, "The biggest problem by far is the lack of skilled pickers—in some cases a labor shortage of as much as 50 percent to 75 percent." One California grower, Toni Scully, asked, "Do people want to maintain the high-quality food supply we have in this country?" She continued, "If they do, then they need to recognize that some agricultural areas need a way to get skilled workers, particularly from Mexico."[18]

On a related note, it is often assumed that most children of undocumented immigrants are also undocumented. In fact, two-thirds of all children with undocumented parents (about 3 million) are U.S.-born citizens who live in mixed-status families, where one parent is undocumented and another is a legal permanent resident or a U.S. citizen. Further, in 2000, only 1.5% of elementary school children (enrolled in kindergarten through fifth grade) and 3% of secondary schoolchildren (grades 6–12) residing in the United States were undocumented. Slightly higher shares—5% in elementary and 4% in secondary schools—had undocumented parents. Therefore, a small percentage of the children of undocumented parents fit into this category.[19]

Also, people are often unclear about the economic impacts of immigration to the United States. For example, one misconception is that immigrants do not pay taxes, particularly those who are undocumented. In fact, immigrants and their businesses contribute $162 billion in tax revenue to U.S. federal, state, and local governments.[20] Further, undocumented immigrants pay the same real estate taxes—whether they own homes or taxes are passed through to rental owners—and the same sales and other consumption taxes as everyone else. The majority of state and local costs of schooling and other services are funded by these taxes. Additionally, the U.S. Social Security Administration has estimated that three quarters of undocumented immigrants pay payroll taxes and that they contribute $6–$7 billion in Social Security funds annually that they will be unable to claim.[21] Further, in terms of income tax payments, a range of studies find that immigrants pay between $90 and $140 billion a year in federal, state, and local taxes.[22] In sum, while undocumented immigrants pay the same taxes as citizens, they do not enjoy many of the same benefits from those taxes as do citizens.

Apart from concerns about taxes, many Americans think that undocumented immigrants come to the United States to get welfare such as food stamps. Often ignored is the fact that undocumented immigrants are ineligible for welfare, food stamps, Medicaid, and most other public benefits—particularly since the passage of the 1996 welfare reforms.[23] And even prior to the 1996 changes, undocumented immigrants who are pregnant do not qualify for federal Medicaid, except in emergencies, labor, and delivery.[24] In all but four states (California, Missouri, New Jersey, and New York), undocumented immigrants do not qualify for prenatal care aid.[25] Moreover, studies show that undocumented men come to the United States almost exclusively to work, not for health-care benefits. In 2003, over 90% of undocumented men worked—a rate higher than that for U.S. citizens or legal immigrants.[26] Moreover, undocumented men are younger, less likely to be in school, and less likely to be retired than other men.[27]

The ratio of immigrant use of public benefits to the amount of taxes they pay is consistently favorable to the United States. In one estimate, immigrants earn about $240 billion a year, pay about $90 billion a year in taxes, and use about $5 billion in public benefits. Other data show that immigrant tax payments total $20–$30 billion more than the amount of government services they use.[28] According to the Urban Institute, in 1994 immigrants and refugees paid approximately $28 million more in taxes than they consumed in services.[29] Many undocumented immigrants pay more income tax than they owe because they are afraid to file and claim a refund. Despite higher poverty rates, immigrants use fewer public benefits than citizens and are less likely to become dependent on welfare. In fact, the National Academy of Sciences found that the average immigrant annually contributes $1,800 more in taxes than he or she receives in benefits. Over their lifetimes, immigrants and their children will each pay an average $80,000 more in taxes than they will receive in local, state, and federal benefits combined.

Another misconception concerning the economic impact of immigrants is that they send all of their money back to their home countries. As noted in the example above, many immigrants find that they need most of the money that they earn to pay rent and other expenses here in the United States. Most estimates show that $7–$8 of every $10 earned by an immigrant in the United States is spent in the areas in which they live, on consumer items and basic necessities.[30]

It is also said that immigrants are a drain on the U.S. economy and take jobs and opportunity away from American workers. However, the largest wave of immigration to the United States since the early 1900s coincided with our lowest national unemployment rate and fastest economic growth. Further, immigrants do not just take jobs—they also create them. While there has been no comprehensive study done of immigrant-owned businesses, we have countless examples. In Silicon Valley, California, companies begun by Chinese and Indian immigrants generated more than $19.5 billion in sales and nearly 73,000 jobs in 2000.[31] *Inc.* magazine reported in 1995 that 12% of the Inc.

500—the fastest-growing corporations in America—were companies started by immigrants. According to a 1997 report by the U.S. Census Bureau, Miami had 121,000 Hispanic-owned firms, which employed 128,000 people and generated receipts of $27 billion. More than half of these businesses were owned by Cuban exiles and their descendants; Cuban-owned firms accounted for more than half of the employees and receipts.[32] Moreover, at the state level it was recently reported that the Texas economy would have suffered without undocumented immigrants. "The absence of the estimated 1.4 million undocumented immigrants in Texas in fiscal 2005 would have been a loss to our gross state product of $17.7 billion," said Texas Comptroller Carole Keeton Strayhorn.[33]

The role of immigrant workers is also misconstrued by many people. During the 1990s, half of all new workers were foreign-born, filling gaps left by native-born workers at both the high- and low-skill ends of the spectrum. Immigrants fill jobs in key sectors and contribute to a thriving economy; the net benefit of immigration to the United States is nearly $10 billion annually. As Alan Greenspan once pointed out, 70% of immigrants arrive at prime working age.[34] That means the U.S. government and taxpayers have not spent a penny on their education or preparation, yet they are transplanted into our workforce and will contribute $500 billion toward our Social Security system over the next 20 years.[35]

It is important to note that immigrants do not increase unemployment among natives. A recent study by economists reported that it is likely that immigration opens up many job opportunities for natives by (1) expanding the demand for goods and services through their consumption; (2) contributing to output through the investment of savings they bring with them; (3) demonstrating high rates of entrepreneurship, which may lead to the creation of new jobs for U.S. workers; (4) filling vital niches at the low- and high-skilled ends of the labor market, thus creating subsidiary job opportunities for Americans; and (5) contributing to economies of scale in production and the growth of markets.[36] Economists believe that it is likely that immigration opens up many job opportunities for natives. Further, there is no such thing as a fixed number of jobs for which an increasing number of people compete; in fact, the number of jobs in America increased by 15 million between 1995 and 2000, according to the Bureau of Labor Statistics.[37] Between 2000 and 2010, more than 33 million new jobs that require only a little or moderate training, representing 58% of all new job openings, will be created in the United States, according to the Bureau of Labor Statistics.

Research on immigration's labor market consequences for minorities suggests little negative impact. In her study of immigration's impact on the wages and employment of black men, the Urban Institute's Maria E. Enchautegui concluded, "The results show that in the 1980s black men were not doing worse in areas of high immigration than in other areas and that their economic status in high-immigration areas did not deteriorate during that decade."[38] A National Academy of Science study, *The New Americans*, while finding that there may be some impact of immigration on some African Americans locally, concluded that "While some have suspected that blacks suffer disproportionately from the inflow of low skilled immigrants, none of the available evidence suggests that they have been particularly hard-hit on a national level."[39] Even in particular sectors of the economy, the evidence of a negative impact of immigrants on natives is limited. A review of studies by Passel and coworkers[40] found that "The majority find no more evidence of displacement than is revealed by the aggregate data. Even studies of more highly skilled occupations (e.g., registered nurses) find no strong evidence of displacement."

As the U.S. population ages, many skilled workers and professionals will retire, leaving gaps for employers. Meanwhile, as jobs in the skilled professions become more attractive, natives will continue the trend of gaining higher levels of education and abandoning lower-skilled jobs. (Today, less than 10% of native-born Americans have not completed high school.) That will create gaps at the lower end of the job market as the demand in health care, hospitality, and other service jobs increases as the U.S. population ages. Further, immigrants will help keep the labor pool from shrinking excessively as the baby boom generation retires. While countries in Europe and elsewhere will experience a shrinking pool of available workers, the United States, due to its openness to immigration, will continue healthy growth in its labor force and will reap the benefits of that growth. Federal Reserve Board Chair Alan Greenspan has stated that "Immigration, if we choose to expand it, could prove an even more potent antidote for slowing growth in the working-age population."[41]

The National Academy of Sciences concluded that "Over the long run an additional immigrant and all descendants would actually save the taxpayers $80,000."[42] States come out ahead. In congressional testimony in 1997, University of California, Berkeley, economist Ronald Lee, the principal author of the fiscal analysis in the National Academy of Sciences study, concluded that a dynamic analysis, with the appropriate assumptions, would likely show that 49 of the 50 states come out ahead fiscally from immigration, with California a close call.[43]

Most economists agree on immigration's benefits. In a poll of eminent economists in the mid-1980s and updated in 1990, 81% of the respondents said that, on balance, twentieth-century immigration has had a "very favorable" effect on U.S. economic growth.[44] Moreover, 56% of the economists polled said that more immigration would have the most favorable impact on the U.S. standard of living, while another 33% said that the current levels of immigration would have the most favorable impact.[45] However, exception is taken to this consensus by economist Jorge Borjas, who found that high-school dropouts were left with a wage loss of 5% over those two decades, some $1,200 a year, given increases in immigrant labor. To many economists as well as lay folk, Borjas's findings confirmed what seemed intuitive all along: Add to the supply of labor, and the price goes down.[46] While some economists concede that "immigrants may be depriving native dropouts of the scarcity value they might have enjoyed, at least in a historical sense, unskilled labor is not in surplus. America has become so educated that immigrants merely mitigate some of the decline in the home-grown unskilled population."[47]

The last major issue of contention and misunderstanding about immigration centers on the issues concerning the numbers and composition of contemporary immigrant populations and their ability and desire to become part of U.S. society. It is common to hear people say that today's immigrants are different from those of a hundred years ago and that there are more of them now. On a recent episode of ABC's *This Week with David Brinkley*, Pat Buchanan referred to "five million illegal immigrants coming into this country," "one, two, three million, invading the Southwest," and finally "two million people walking across your border." In response, the *New Republic* pointed out that "the actual annual inflow of illegal migrants by air, sea and land is approximately 300,000 according to the Immigration and Naturalization Service." And while the percentage of the U.S. population that is foreign-born now stands at 11.5%, in the early twentieth century it was approximately 15%. The number of immigrants living in the United States remains relatively small as a percentage of the total population.[48] The annual rate of legal immigration today is low by historical measures. Only three legal immigrants per 1,000 U.S. residents enter the United States each year compared to thirteen immigrants per 1,000 in 1913.[48a] The 2000 Census found that 22% of U.S. counties lost population between 1990 and 2000. Rather than "overrunning" America, immigrants tend to help revitalize demographically declining areas of the country, most notably urban centers.[49]

Similar to accusations about today's immigrants, those of a hundred years ago initially often settled in monoethnic neighborhoods, spoke their native languages, and built up newspapers and businesses that catered to their fellow émigrés. Little Italy in New York and Chinatown in San Francisco are examples of ethnic enclaves built by previous waves of immigrants that still exist today. They also experienced the discrimination that today's immigrants face and integrated within American culture at a similar rate. If we view history objectively, we remember that every new wave of immigrants has been met with suspicion and doubt and yet, ultimately, every past wave of immigrants has been vindicated and saluted.[50] The Irish, Polish, Japanese, and Italians were discriminated against because of their religious beliefs and, for the latter groups, their lack of English proficiency.

Some pundits also argue that immigrants do not want to learn English or become Americans. Within ten years of arrival, more than 75% of immigrants speak English well; moreover, demand for English classes at the adult level far exceeds supply. More than 33% of immigrants are naturalized citizens; given increased immigration in the 1990s, this figure will rise as more legal permanent residents become eligible for naturalization in the coming years. The number of immigrants naturalizing spiked sharply after two events: enactment of immigration and welfare reform laws in 1996 and the terrorist attacks in 2001.[51]

Most immigrants identify with the United States of America. "Nearly 70 percent of foreign-born Hispanics say they identify more with the United States than with their country of origin," according to a New York Times/CBS News poll. Only 16%, including those here fewer than 5 years, said they identify more closely with their native country. Immigrants believe in the American Dream.[51a] A CNN/USA Today poll reported that more immigrants than natives believe that hard work and determination are the keys to success in America and that fewer immigrants than natives believe that immigrants should be encouraged to "maintain their own culture more strongly."[52] "A poll of Hispanics finds they are far more optimistic about life in the United States and their children's prospects than are non-Latinos," according to an August 2003 New York Times/CBS News poll.[53]

In San Diego, 90% of second-generation immigrant children speak English well or very well, according to a Johns Hopkins University study—in Miami, the figure is 99%.[54] Data from fiscal year 2000 indicate that 65% of immigrants over the age of five who speak a language other than English at home speak English "very well" or "well."[55] The children of immigrants, although bilingual, prefer English to their native tongue at astounding rates. In fact, the grandparents and parents of immigrant children have expressed some concern that their youngsters are assimilating too quickly. Immigrants learn English. Only 3% of long-term immigrants report not speaking English well, according to the National Academy of Sciences.[56] These data demonstrate that immigrants want to become proficient in English.

In other areas as well, immigrants show positive demographic characteristics. A Manhattan Institute report showed that immigrants are more likely than are the native-born to have intact families, to have a college degree, and to be employed and they are no more likely to commit crimes.[57] According to the New Immigrant Survey, which measures only legal immigrants, "The median years of schooling for the legal immigrants, 13 years, is a full one year higher than that of the U.S. native-born."[58]

Further, foreign-born expertise aids U.S. research and development. Foreign-born scientists and engineers make up 28% of all individuals with

PhDs in the United States engaged in research and development in science and engineering, helping to spur innovation.[59] Immigrant entrepreneurs create jobs for U.S. and foreign workers, and foreign-born students allow many U.S. graduate programs to keep their doors open because these students pay out-of-state tuition. Foreign students and their dependents contributed more than $12.85 billion to the U.S. economy during the 2002–2003 academic year, according to a conservative estimate by the Association of International Educators.[60] Further, according to Allan E. Goodman, president and CEO of the Institute of International Education, "International educational exchange has never been more important for the United States. Foreign students bring intellectual, economic and cultural benefits to our campuses and communities."[61] However, international student enrollment growth has been in decline as a result of delays and denials pertaining to visas in the post-9/11 era. In turn, U.S. graduate programs have been adversely affected. Countries such as Canada, Australia, New Zealand, and Great Britain are competing more fiercely and successfully than ever before for foreign students in the hopes of supplanting the United States from its position as the preferred destination for international students.

Finally, our understanding of the meaning of American patriotism would not be complete without considering the pride and commitment immigrants demonstrate on behalf of the United States. According to the U.S. Department of Defense, more than 60,000 immigrants serve on active duty in the U.S. armed forces, nearly 5% of all enlisted personnel on active duty overall and nearly 7% of U.S. Navy enlisted personnel.[62] Historically, immigrants have made significant contributions to the defense of America. More than 20% of the recipients of the Congressional Medal of Honor in U.S. wars have been immigrants.[63] Approximately 500,000 immigrants fought in the Union Army during the Civil War. A special regimental combat team made up of the sons of Japanese immigrants was the most decorated of its size during World War II. Further, major U.S. weapons, such as a more advanced ironclad ship, the submarine, the helicopter, and the atomic and hydrogen bombs, were developed by immigrants.

On July 3, 2002, President Bush recognized the recent contributions of immigrants in the U.S. armed forces by signing an executive order that provided for "expedited naturalization" of noncitizen men and women serving on active duty since September 11, 2001. The order granted some 15,000 members of the U.S. military who served fewer than three years the right to apply for expedited citizenship in recognition of their service. This follows a pattern of recognition of the military service of immigrants from previous conflicts. After the passage of Section 329 of the Immigration and Nationality Act, 143,000 noncitizen military participants in World Wars I and II and 31,000 members of the U.S. military who fought during the Korean

War became naturalized American citizens, according to White House statistics.[64] At a time when Americans value patriotism more than ever, immigrants demonstrate that they are a part of this spirit through their service in the military. Paul Bucha, president of the Congressional Medal of Honor Society, has stated, "I put to you that there is a standard by which to judge whether America is correct to maintain a generous legal immigration policy: Have immigrants and their children and grandchildren been willing to fight and die for the United States of America? The answer right up to the present day remains a resounding 'yes.' "[65]

Recent Legal Changes

Legislative change in immigration policy is as inevitable as the ever-changing economic and political climate of the United States. There have been more than ten major changes in the area of immigration policy since the mid-1990s. This section reviews some of these major changes and discusses the impact of each. For example, in 1996 the Illegal Immigration Reform and Immigrant Responsibility Act was passed by Congress. This legislation created a pilot project for telephone verification of the migration status of potential workers and bolstered the Border Patrol by adding guards and barriers in high-traffic areas. As a result, the Border Patrol is now the largest federal law enforcement agency in the country.

In the same year Congress approved the 1996 Anti-Terrorism and Effective Death Penalty Act. This act states that members of terrorist organizations cannot seek asylum in the United States and allowed for faster deportation for nonviolent crimes, including crimes committed years ago. This policy enabled state and local police to arrest illegal immigrants. While the Supreme Court has ruled that immigration officials cannot hold migrants indefinitely, it has failed to say exactly how long is acceptable. This legislation, therefore, has contributed to the ambiguity concerning the rights of noncitizens in the areas of questioning by authorities, coercion, and so on. One specific illustration of this is that immigrants claiming political asylum remain in legal "limbo" until their cases are decided, which can result in years of detention—and will likely now be worse for those from "questionable" nations.

The 2001 Patriot Act also impacted immigration policy as it provided unprecedented new powers to the U.S. attorney general to detain noncitizens certified as a threat to national security. While on its face this change in policy seems innocuous, the act does not provide guidance on what process the attorney general must follow in making and reviewing the decision to certify an individual as a suspected terrorist. The law fails to provide guidance to the courts on what evidence they should consider in assessing the reasonableness of the attorney general's decision during the process of judicial review. Further, the act is ambiguous on the question of whether detainees will have access to the evidence on which such decisions are based and the standards for review of such evidence. Finally, the sunset provisions do not apply to the detention provisions and therefore do not need to be readdressed in the future.

In 2002 Congress passed the Enhanced Border Security and Visa Entry Reform Act. Major provisions of the act led to changes in enforcement and the processes of visa approval. For example the act required the foreign student–tracking system to track the acceptance of aliens by educational institutions, the issuance of visas to the aliens, and other details regarding foreign students. It also barred nationals of countries that are state sponsors of terrorism from receiving temporary visas unless they are determined not to pose a threat to U.S. national security. The act authorized an additional 200 inspectors and 200 investigators at the INS for each of the fiscal years 2003 through 2006; increased the pay and training of INS personnel, including Border Patrol agents; and authorized $150 million for improved border control technology. However, despite a request for extension by the Bush administration, in 2002 Congress voted down the renewal of Section 245i—which would have continued for the allowance of insufficiently documented immigrants to stay in the United States while filing required paperwork to gain legal status. While Section 245i was not an amnesty program, a person who could be approved by immigration authorities on a petition (by a family member or by an employer) could have filed an application for a resident card inside the United States, even if she or he was in the United States without any permission to enter or with an expired permit.

In 2003, all activities of the INS were transferred to the Department of Homeland Security. Shortly following this development the INS was dismantled and the USCIS was created. This transition was more significant than a simple name change: Administrative processes and policy implementation patterns were altered significantly. Despite the shift to include security in the national immigration debate, and therefore various shifts in policy, no security expert since September 11, 2001, has said that restrictive immigration measures would have prevented the terrorist attacks—rather, they have stated that the key is effective use of good intelligence. It is important to keep in mind that most of the 9/11 hijackers were in the United States on legal visas. Further, since 9/11 the myriad measures targeting immigrants in the name of national security have netted no terrorism prosecutions. In fact, some say that several of these measures could have the opposite effect and actually make us less safe as targeted communities of immigrants are afraid to come forward with information.[66]

The discussion of contemporary legislative changes demonstrates the rapid, impactful, and often confusing nature of immigration policy in the United States. It is important to keep in mind that it is generally agreed that U.S. immigration policy is governed by five broad goals: (1) the social goal of family unification, (2) the economic goal of increasing U.S. productivity and standard of living, (3) the cultural goal of promoting diversity, (4) the moral goal of promoting human rights, and (5) the national and economic security goal of preventing illegal immigration. Critiques of immigration often overlook the noneconomic goals.

The policy context encompasses not just the nation's immigration policies, which determine who comes and in what numbers, but also the nation's immigrant policies (the federal, state, and local policies that influence the integration of immigrants after they have arrived). U.S. immigration policy is set by the federal government and has been both inclusive and well-defined. U.S. immigrant policy, by contrast, is made up of scattered, unlinked provisions and programs that fall, largely by default, to state and local governments.

Public Opinion About Immigration and Pending Immigration Legislation

Throughout 2005 and 2006, numerous polls have been conducted across the United States on the topic of immigration, and their results have been remarkably consistent. "Americans continue to take pride in the United States' heritage as a nation of immigrants."[67] In "Immigrant Nation," Jacoby reports that while many people are uneasy about the current influx of foreigners, "between two-thirds and three-quarters in every major poll...would like to see Congress address the problem [of immigration] with a combination of tougher enforcement and earned citizenship for the estimated 12 million illegal immigrants already living and working here."[68] While public opinion concerning immigration seems clear, gridlock has been the rule on the issue in Congress.

Most recently the immigration debate has focused on two major pieces of legislation written in 2005, one originating in the U.S. House of Representatives and the other originating in the U.S. Senate. HR 4437, sponsored by Representative F. James Sensenbrenner (R-WI)—also called the Border Protection, Antiterrorism, and Illegal Immigration Control Act of 2005—proposed several sweeping changes to immigration policy. For example, it intended to criminalize organizations and individuals assisting undocumented immigrants, criminalize undocumented immigration status, grant state and local law enforcement agencies "inherent authority" to enforce immigration laws, further the erosion of due process for noncitizens, and expand the detention of immigrants. Among other changes, the bill also proposed construction of a 700-mile fence along the U.S.–Mexican border. In December 2005, the House approved the bill by a vote of 239 to 182. While the bill failed to gain approval in the U.S. Senate, it did spark major debate and political activism surrounding immigration policy. Millions of people across the country protested the legislation at rallies, demonstrations, and marches and through boycotts. For example, on May 1, 2006, "A Day Without Immigrants" was organized across the country, where immigrants and those who opposed the bill were encouraged to stay home from work and school and refrain from making any purchases. Massive marches were held across the United States, with more than a million participants. According to reports by the Associated Press, the economy was impacted by these events as several major companies closed for the day or worked at limited capacity.[69] For example, Tyson Foods closed a dozen plants, Perdue Farms closed eight of fourteen chicken plants, Goya Foods suspended delivery everywhere except Florida, and some restaurants operated by McDonald's Corp. worked with limited crews. The long-term impact of the response to the Sensenbrenner bill is yet to be determined.

Senate bill S2611, entitled the Comprehensive Immigration Reform bill, was sponsored by Arlen Specter (R-PA). The bill was intended to require new investment in border security and technology but to allow employers to hire foreigners under a temporary visa program if they can prove they are unable to hire American workers for the same job. Under this bill, temporary visa-holders would be able to change jobs and immigrants could apply to stay in the United States. These programs would require the issuance of tamper-proof identity documents and would allow undocumented immigrants already here to regularize their status. However, these immigrants would have to go to the end of the line, and only after paying a hefty fine, staying employed for a prescribed period, and paying back taxes could they be eligible for regularization of their status. In May 2006, the bill passed the Senate by a vote of 62–36, but it died in the House of Representatives.

As the comprehensive House and Senate bills failed to become law, some legislators have decided to change their strategy in this policy area by sponsoring and supporting narrower bills. One example of this strategy is the Secure Fence Act of 2006 (HR 6061), which was sponsored by Representative Peter King (R-NY). This law directs the secretary of homeland security to take appropriate actions to achieve operational control over U.S. international land and maritime borders. This legislation was passed by both houses of Congress in September 2006 and amends the Illegal Immigration Reform and Immigration Responsibility Act of 1996 to direct the secretary to provide at least two layers of reinforced fencing as well as additional physical barriers, roads, lighting, cameras, and sensors extending 700–800 miles across the U.S.–Mexican border.[70] To date, no funding for this project has been appropriated by Congress.

While we cannot predict the future of immigration policy, some scholars argue that the future of the contemporary immigration debate will change with partisan shifts in Washington, D.C. The Democrats retook control of the Congress in January 2007 for the first time in twelve years, and if they are able to maintain this position of power some are hopeful that progressive immigration reform will be made. Other scholars argue that the results of the 2006 midterm elections will not be enough to change the discourse, and still others point to the changes of the mid-1990s, during the Democratic administration of President Bill Clinton, and say that neither Democrats nor Republicans are immigrant-friendly or looking for a positive solution to problems of the economy and security as they relate to immigration.

Conclusions: Immigration, Citizenship, and Security Issues

Immigration is emerging as a pivotal issue—like race, taxes, and crime—that defines political conflict over the basic values of our society. It is an issue that evokes cultural, religious, and economic anxieties; concerns about the preservation of natural and public resources; and even fears of personal safety. After years of comparative obscurity, pressures are mounting again for immigration policy reform. As public debate intensifies, it is characterized increasingly by disagreement over facts as well as policy. Agreement about facts does not imply policy agreement. But a generally accepted factual base and framework for thinking about immigration issues can provide a common starting point from which to assess different policy alternatives.

One ethnic group or race has not defined the cultural heritage of the United States. Nor is this country reserved for any one ethnic group—although some have often tried to claim it to the exclusion of others. Historically, the United States is a nation of immigrants. With the exception of Native Americans, most Americans are in this country as voluntary or involuntary descendants of immigrants, with ancestors coming from every part of the globe; all have shaped and contributed to the development of this country. Therefore, the importance of allowing people to make better lives for themselves and their descendants, as well as continuing to make important contributions to the progress of the United States, should be understood. While most citizens seem to agree with these premises, the challenge is for Congress and the president to translate these ideas into legislation that will address the systematic and individual-level concerns regarding the nation's immigration policy.

DISCUSSION QUESTIONS

1. Some people argue that all undocumented immigrants should be arrested and deported, while others argue that each case is unique and should be evaluated on its own merits. In Miguel's case described above, what do you think is the best course of action?
2. In the past, most immigrants came to the United States from Europe, and today most immigrants come from Asia and Latin America. Why have we seen this change in contemporary times? What impact do you think this shift has on the United States?
3. Public opinion regarding immigrants and immigration policy has ebbed and flowed over time. What factors drive public attitudes about immigration and immigration legislation today?
4. In this chapter, many misconceptions about immigration and immigrants were addressed. Why do these misconceptions exist? How can we be better informed, as voters and as residents, so that misinformation plays less of a role in our beliefs and decision making about immigration?
5. Debate whether immigration to the United States should be considered a right or a privilege.

Major Legislative Milestones in U.S. Immigration History
Chinese Exclusion Act (1882)
- Suspends immigration of Chinese laborers for 10 years
- Bars Chinese naturalization
- Provides for deportation of Chinese illegally in United States

Immigration Act of 1891
- First comprehensive law for national control of immigration
- Establishes Bureau of Immigration under Treasury
- Directs deportation of aliens unlawfully in country

Immigration and Naturalization Act of 1924
- Imposes first permanent numerical limit on immigration
- Establishes the national origins quota system, which resulted in biased admissions favoring northern and western Europeans

Immigration and Naturalization Act of June 27, 1952
- Continues national origins quota
- Quota for skilled aliens whose services are urgently needed

Immigration and Nationality Act Amendments of October 3, 1965
- Repeals national origins quotas
- Establishes seven-category preference system based on family unification and skills

- Sets 20,000 per country limit for Eastern Hemisphere
- Imposes ceiling on immigration from Western Hemisphere for the first time

Immigration and Nationality Act Amendments of 1976

- Extends 20,000 per country limits to Western Hemisphere

Refugee Act of 1980

- Sets up first permanent and systematic procedure for admitting refugees
- Removes refugees as a category from preference system
- Defines refugee according to international vs. ideological standards
- Establishes process of domestic resettlement
- Codifies asylum status

Immigration Reform and Control Act of 1986

- Institutes employer sanctions for knowingly hiring illegal aliens
- Creates legalization programs
- Increases border enforcement

Immigration Act of 1990

- Increases legal immigration ceilings by 40%
- Triples employment-based immigration, emphasizing skills
- Creates diversity admissions category
- Establishes temporary protected status for those in the United States jeopardized by armed conflict or natural disasters in their native countries

SOURCES: Maldwyn Allen Jones. 1992. *American Immigration*. University of Chicago Press.; U.S. Immigration and Naturalization Service, (1991), Statistical Yearbook of the Immigration and Naturalization Service. 1990. Washington, D.C. U.S. Government Printing Office.

Chapter 5

Bridging the Cultural Divide

Accommodating Religious Diversity

Jocelyn Sage Weiner
Clyde Wilcox

When the first Somali families began to trickle into the town of Lewiston, Maine, in the fall of 2001, their presence was noticeable immediately.[1] After all, Lewiston, a struggling mill town with a population of around 35,000, was 96% white and heavily Catholic. In Maine, if a family has not lived in the state for at least three generations, they are commonly viewed as being "from away"; and the black, Muslim Somali immigrants were some of the "furthest away" that Lewiston residents had ever seen.[2] The first Somalis came to Lewiston, lured by the town's good school system, safe streets free of drugs and crime, affordable and available housing, and generous social services. The positive reports sent back to family and friends living in other parts of the United States—predominantly in unsafe housing projects in Georgia—created a massive wave of immigration into Lewiston, with about 1,000 Somalis arriving within the first year. The city and state provided welfare to the new arrivals, public and subsidized housing was found, and many organizations sprung up to help acclimate the Somalis to their new environment, to provide them with jobs and English-language training, and to help their children adjust to their new schools. Yet, the strange dress, customs, and religion of the new arrivals kept the growing Somali community distinct from the locals, and competition over welfare resources and rumors about preferential treatment fueled confusion and resentment among many native Lewiston residents. The face of Lewiston, Maine, was changing, and people were not entirely sure how to respond.

The mayor of Lewiston tried to provide an answer to the situation. Without prior consultation, Mayor Laurier Raymond sent a letter to the Somali community, pleading with them to halt further immigration to the city. His claim that the city was "maxed out, financially, physically, and emotionally" set off a media frenzy that made Lewiston internationally known. The small town—known previously, if at all, for once producing a quarter of all the textiles in the United States and for hosting a 1965 title fight between Muhammad Ali and Sonny Liston which lasted one round—was now featured on major news networks as a symbol of a changing and conflicted America. The attention was fueled, in part, by the World Church of the Creator, a white supremacist group, which announced that the organization would hold a rally in Maine to support the citizens of Lewiston against the "Somali invasion."[3]

Lewiston residents were shocked at the amount of press coverage and chagrined that the white supremacist group was coming to their community, and they responded with typical insular strength and pragmatism. The general feeling was, "Yes, it's a problem, but it's our problem, and we're going to deal with it ourselves." In the wake of the letter, the Lewiston religious community organized a "community friendship walk," which began at the Calvary United Methodist Church on Sabattus Street and ended at the makeshift mosque on Lisbon Street. The marchers carried a banner depicting a Christian cross, a Muslim crescent, and a Jewish star, with the words "We Are All Friends" written across it. The Holy Trinity Greek Orthodox Church hosted an event with the governor of Maine and the Somali community, with Father Ted Toppses noting that the aim was "reversing the tide of hate and supporting the Somali community." The Many and One coalition, headed by prominent community and religious leaders, was formed to organize a prodiversity rally on the same day as the World Church gathering. Although no one knew for sure what would happen, on the day of the two rallies, around thirty people showed up to the white supremacist gathering, while over 4,000 attended the overflowing prodiversity rally at Bates College.[4] The people of Lewiston, Maine, had spoken—they were going to confront the new diversity on their own terms and work through it together.[5]

Introduction

In this chapter, we will discuss the religious diversity of the United States, in all its historical, social, and political implications. Beginning with a vignette from the November 2006 elections, we will look at the crucial role religion has played throughout this country's history. Next, we will investigate the religious diversity of today, contemplating whether the United States can best be described as a country dominated by its Judeo-Christian heritage; as one with several major traditions, such as black Protestants or Catholics; or as a kaleidoscope of religions, ranging from the hundred (or more) different Christian denominations to communities of Sikhs, Jains, and Zoroastrians.

How will the new diversity change the character of American public life? We will explore this question next, focusing on the intersection of religious diversity and public opinion, public policy, social interaction, and personal responses. We will look at how Americans respond to survey questions on minority religions and how these attitudes relate to public policy questions, such as the role of religion in schools and the ways in which religious groups should use their freedoms of expression and assembly. We will pay special attention to the effect of personal interactions on opinions and attitudes. Can we expect greater tolerance if more Americans meet people of diverse faiths, or will more conflict result?

Next, we will examine the role of political mobilization by the party system in the United States. How does religion affect American electoral politics and policy making? We will investigate how politicians and their parties have combined religious appeals with other salient issues in an effort to win the votes of particular communities. Last, we will speculate on the future of religious diversity in America and the ways in which political parties, local and federal government, and social communities will seek to address the changing landscape.

That such a small town as Lewiston could make international headlines and attract more than 4,000 people to a prodiversity rally shows the extent to which the new religious diversity has become so important to the political, social, and cultural fabric of the United States. This diversity is shaping and reshaping the landscape of thousands of communities in the United States, just like Lewiston. In each community experiencing this rapidly changing landscape, the question remains: How maxed out are we, financially, physically, and emotionally? Do we still have more to give to accommodate the new arrivals who are changing the way we look at our communities and ourselves? Sometimes we face decisions as stark as Lewiston's, with the choice of which rally—exclusionist or pluralist—we should attend. Yet, often these choices are muted gradations, and each decision along the way of how to respond to the new diversity carries with it implications for redefining America. How we navigate these choices will determine how melodious—or discordant—our national symphony will remain.

Religious Diversity in the United States: A Historical Perspective

When I raise my hand to take the oath on Swearing In Day, I will have the Bible in my other hand. I do not subscribe to using the Quran in any way.

Virginia Representative Virgil Goode

He has a lot to learn about Islam.

Minnesota Representative Keith Ellison, the first Muslim elected to the U.S. Congress

In November 2006, the voters of the Fifth Congressional District of Minnesota elected the nation's first Muslim representative to the U.S. House of Representatives, Keith Ellison. All members of Congress swear an oath to support the Constitution, and then in a later private ceremony with the Speaker they swear another oath, in which they generally place their hands on sacred scriptures of their faith tradition. The vast majority of members swear on the Christian Bible, but in the past, a few members have used no religious text, some have used Jewish scriptures, and some have used the Book of Mormon. Ellison's announcement that he would use the Quran for his oath provoked angry comments from a variety of sources, including one member of the U.S. Congress and a member of the United States Holocaust Memorial Council.

Virginia Representative Virgil Goode, in a letter to his constituents, warned that Ellison's election was a portent of things to come. "I fear that in the next century we will have many more Muslims in the United States if we do not adopt the strict immigration policies that I believe are necessary to preserve the values and beliefs traditional to the United States of America and to prevent our resources from being swamped." Goode's comments were quickly repudiated by many political leaders, including Virginia's senior Senator John Warner, who announced his support for Ellison's use of the Quran.[6] Other Republican lawmakers, however, found it prudent to duck comment.

The 2006 election of the first Muslim and the first two Buddhists to the U.S. Congress highlights the growing religious diversity in America, and Goode's comments highlight the backlash against that diversity. Over the past few decades, immigration has dramatically reshaped the contours of religious life in America's largest cities as well as in smaller communities. The 1965 change in immigration laws allowed for an influx of immigrants from all over the globe that has brought new religious communities, such as Muslims, Sikhs, and Hindus, to a nation with a Judeo-Christian tradition.[7] This diversity has radically changed the religious landscape of the United States, to the point where Eck[8] claims that we see "a new America."

Muslims, Hindus, Sikhs, Buddhists, and adherents of other faiths are now active participants in politics, public schools, and social life. Christian denominations are more ethnically diverse, and many Christian churches in major cities now house multiple congregations who worship in different languages. Thus, the religious face of America is changing as new religious groups increase in numbers and visibility and immigrant communities redefine the politics and culture of existing religious bodies.

Consider, for example, the suburbs of Washington, D.C. One study of a ten-mile stretch along New Hampshire Avenue in Montgomery County showed myriad religious institutions. This short stretch included a synagogue, a mosque, a Cambodian Buddhist temple, a Hindu temple, a Unitarian church, and 29

Christian churches, including three Catholic (one of which is Ukrainian), one Ukrainian Orthodox church, two Seventh-Day Adventist churches, two Jehovah's Witness Kingdom Halls, and 21 Protestant churches. The Protestant churches included mainline Protestants, such as Presbyterian, United Methodist, and Lutheran, as well as a large and growing nondenominational Bible church. Some of the Protestant and Catholic churches served particular immigrant communities, including the Choong-Moo Evangelical Church of Washington, the Sung Hwa Presbyterian Church, and the Our Lady of Vietnam Roman Catholic Church. These diverse religious groups joined forces to lobby government about zoning regulations affecting religious institutions, and congregations worked together to remove graffiti from a nearby mosque.[9]

Yet, a census of the actual churches in an area can undercount religious diversity, for in areas with high property values sometimes multiple congregations share the same building. One small Presbyterian church in Wheaton, Maryland (another D.C. suburb), houses four different congregations, speaking three different languages. Sunday services start with a worship service of relatively sedate, older, mostly white Presbyterians, followed by an affluent and younger congregation of Taiwanese Presbyterians who worship in Chinese. Later in the day, the New Baptist Creation Church, an African American congregation headed by a female pastor, meets for an exuberant service. In the late afternoon, the Iglesio Pentecostal Christo Rey (Christ the King Pentecostal Church) holds a Spanish-language service that attracts immigrants from El Salvador, Nicaragua, and Guatemala and often lasts more than four hours.[10]

There is no doubt that many American cities, large and small, have witnessed an increase in religious diversification in the past few decades. This wave of religious diversification is but the latest in a series that stretches to the founding of the United States. Each of these waves led to accommodation of religious diversity and further disestablishment of dominant religious traditions.[11] They also led to marked resistance and intolerance by those who wished to preserve the existing religious order.[12]

During the period of colonial settlement, a diverse collection of Christians settled different colonies. Baptists settled in Georgia, Puritans in Massachusetts, and Quakers in Pennsylvania. The early colonies meted out severe punishment to those who did not share their faith traditions. At the time of the founding and several decades beyond, some states had established churches and some had religious tests for public office. Yet, the national Constitution barred religious tests for national office, forbade an establishment of religion, and guaranteed the free exercise of religion. This recognition of the diversity of the new nation met with opposition, and there were efforts to amend the constitution to create an establishment of Protestantism.[13]

The first century of the new nation might be termed a "period of Protestant hegemony."[14] Yet, in the late 1800s and early 1900s, a wave of immigration brought large numbers of Catholics and Jews to the United States. This new diversity brought accommodation—leading national universities became less sectarian, and many states allowed Catholic churches to build schools and educate children outside of the public school system. This new diversity also brought backlash, however, as the Ku Klux Klan mobilized in the South and Midwest to oppose Catholics and Jews.[15] Moreover, some of the impetus for the campaign for Prohibition came from Protestants seeking to reestablish the primacy of their moral order.[16]

During this same period, Protestantism splintered, first through disagreements over slavery during the Civil War and then over disagreements over doctrine that led to the rise of fundamentalist and Pentecostal Christianity in the early 1900s.[17] New denominations formed and older denominations split. However, throughout the early twentieth century, the United States was numerically a Christian nation and culturally one that shared a Judeo-Christian tradition.

A number of scholars have argued that this Judeo-Christian consensus was essential to the formation and stability of American democracy.[18] Reichley[19] suggests that both Christianity and Judaism, through different paths, developed a set of theistic–humanist values that serve to underpin democracy. As he argues,

> Theistic-humanism solves the problem of balancing individual rights against social authority by rooting both in God's transcendent purpose, which is concerned for the social welfare of each human soul. This does not, of course, provide a formula for settling all, or even most, or even any social problem. But it does create a body of shared values through which problems can be mediated.[20]

By the 1960s, the United States was in the midst of a flowering of religious experimentation. Many younger Americans were attracted to spiritual experiences outside the established church boundaries. "Spiritual shoppers" experimented with elements of Hinduism, Buddhism, and Native American religions, often blending these faith traditions.[21] By the 1990s, a new wave of diversification was under way as Hindus, Sikhs, Buddhists, Muslims, and others built temples, held marches, and formed student associations in county high schools. By the beginning of the twenty-first century, Eck[22] declared, "Nowhere, even in today's world of mass migrations, is the sheer range of religious faith as wide as it is today in the United States."

The new diversity is seen in many facets of American politics and society. It is seen on the streets of Lewiston, Maine, where intermixed with boarded-up brick buildings from the mill-town days we see Somali grocery stores and restaurants and a makeshift mosque and Islamic center. It is seen in school policies throughout the United States, which now allow time for daily prayers and modifications of dress codes to accommodate Muslim head coverings and Sikh daggers.[23] And it is seen in government actions that range from the Postal Service issuing stamps representing the Chinese New Year, Kwanzaa, and Eid to the White House hosting an Iftaar dinner or a Diwali celebration. Courts, government agencies, and civil society organizations have also accommodated this growing diversity, such as protecting the rights of immigrant churches like the Church of the Lukami Babalu Aye (a Santerian congregation) or excusing pupils from physical education classes during Ramadan. However, the new religious diversity has also sparked a backlash, exemplified by the comments of Representative Goode (see earlier), which is connected to the broader mobilization against immigration.

Religious Diversity in the United States Today: The One, the Few, or the Many?

How diverse is American religion today? Religion in the United States today might be conceived, as once noted in a different context, as "the one, the two, or the many."[24] That is, it is possible to speak of a dominant religious tradition, of a relatively limited number of large religious groupings, or of myriad faiths.

The "one" would refer to the Christian majority or to the Judeo-Christian tradition. Observing the United States in the early 1800s, Alexis de Tocqueville wrote, "Christianity...reigns without obstacle, by universal consent."[25] His claim was echoed more recently by politicians such as Mississippi Governor Kirk Fordice, who proclaimed in 1992 that the United States was a Christian nation.[26]

By the numbers, Christians clearly constitute a sizable majority in the United States. Figure 5.1 shows the percentage of adherents to various religious traditions from the National Election Study in 2004.[27] This graph shows that 75% of Americans belong to Christian religious traditions, that another 15% are secular, and that all other faith traditions add to up 10%—including 3% who are listed as "unknown." In comparative perspective, the portion of practicing Christians in the United States is higher than in most European nations with official state churches. The percentage of Americans who fit the broader Judeo-Christian tradition is fully 78%—nearly as high as the percentage of Indians who are Hindu. Clearly, it is possible to describe America as having a single dominant religious tradition.

In other ways, we might conceive of the United States as composed of a "few" dominant religious traditions. Within the Judeo-Christian majority are important fissures, making it possible to say that all Americans belong to

Religious Families in the U.S., 2004

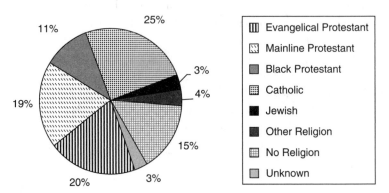

Figure 5.1. Religious families in the United States, 2004.

SOURCE: Adapted from Wald and Calhoun-Brown (see note 27). Data from the National Election Study 2004 (Steensland et al., see note 73).

a "minority religion."[28] White evangelical Protestants, white mainline Protestants, black Protestants, Catholics, and Jews all exert significant political and social influence; but they disagree on theology, moral rules, and politics. White Evangelical Protestants are now the largest segment and represent a growing share of the population; further, they have formed the core of the Republican base in recent elections and have pushed for conservative moral, economic, and foreign policy.[29] White mainline Protestants were once the political establishment in the United States, and they retain considerable resources but constitute a declining portion of the population: The six largest mainline Protestant denominations lost nearly 6 million members between 1965 and 1990.[30] These mainline Protestants are considerably more moderate on social policy, economics, and foreign policy and have moved to the Democratic Party in recent years.

Black Protestants attend mostly Evangelical churches, but they interpret Scriptures quite differently from white Evangelicals in many cases and, thus, are frequently on opposite sides of political arguments.[31] Black Protestants tend to be conservative on moral issues but to take liberal positions on economic and foreign policies and are a reliable part of the Democratic constituency.[32] Catholics are a growing share of the population and represent a tradition caught in the middle of political struggles. In recent years, the most devout younger Catholics have moved to the Republican Party, while the most devout older Catholics have remained staunch Democrats.[33] Finally, Jews are far more important to American culture and politics than their numbers would suggest and constitute a reliable liberal bloc within the Democratic Party.[34] Thus, the "few" would include white Evangelical Protestants, white mainline Protestants, black Protestants, Catholics, and Jews—groups that form shifting alliances on different moral and political issues.

Yet, in a very real sense, America is characterized by "many" religions. Among the Judeo-Christian majority are literally hundreds of denominations, with important distinctions. The combined 1990–2000 National Election Studies show more than 120 denominations with at least one member.[35] Further, individual congregations within these denominations may take positions that differ from the official doctrine, sometimes leading to official fissures and sometimes not.

Catholics comprise 25% of the population but have long been divided along ethnic lines, and today new Latino immigrants are joined by Catholics from Vietnam, Indonesia, and elsewhere. Latino Catholics now comprise 35% of adult Catholics and often take different positions on issues from other Catholics.[36]

Evangelical Protestants are divided theologically and along denominational lines, and many are now found in large megachurches outside of regular denominations. Evangelicals have also become more ethnically diverse, with immigrants from Africa and Asia, especially with large Latino Pentecostal congregations.[37] In the past, antagonism between contending theological communities had blocked political cooperation,[38] but today there is evidence that theological particularism has declined among Evangelicals.[39]

Mainline Protestants are also divided along denominational lines, although these seem less important today than a generation ago.[40] Mainline Protestants have also become more ethnically diverse, and, in this case, Nigerian Episcopalians and Korean Presbyterians may have different views on sociomoral issues facing the country. Mainline Protestant denominations are frequently internally divided on social issues—one salient example is the internal conflict experienced by the Episcopal, Presbyterian, and Methodist churches over the issue of gay rights in recent years.[41]

Jews are divided within their tradition into movements such as Ultra-Orthodox, Orthodox, Modern Orthodox, Conservative, Reform, and Reconstructionist, each with its own approach to social and political issues. Interdenominational debates on intermarriage, the role of women, and support for the state of Israel are prevalent. There is also intradenominational debate, such as the recent Conservative rabbinical ruling on the treatment of homosexual Jews. In December 2006, the Committee on Jewish Law and Standards, a group of Conservative rabbis that interprets Jewish law and traditions, sanctioned three different opinions on the matter: one that allows homosexual clergy and commitment ceremonies, albeit with a prohibition of sexual activity;

one that upholds the ban on homosexual clergy and commitment ceremonies; and one that calls for reparative therapy for homosexuals.[42] Each Conservative congregation chooses which opinion to follow, which highlights the divisions found within the denominational movement.

Among faiths outside of the Judeo-Christian majority, there are also key distinctions. American Muslims divide not only along Sunni/Shiite lines but also along lines of nationality.[43] In Fairfax County, Virginia, outside of Washington, D.C., the 150,000 Muslims include immigrants from Iran, Iraq, Pakistan, Afghanistan, India, Lebanon, Palestine, and other areas. These national divisions hinder a collective political voice for this growing religious minority.[44] Buddhists are also divided somewhat along lines of nationality and of doctrine, and the United States is home to a long list of other faiths, including Sikhs, Hindus, Zoroastrians, Wiccans, and others.[45]

The growth in the number of Americans whose faith tradition is non-Judeo-Christian has drawn the most attention and the greatest backlash. By the numbers, these faith traditions total fewer than 4% of Americans. Yet, the difference is felt, not in pure *numbers* but rather in the increased *visibility* of these religions.[46] There are substantial concentrations of these new religious groups in various cities and suburbs. New York City is home to some 450 mosques and other Islamic religious centers, as well as 13 private Islamic schools. There are sizable Hindu temples in Atlanta, Pittsburgh, Cleveland, Houston, Sacramento, Portland, Los Angeles, Chicago, New York, and Seattle and in smaller towns such as Littleton, Colorado, and Allentown, Pennsylvania.[47]

Moreover, the United States has a large population, so a small percentage of the population translates into a large number of people. Estimates of the number of religious adherents are unreliable for many reasons, resulting in widely varying estimates of the various minority religious populations, without much scholarly consensus. For example, estimates place the Muslim community in the United States as ranging from approximately 1.2 million to 7 or 8 million.[48] The Pluralism Project estimates that there are 3–6 million Muslims (approximately 2.0% of the population), 2–4 million Buddhists (1.0%), 1.2 million Hindus (0.4%), 200,000 to 1 million pagans (0.2%), 100,000–800,000 Baha'i (0.2%), 250,000 Sikhs (0.08%), 25,000–75,000 Jains (0.02%), and 18,000 Zoroastrians (0.01%).[49]

To put these numbers in context, Muslims are at least as numerous as Episcopalians and perhaps as numerous as Lutherans, there are more Sikhs than Quakers, and there are as many Buddhists as members of the Assembly of God. Moreover, regardless of the precise count of Muslims or Buddhists, there is widespread agreement that these numbers are growing rapidly. Wuthnow[50] reports that two-thirds of America's Islamic mosques have been built since 1980 and that 70% of Buddhist temples have been constructed since 1985.

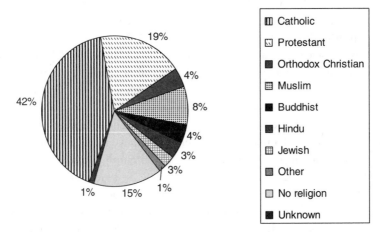

Religious Preferences of Adult Immigrants, 1996

Figure 5.2. Religious preferences of adult immigrants, 1996.
Source: Jasso et al. (see note 74) and New Immigrant Survey (see notes 18 and 51).

Figure 5.2 shows that most of this growth has come from immigration. The New Immigrant Survey,[51] conducted by scholars at Princeton University, provides estimates of the religious preference of adult immigrants. In 1996, the year of the pilot study, a majority of new immigrants were Christian, with a heavy skew toward Catholics. However, Buddhists and Hindus make up approximately 4% and 3.5% of the new immigrants—far higher than their representation in the population. Muslims constituted fully 8% of new immigrants. Taken together, religious traditions outside the Judeo-Christian tradition, which constitute less than 4% of the current U.S. population, may total as many as 16% of new immigrants.

How will this new diversity change the character of American public life? In some countries, differing faiths coexist in harmony—witness the syncretism between Buddhism and Shinto in Japan. In other countries, such as India, there is a longer history of religious conflict. And in Europe, immigration is changing the religious character of societies and provoking a backlash among the Christian majority. To know what is in store for the United States, let us consider first the public response and then the political mobilization by the parties.

Public Response to Religious Diversity

How has the American public reacted to the new diversity? It is difficult to disentangle reactions to religious diversity from broader reactions to immigration. To many Americans, religious diversity is intertwined with diversity in race and ethnicity, in language, in attire, and in cuisine. Yet, there have been a number of surveys of American attitudes toward non-Judeo-Christian religious traditions in the United States, which can provide us with some important insights.

These surveys suggest a certain level of ambivalence on the part of most Americans. Americans tend to be supportive of minority religions in the abstract but to have more difficulty when confronted with concrete worship practices— a common finding in surveys of civil liberties attitudes. The ambivalence is understandable because the United States has a well-established tradition of religious freedom, but a majority of Americans believe that their own religious views are not merely a preference but, in fact, the only ultimate truth. Thus, tolerance for seemingly strange religious practices is different in kind from tolerating strange-smelling foods or strange-looking clothing.

The Williamsburg Charter survey, conducted in 1988 in the early days of the latest wave of diversification, reported that most Americans were comfortable with both the display of the Nativity scene on public land at Christmas and the display of the Jewish menorah at Chanuka.[52] Yet, although 93% supported providing military chaplains in general, only 63% supported providing Buddhist chaplains. Large numbers of the general public and many types of elites agreed that the government should require the teaching of Judeo-Christian values in public schools.[53] There was widespread support for limiting religious activity by various groups, including barring Hare Krishna from soliciting at airports, preventing supporters of Reverend Moon from publishing a newspaper, and banning Satan worship.

In a survey of residents of the Washington, D.C., metro area in November 1993, fully 96% agreed that everyone should be allowed to practice their own religion, even if it seems strange to others. Yet, only 82% agreed that children should be allowed to wear religious headgear in the local schools, suggesting that 14% of Washington area residents had a rather impoverished conception of the weird. Sizable minorities supported barring fundamentalist ministers from preaching on college campuses and prohibiting Native Americans from using peyote in religious ceremonies. Only 28% would support allowing animal sacrifice in religious services such as those of the Santerians.[54]

More recently, the Religion and Diversity Survey contacted a random sample of nearly 3,000 Americans and included many questions about religious diversity and about diversity and immigration more generally.[55] Here, we present the survey results by major religious tradition, isolating white Evangelical and mainline Protestants, black Protestants, Catholics, Jews, and those who are not affiliated with a religion. We do not show in our tables the relatively small numbers of Hindu, Muslim, Sikh, Buddhist, and other religious respondents because they are too few for reliable estimates. Note that the number of Jews in the tables is also small, so those results should be interpreted with caution.

RELIGIOUS DIVERSITY AND PUBLIC OPINION

In Table 5.1, we show responses to general questions about the religious traditions of the United States, the new diversity, and whether different religions possess insights into God's truth. In the top part of the table, we see that large majorities of Christians believe that the United States is founded on Christian principles, that the country is strong because of its faith, that the democratic system of government is based on Christianity, and that the United States remains, basically, a Christian society. Yet, very large majorities also believe that religious diversity is good for the country.

However, sizable minorities believe that new religious groups pose a threat to traditional American values. Further, many respondents state that Buddhists and Muslims believe in different things from Christians, while also stating that all religions contain the same basic teachings. Many respondents say simultaneously that all religions are equally good ways to know God's will and that Christianity is the only way to have a true relationship with God.

The seeming inconsistency in these responses suggests considerable ambivalence. It appears in part because the survey asks respondents to agree to various statements about which they have not given much thought. Thus, respondents might well believe that the new diversity is good for America and that it poses a threat to their way of life but not pause to consider the tension between those two beliefs.[56]

This ambivalence is not uncommon—Americans hold ambivalent attitudes on many issues, such as abortion, gay rights, and the Iraq War. This ambivalence may result from the belief by Christians that theirs is the one true faith coupled with the unwillingness to state openly that other faiths are wrong. Yet, it also suggests that many Americans may be potentially responsive to elite manipulation of symbolic language and that reactions to the nation's growing diversity may well depend on how political issues frame the phenomenon. We will return to this point later.

Across the faith traditions, responses to these questions are generally similar. White Evangelicals are the most likely to state that the United States was founded on Christian principles and that democracy was based on Christianity, but they are slightly less likely to think the nation is strong because of its faith—as many believe that this faith has weakened. They are more likely to see a threat from new religious groups and slightly less likely than most other groups to value religious cooperation. They are especially likely to believe that Christianity is the one true faith. Mainline Protestants and Catholics are more

TABLE 5.1. Religious Diversity and Public Opinion

	Evangelical Protestant	Mainline Protestant	Black Protestant	Catholic	Jewish	Unaffiliated
Religion in the United States						
U.S. is founded on Christian principles	91%	91%	78%	80%	47%	70%
U.S. is strong because of its faith	81%	88%	83%	84%	57%	59%
U.S. democratic government is based on Christianity	70%	64%	59%	57%	22%	43%
U.S. is basically a Christian society	79%	84%	77%	74%	60%	67%
Religious diversity is good for the U.S.	83%	93%	87%	91%	94%	87%
New religious groups are a threat to traditional values	48%	37%	41%	33%	32%	23%
As a result of new groups						
People will think harder	83%	78%	81%	73%	56%	79%
Your faith will be stronger	75%	69%	80%	69%	42%	48%
Christianity will be stronger	64%	59%	63%	56%	19%	48%
Greater understanding between religions is desirable	75%	84%	76%	76%	85%	82%
Cooperation among religious leaders is desirable	79%	92%	76%	83%	97%	85%
Christian and Muslim beliefs are fairly different	74%	56%	81%	61%	72%	51%
Christian and Buddhist beliefs are fairly different	77%	63%	77%	64%	70%	63%

God's word is revealed in sacred texts besides the Bible	30%	50%	41%	53%	45%	56%
All religions contain some truth	72%	83%	80%	89%	74%	85%
All religions are equally good	37%	59%	56%	81%	64%	76%
All religions teach the same thing	26%	72%	36%	54%	53%	59%
Christianity is the only way to have a true relationship with God	71%	46%	70%	34%	0%	17%
Christianity is the best way to know God	81%	67%	80%	54%	2%	25%
Number of respondents	849	366	188	689	58	504

SOURCE: Religion and Diversity Survey, 2002–2003 (see note 59).

open to diversity, and those unaffiliated with any church are even more open. These results have important implications for the future politics of religious diversity, as we will argue below.

RELIGIOUS DIVERSITY AND PUBLIC POLICY

Table 5.2 shows attitudes relating to public policy questions. One of the most frequent challenges that new religious groups face is winning zoning ordinances in order to build temples, mosques, and other places of worship. Christian churches face similar problems in some cases because residents fear that they will bring traffic, noise, and other unwanted problems to the neighborhood. Most Americans appear largely indifferent to whether Muslims or Hindus build centers of worship in their communities. Few would object strongly to the presence of these new congregations, but even fewer would welcome them.

The survey shows strong support for the government collecting information about religious groups in the United States. Support for this kind of activity is highest again for Muslims. Yet, majorities of all Christian groups favor gathering information about all kinds of non-Christian groups. The survey also included a question that asked if the government should gather information about "some" Christian groups, and a majority of all groups except Jews favored this. This question appeared in the survey after all of the others, and this may have inflated the number of positive responses. It is possible that this represents a groundswell of support for funded social science research into religion in America, but more likely it suggests that Americans want the government to investigate any group that could potentially be dangerous and that majorities see various religious groups—including some Christian groups—as potentially dangerous.[57]

Finally, the survey asked if the U.S. government should make it illegal for various religious groups to meet. This strongly worded statement invited respondents to agree with a policy that would clearly violate the Constitution and basic religious liberty, so it is reassuring that only a small minority favored such actions. However, it is also worth noting that 20%–30% of white Evangelicals, black Protestants, and Catholics favored each set of laws.

In sum, the data in Table 5.2 show that the ambivalence seen in public responses to religious diversity carry over to questions of public policy. Although few respondents object to new centers of worship in their communities, even fewer are in favor of them. The responses also showed support for policies that would infringe on constitutionally protected rights of privacy and religious liberty. Particularly with regard to Muslims, support for these types of infringements is quite high. These types of results suggest the possibility of a potent backlash against the new diversity that might be mobilized politically, which we will discuss in the next section.

TABLE 5.2. Religious Diversity and Public Policy

	Evangelical Protestant	Mainline Protestant	Black Protestant	Catholic	Jewish	Unaffiliated
What if this religious group were to build a worship building in your community?						
Muslims						
Bother a lot	25%	16%	18%	19%	30%	10%
Welcome	9%	14%	13%	15%	17%	29%
Hindus						
Bother a lot	22%	10%	15%	11%	19%	7%
Welcome	10%	19%	18%	18%	26%	25%
The government should gather information about...						
Muslim groups	71%	63%	55%	64%	56%	60%
Buddhist groups	58%	50%	51%	53%	39%	47%
Hindu groups	62%	54%	55%	54%	41%	52%
Some Christian groups	57%	51%	54%	53%	39%	52%
The government should make it illegal for this religious group to meet...						
Muslims	30%	19%	26%	25%	18%	21%
Buddhists	26%	16%	26%	23%	14%	16%
Hindus	27%	17%	22%	22%	14%	19%
Number of respondents	849	366	188	689	58	504

SOURCE: Religion and Diversity Survey, 2002–2003 (see note 59).

RELIGIOUS DIVERSITY AND SOCIAL INTERACTION

In Table 5.3, we focus on social interactions and religious diversity. The data at the top of Table 5.3 show that a majority of Americans claim to have had at least some contact with Muslims, Hindus, and Buddhists but that only a minority claim to have had a fair amount of contact. Most Christians and unaffiliated Americans claim to have had significant contact with Jews. Black Protestants stand out as more likely than other Christian groups to have had contact with Muslims, presumably because of the Nation of Islam.

In the middle of the table are the results of three questions that asked if respondents would welcome a "stronger presence" by each religious group. Here, there is a clear distinction between attitudes toward Muslims and other religious groups, which may be because the survey was conducted after September 11, 2001. These data suggest that most Americans are comfortable with the idea that these new religious communities will grow—overall, two-thirds are welcoming of a greater presence by Hindus and Buddhists. Again, white Evangelicals stand out as less welcoming, but almost half would welcome a greater presence of Hindus and Buddhists.

Respondents were also asked how they would react if their child were to marry a member of another faith tradition "with a good education and who came from a good family." White Evangelicals stand out as likely to object to their child marrying a Muslim or a Hindu, but the surprising finding is that nearly 50% or more of most groups claim that they would not object at all to the marriage.

So, taken together, the data in Table 5.3 suggest a public that has had limited contact with new religious communities but states that it is open to greater participation and even family relationships. Of course, the tolerant response is socially and normatively acceptable, and it is possible that these numbers overstate religious tolerance. Moreover, sizable minorities of each community would object to a stronger presence of these groups in the public sphere or their child marrying someone from these faiths.

RELIGIOUS DIVERSITY AND PERSONAL RESPONSES

As American religious diversity grows, more Americans will have the opportunity to meet someone from a different faith tradition. There is a considerable literature that suggests that, under certain circumstances, exposure breeds tolerance—especially when individuals meet and only later discover their difference.[58] One of our mothers met a Muslim woman who was caring for one of our children and stated later that she was "a wonderful Christian woman." If more Americans meet more Hindus, Sikhs, Muslims, and those of other faiths, is the result likely to be more tolerance?

TABLE 5.3. Religious Diversity and Social Interaction

	Evangelical Protestant	Mainline Protestant	Black Protestant	Catholic	Jewish	Unaffiliated
Contact with religious minorities						
Muslims						
None	36%	35%	28%	37%	16%	25%
A fair amount or more	21%	20%	37%	20%	44%	27%
Hindus						
None	45%	46%	52%	41%	29%	32%
A fair amount or more	12%	12%	8%	15%	19%	21%
Buddhists						
None	48%	45%	54%	47%	28%	34%
A fair amount or more	10%	14%	11%	12%	19%	23%
Jews						
None	12%	9%	24%	15%	0%	12%
A fair amount or more	53%	59%	45%	57%	100%	59%
Would you welcome this religious group becoming a stronger presence in the U.S.?						
Muslims	41%	48%	62%	54%	51%	66%
Hindus	49%	58%	62%	63%	77%	74%
Buddhists	49%	58%	58%	65%	75%	83%

(continued)

TABLE 5.3. (*Continued*)

	Evangelical Protestant	Mainline Protestant	Black Protestant	Catholic	Jewish	Unaffiliated
If your child were to marry a member of this faith with a good education and who came from a good family...						
Muslim						
Object some/strongly	61%	36%	33%	29%	34%	14%
Not object at all	25%	48%	51%	50%	34%	75%
Hindu						
Object some/strongly	48%	36%	33%	29%	34%	14%
Not object at all	31%	50%	47%	55%	33%	77%
Number of respondents	849	366	188	689	58	504

Source: Religion and Diversity Survey, 2002–2003 (see note 59).

We explored the potential of increased contact with other faiths in our own study.[59] Specifically, we looked at the sources of two divergent responses to religious diversity—first, the support for a ban on religious meetings by Muslims, Hindus, and Buddhists and, second, the welcoming of increased influence by these groups.[60] By using multiple regression techniques, we were able to control for various demographic and attitudinal factors and to establish which characteristics help to determine a person's response to the two scenarios.

We looked first at the influence of a person's religion on his or her responses to these scenarios. Religion may affect attitudes both due to the religious tradition, which may inculcate certain values and behaviors in its members, and due to the intensity or exclusiveness of the religious beliefs. White Evangelical Protestants and Jews are less likely than other religions to welcome increased influence in the United States by non-Judeo-Christian groups, but they are not more likely to favor a ban on these groups' religious meetings. Not surprisingly, those who identified themselves as a member of a non-Judeo-Christian group were more likely to oppose a ban on these religious meetings. The other religious groups surveyed (black Protestant, mainline Protestant, and Catholic) were not distinctive in their reactions to these two scenarios, once the other factors were controlled.

The intensity or exclusiveness of a person's religious beliefs also affects his or her responses to religious diversity. Those who believe that Christianity is the only way to attain a personal relationship with God are far more likely to oppose increased influence by non-Judeo-Christian groups and to favor bans on their religious meetings than those who do not follow such an exclusivist religious ideal.

Besides religion, a person's gender, age, and educational level may also affect his or her responses to religious diversity. Our study found that, on average, older Americans are less likely than younger Americans to welcome the increased influence of non-Judeo-Christian religious groups, but they are not more likely to favor bans on religious meetings. For example, a 25-year-old, on average, would be 15% more likely to welcome the influence of these religious groups than would the average 50-year-old. Those with higher levels of formal education are more likely to welcome increased influence and to oppose bans on religious free exercise. This means that a person with a college education would be about 18% more likely to welcome other faiths than a person with a high school education and about 13% more likely to oppose a ban on their meetings. Whether the person was male or female did not matter to the analysis. Both the findings that younger Americans are more tolerant of religious diversity and that higher education results in increased tolerance are consistent with the literature and with common sense.

How one feels about safety and security can also affect the response to religious diversity. Americans who are most worried about another terrorist attack are significantly less likely to welcome increased influence by religious minorities and more likely to favor banning religious meetings by groups outside of the Judeo-Christian tradition. The opposite relationship also holds true in that the respondents least worried about another terrorist attack are more likely to welcome the new religious diversity and to oppose banning religious meetings.

What about the role of personal contact and social interactions in responses to religious diversity? Putnam[61] and others have explored how social capital—social networks and the norms of trust and reciprocity that arise from them—help or hinder the civic quality of communities. There are two types of social capital: *bonding social capital* refers to connections between "similar" people, which may reinforce exclusive identities and homogeneous groups, while *bridging social capital* refers to cross-cutting connections between various groups, which can generate a broader sense of identity and community. In our analysis, we tested both forms of social capital to determine their effects on a person's response to religious diversity.

We find that the more neighbors a person knows, the less likely he or she is to welcome increased influence by non-Judeo-Christian groups and the more likely to favor banning their religious meetings. For example, those respondents who report knowing "almost all" of their neighbors are around 14% more likely to oppose increased influence by "other" religions and 8% more likely to favor bans on their religious meetings than those who respond that they know "nobody" from their neighborhoods. This finding may be an example of bonding social capital at work as the tighter-knit communities may be more homogeneous and therefore less likely to support religious diversity.

As for bridging social capital, we find that those who have encountered members of other faiths are significantly more likely to welcome their increased influence in the United States and to oppose banning their religious meetings than those who have not had any contact with these groups. The level of contact also matters as those with high amounts of contact with other faiths are more tolerant and welcoming than those with low amounts of contact. For example, respondents who claimed to have "a great deal or a fair amount" of contact with non-Judeo-Christian groups were around 13% more likely to welcome increased influence by these groups than were those who reported "only a little or almost none" and about 25% more likely than those who reported no contact. We see the same pattern when it comes to banning religious meetings as those with the most contact were about 3% more likely to oppose these bans than those with minimal contact and about 6% more likely than those with no contact. The effect is greatest within specific groups—that is, those who have contact with Muslims are more favorable toward Muslims. There is, however, a diffusion effect so that those who have encountered Muslims are also supportive of allowing Hindus and Buddhists a greater place in the public sphere and vice versa. Here, we see that bridging social capital—social connections between different religious groups—helps to create a more tolerant and welcoming society.

Further analysis suggests that this personal contact works primarily to lessen negative stereotypes about various faiths. The survey invited respondents to rate members of various religious traditions on adjectives such as "closed-minded," "violent," "peaceful," "fanatical," "appealing," and "strange." Those who knew Muslims were far less likely to hold negative stereotypes than those who did not, and this was true for Hindus and Buddhists as well. Moreover, knowing a Muslim reduced negative stereotypes of Buddhists.

Yet, our additional analysis suggests that not everyone benefits equally from contact with those who have different faiths. White Evangelical Christians were much less affected by knowing someone of a different religious tradition than were other Christians. Further, those who believed that Christianity is the only way to have a personal relationship with God gained practically nothing from knowing someone from a different faith tradition. It appears that interreligious contact changes attitudes among those who are open to new information but not for everyone. For some, walking into a Hindu temple and seeing a statue of Ganesh in the doorway may lead to more tolerance; but to others, it is simply a reminder that Hindus are not followers of Christ.

Contact, however, can happen in unusual circumstances, and repeated contact can have a cumulative effect. In the 1950s, most white Evangelicals were vehemently anti-Catholic, but years of working together with conservative Catholics in political battles have created not only warm political relations but also an openness by Evangelicals to Catholic theology. Muslims have been involved in the coalition opposing same-sex marriage in the United States; and if they join with conservative Christians on other social issues, over time the impact might be considerable.[62]

The Politics of Religious Diversity

Although America is a secular state, religion plays an important role in its politics. Religion has always played an important part in American electoral politics as parties compete to win the votes of religious constituencies. Religion has also played a role in policy making as religious groups build coalitions to formulate and enact policies at the national, state, and local levels of government. Electoral politics and policy making are connected, for groups that are critical elements in a party's electoral coalition are more likely to win policy concessions if that party wins office.

Political parties in the United States have appealed both to minority religious constituencies and to the backlash that their presence provokes. These political appeals are seldom based on religion alone. Rather, politicians and parties combine religious differences with issues of race and ethnicity, social class, regional politics, and other salient cleavages in an effort to appeal to particular communities, both minority and majority. In 1928, Democrats nominated Catholic Al Smith for president and Evangelical Protestants were very visible at the Republican nominating convention, advocating immigration limits on the number of new Catholics and Jews. For most of the early part of the twentieth century, Democrats welcomed Catholic and Jewish candidates and voters, whereas the Republican Party represented the mainline Protestant establishment. White Evangelicals identified as Democrats because of regional politics but began voting for Republican presidential candidates early in the second half of the century. Black Protestants voted for Democratic candidates, and churches were a source of voter registration drives to increase turnout.[63]

In the 1980s, the religious alignment shifted as Republicans began to target white Evangelical Christians and then, a few years later, conservative white Catholics. Political organizations such as the Moral Majority and, later, the Christian Coalition were formed to help Republican candidates and party committees identify sympathetic churches and members and target them with specially tailored communications.

By 2000, a new religious alignment had solidified with white Evangelical Protestants as the single most loyal part of the Republican Party and with highly observant conservative Catholics and the more observant white mainline Protestants also supporting Republicans.[64] George W. Bush sought to win the votes of conservative Christians through issues such as abortion and opposition to same-sex marriage but also with subtle religious language, including quoting lines of well-known Evangelical hymns. His campaign also obtained membership lists from many conservative congregations and used them to send narrowly targeted appeals through the mail.[65] Less committed Christians, black Protestants, and Jews were all solidly in the Democratic camp. Muslims appear to have moved to the Democratic Party after 2001,[66] and this is especially true of Muslims who experienced discrimination after September 11, 2001, and those who believe that the war in Iraq is a war on Islam.

Both political parties have built financial networks within various religious minorities, such as among Hindus and other religious groups.[67] However, less is known about party appeals to religious minorities for votes or about the voting patterns of smaller religious communities because surveys do not capture them in sufficient numbers to generate reliable estimates.

Yet, the two-party political system of the United States does not easily fit the multiparty religious system. Republican positions on abortion and same-sex marriage fit the official position of the Catholic Church, but their positions on the welfare state, the death penalty, and even the war in Iraq do not. Black Protestants are drawn to the Democratic Party for its positions on social justice issues, but the most observant members are conservative on abortion and gay rights. Muslims might support Republican positions on gay marriage but oppose the Iraq War. Buddhists might reject Republican tax cuts for the wealthy but be drawn to the party on issues such as abortion.

How might this party system adapt to fit new religious groups outside of the Judeo-Christian tradition? It is difficult to predict how the parties will react to growing diversity over the next few decades. One possibility is that the current cleavage around religiosity will continue. Orthodox Muslims, Hindus, Sikhs, and Buddhists may support the Republican Party, which will oppose secularism, while less observant Muslims, Hindus, Sikhs, and Buddhists support the Democrats. This particular alignment reflects Ralph Reed's[67a] call for a coalition of "people of faith" regardless of the content of that faith. Yet, white Evangelicals are a core constituency of the Republican Party, and they are the least open to new religious groups. Political parties spawn unusual coalitions, but this one would be difficult to maintain.

Also, it is possible that both parties will appeal for the votes of the new religious groups. George W. Bush focused his reelection campaign on energizing white Evangelicals, but he also prayed with Hindus and publicly stated that Muslims and Christians worship the same God.[68] In this scenario, both Republicans and Democrats will bid for the votes and support of new religious communities.

Finally, it is possible that the new politics of religion will closely resemble the old politics of religion. In the early 1900s, Democrats welcomed new religious immigrants and Republicans embraced resistance and backlash to these groups. The Democratic Party's more inclusive ideology may make it more attractive to new religious groups, and Republicans may find this diversity a useful tool to mobilize an Evangelical religious base. The silence by many Republican leaders in the aftermath of Representative Goode's comments suggests that at least some are considering this strategy, which would mesh well with the Republican Party's opposition to immigration in the 2004 and 2006 elections. Republican Senator Sam Brownback, who explored a presidential bid in 2008, sounded these themes in endorsing the idea of an "attack on Christmas."[68a]

The partisan strategies may well have an impact on public response to new religious diversity. If candidates of both parties carefully cultivate votes among Muslims, Sikhs, Hindus, and other religious groups, then ambivalent Americans will receive a message that they are valuable new additions to our democracy. If one party or the other embraces a backlash against these groups, the attitudes may well polarize along partisan lines.

The Future of Religious Diversity

Already in 2006, the new religious diversity has consequences—for government, for private business, and for social life. These new religious communities, unlike their Catholic and Jewish predecessors, are not following exclusionary or assimilating paths. Rather, the new religious diversity in America is pluralizing, demanding the "right to be different, not just in dress and public presentation, but in religion and creed, united only by participation in the common covenants of citizenship."[69]

School districts across the country have found ways to accommodate religious diversity—allowing Muslims, Hindus, and Sikhs to wear distinctive clothing; excusing Muslims from the cafeteria during Ramadan; and, in some cases, excusing Muslims from active physical education courses in the afternoon during that extended fast. Employers have found themselves faced with a wide array of religious holidays, dietary restrictions, and other requests.

New religious groups have created challenges for religious accommodationists who have long argued for public displays of unifying religious symbols. For many years, the Christian majority in the United States has supported the display of the Nativity scene on public lands and then displayed the Jewish menorah as a gesture to religious inclusion. Yet, to be truly inclusive, many communities would now need to display, for example, a statue of the Buddha or Ganesh,; and the Ten Commandments, so often fought over outside of courthouses in the South, are not part of Buddhist or Shinto tradition.

Thus far, responses to the new diversity have given reason to despair and to hope. After September 11, hate crimes against religious minorities of all kinds increased dramatically. One of us flew soon afterward beside a Sikh wearing a huge button, easily readable from 30 feet, proclaiming, "A PROUD SIKH AMERICAN." Mosques were defaced—but then religious communities combined to scrub off the graffiti or to collect funds to repair damages.

In 1940s America, it was difficult to believe that animosity between Protestants, Catholics, and Jews would ever abate. This conflict was portrayed poignantly in the 1947 Oscar winner for Best Picture, *Gentleman's Agreement*.[70] In this movie, Phil Green, played by Gregory Peck, is a journalist assigned to do an undercover story about anti-Semitism by pretending he is a Jew. Over the breakfast table, Phil attempts to explain his new role to his young son Tommy.

> TOMMY: What are Jews, anyway? I mean, exactly.
> PHIL: Well…well, you remember last week, when you asked me about that big church?

TOMMY: Sure.

PHIL: And I told you there were lots of different churches?

TOMMY: Yeah...

PHIL: Well, the people who go to that particular church are called Catholics, see, and there are people who go to other churches and they're called Protestants, and there are others that go to still different churches and they're called Jews, only they call their kind of churches synagogues or temples.

TOMMY: And why don't some people like those?

PHIL: Well, that's kind of a ... something to explain, son. Some people hate Catholics, and some hate Jews.

TOMMY: And no one hates us 'cause we're Americans!

GRANDMOTHER: [Hmmmph.]

PHIL: Well, no, no, that's another thing again.

This exchange is a perfect example of the diversity and conflict between the three religions immediately following World War II. It would have been hard for a 1947 audience to imagine that this animosity would be resolved quickly, if at all.

Yet, recent surveys have shown that the historical animosity toward Catholics and Jews has been largely eradicated. This change in attitudes reflects the growing acceptance of and cooperation within the two families, including initiatives by religious elites to find common ground on important issues.[71] These results "strongly suggest that the United States has the capacity to overcome historical religious divisions and prejudices."[72]

It is difficult to say whether tensions over the new religious diversity will one day seem as antiquated as the religious prejudice that the movie addressed. Yet, as we have discussed, there are signs that communities are adapting to and often overcoming differences in religion, ethnicity, and even language. These interactions are reshaping the social, cultural, and political landscape of the United States, with vast implications for how we view each other and ourselves.

Conclusion

This chapter has discussed the religious diversity of the United States, from colonial times to the present. From this historical look, it is clear that the place of religion in public life has always been a source of lively debate, heated conflict, and measured compromise. The new religious diversity is continuing this trend as America changes from a country dominated by its Judeo-Christian heritage to a multifaceted kaleidoscope of religious communities.

The new religious diversity has changed the character of American public life in a multitude of ways. Public opinion is often inconsistent when it comes to assessing the impact of religious diversity on the United States, with people believing both that America benefits from being a Christian society and that religious diversity has a positive effect. This ambivalence is also seen in the support for public policies that violate constitutional rights of privacy and religious freedom, which suggests the possibility of a potent backlash against minority religious groups that may be mobilized for political gain.

The importance of social interactions and personal contacts becomes even more crucial when these types of policies and opinions are publicly debated. Our analysis depicts a public, albeit with limited contact to the new religious diversity, which appears open to greater interaction and family relationships. By controlling for various demographic and attitudinal factors, we are able to determine that having contact with other faiths is a crucial part of feeling welcoming toward minority religions and supportive of their rights. "Contact" is a tricky concept to define, and not everyone benefits equally from these types of cross-cutting social interactions. However, the warming relations between previously opposed Evangelical and Catholic religious groups gives hope that repeated contact with non-Judeo-Christian religions will produce increased tolerance and understanding.

We also explored the politics of religious diversity, noting that religion has always played an important role in American electoral politics and policy making. The multifaceted religious community of the United States is not easily categorized by the two-party political system, and it is difficult to predict future political reactions to the growing religious diversity. It is worth paying attention to the partisan strategies as these choices will impact the public response to minority religious groups in the future.

Will tensions over the new religious diversity appear as archaic as the prejudice of the 1920s? The answer to this question, albeit incomplete, is being expressed through the daily actions of political parties, local and federal government, social communities, and personal relationships. The ways in which we seek to address the changing religious landscape of the United States will ultimately determine the melodic nature of our national symphony, the notes of which are being written every day.

DISCUSSION QUESTIONS

1. The Religion and Diversity Survey results highlighted the considerable ambivalence of many Americans when confronted with the consequences of the new religious diversity. In your opinion, why do Americans respond in contradictory ways

to these types of survey questions? What do these responses portend for the future accommodation of increased religious diversity in the United States?

2. Throughout this chapter, we stressed the cyclical nature of the religious history of America. What can we learn from the struggles of Protestants in colonial times and the immigration battles of the 1920s that is relevant for today?

3. The importance of certain types of personal interactions and relationships was highlighted in our discussion of the survey results. Can you think of some examples of bonding and bridging social capital that could help or hinder tolerance for religious diversity?

4. In our discussion of the politics of religious diversity, we outlined three possible partisan strategies for future elections. In your opinion, which of the three is the most plausible? What are the benefits and costs of implementing this strategy?

5. The story of Lewiston, Maine, and its Somali immigrants serves as an example of the type of change that is occurring in small towns and communities throughout the United States. Think about the town's story in relation to the various processes we have discussed in this chapter, such as the public response and political reactions. What can we learn from Lewiston about the power of local communities to accommodate and adapt to new diversity?

Chapter 6

"Measured Sovereignty"

The Political Experiences of Indigenous Peoples as Nations and Individuals

David E. Wilkins

In the summer of 2007, on the lands of the Lummi Nation located in Washington State, delegates from a number of indigenous nations from the United States (Lummi Nation, Confederated Tribes of the Colville Reservation, Akiak Native Community, Makah Tribe), Canada (Sucker Creek First Nation), Australia (Ngarrindjeri Nation), and New Zealand (Te Runanga O Ngati Awa) forged an international diplomatic accord called the "United League of Indigenous Nations Treaty." This treaty was the culmination of three years of consultations, said Alan Parker, a native professor at Evergreen State College. Parker stressed that "we do not need some other government's permission to enter into treaty agreements with the other to establish alliances."[1]

The preamble to this international document, signed August 1, 2007, stated the following:

> We, the signatory Indigenous Nations and Peoples, hereby pledge mutual recognition of our inherent rights and power to govern ourselves and our ancestral homelands and traditional territories. Each signatory nation, having provided evidence that their respective governing body has taken action in accordance with their own custom, law and or tradition to knowingly agree to and adopt the terms of this treaty, hereby establish the political, social, cultural and economic relations contemplated herein.[2]

The signers of this document pledged to exercise their individual and collective sovereignty "without regard to existing or future international political boundaries of

non-Indigenous nations"; to work on political, social, cultural, and economic unity
among all the signing nations; to recover aboriginal lands; to protect cultural
properties including sacred songs; to share and practice traditional ecological
knowledge; to engage in mutually beneficial trade and commerce between
the respective nations; to protect the human rights of indigenous peoples from
violations such as involuntary servitude and human trafficking; to develop better
communications; and to ensure scholarly exchanges and joint study of strategies
of self-determination. And each of the signers agreed that his or her nation would
appoint an individual who would be responsible for all treaty matters and create an
inter-Nation coordination office to aid in the assembling of data needed to address
the issues and concerns raised by protocol.

Importantly, one of the key principles spelled out by the indigenous leaders
emphatically declared that "no other political jurisdiction, including nation-states
and their governmental agencies or subdivisions, possess [sic] governmental power
over any of our Indigenous nations, our people and our usual, customary and
traditional territories."³ This accord was witnessed by many other Native leaders
from various nations, who, while expressing support for the principles and concepts
outlined therein, expressed that they would need time to study and discuss the
document within their respective communities before adding their names.

Introduction

On June 18, 2001, in Washington, D.C., Jack Abramoff, a powerful Washington
lobbyist, met with Michael Scanlon, a former congressional communications
director, to secretly discuss a partnership centered around a firm known as "Capi-
tol Campaign Strategies" (CCS). Their strategy, later labeled as "Gimme Five,"
was designed to put in $5 million a year to CCS, revenue that was to be secured
from several Indian nations that had grown wealthy through gaming operations.
Later, the expression "Gimme Five" was understood as entailing major kickbacks
to Abramoff from payments made by any of Scanlon's American Indian clients
to Scanlon. By late 2004, six Native nations—the Coushatta Tribe of Louisiana,
the Mississippi Band of Choctaw, the Saginaw Chippewa of Michigan, the Agua
Caliente Band of Cahuilla Indians of California, the Tigua Indians of Ysleta del
Sur Pueblo of El Paso (Texas), and the Pueblo Sandia Tribe of New Mexico—
had become deeply ensnared in a complicated set of financial arrangements with
Abramoff and Scanlon. The Native nations had paid the two men more than $66
million in an effort to gain political influence in Washington, D.C., that would benefit their own nations, sometimes to the outright detriment of other tribal nations.⁴

The Senate Committee on Indian Affairs, later joined by the Justice Department, the Federal Bureau of Investigation, and the Department of the Interior,
then conducted a two-year investigation at the tribes' behest. The investigations

led to Scanlon's guilty plea in November 2005 for conspiring to defraud the tribes and Abramoff's conviction in early 2006 of, among other things, conspiracy to commit mail and wire fraud.

These two stories evidence a startling and complicated reality about indigenous peoples in the United States. On the one hand, as the original self-governing nations (the first sovereigns, if you will) of North America, they maintain a governmental, cultural, and landowning status that is unique among ethnic groups, a status that is not beholden to the U.S. Constitution. On the other hand, as a result of various federal policies of assimilation, Native nations and their individual citizens/members—who over time received the franchise in state and federal elections—have become more active in the American political process and are increasingly functioning more like highly motivated and well-financed interest groups anxious to wield influence over not only their own nations' political systems but those of the states and federal government as well. Native nations, in short, have both an extraconstitutional and a preconstitutional status since their rights originate outside the U.S. Constitution and obviously predate the American Republic. Over time, however, the individual members of these original governments (though not the nations themselves) have also acquired a constitutional status, and they are entitled to participate as fully as any other American in local, state, and federal political events.

Thus, the 560+ indigenous nations, totaling approximately 4.5 million people in 2006, the preexisting and ongoing sovereigns of North America, occupy a distinctive legal, political, cultural, and economic status in relation to one another, other domestic racial and ethnic groups, the American public, and, of course, the latter-day polities—the federal and state governments—that formed in their midst. Despite their separate sovereign status, since the late 1800s, but especially since the Indian Naturalization Act of 1924,[5] the individual citizens of Native nations were incorporated as citizens of the United States and today may exercise the franchise in all three polities: their tribal nation, the state they reside in, and federal elections.

This treble citizenship status, when combined with the ongoing extraconstitutional status of Native nations, raises profound intergovernmental issues that create confusion and generate ambiguity about the precise nature of the rights of Native peoples in their efforts to retain and exercise their inherent sovereignty, while still participating in the political affairs of non-Indian governments. The confusion has been heightened in recent years because of the significant impact of gambling revenues, which have helped ease the profound economic problems of some tribal nations, while at the same time serving to exacerbate (but in some cases easing) political tensions between Native nations and non-Indian governments.

This chapter will examine these dynamic issues and offer insights on where these complex contemporary political developments might be leading Native nations and their treble citizens in their intragovernmental situation and in their intergovernmental relations with local, state, and federal governments.

Original Peoples, Original Governments

The unique identities of the 560+ Native nations are more a product, according to Vine Deloria, Jr., of "historical process and political ideology rather than racial and cultural homogeneity."[6] The generic terms "American Indian," "Native American," and, more recently, "indigenous people" are comparable to the broad concepts of "Asian," "European," and "African" in that they refer to a large number of diverse peoples who inhabit a continental landmass rather than a single nationalistic entity with homogenous roots.

The Western social science, scientific, and legal communities have long sought to depict Native nations as a culturally, racially, and legally unified population based on their alleged migration across the Bering Strait land bridge and the cultural and normative commonalities allegedly shared by these diverse peoples. The Bering Strait arrival account, however, has been universally denounced by Indian nations, which have their own creation and migration accounts; and the tremendous array of cultures, political and economic systems, and language groups wielded by these nations argue against a single racial identity or migratory route.

This profound degree of indigenous diversity—hundreds of distinctive Native nations, speaking a multitude of languages, wielding radically different governing systems, and inhabiting a variety of landscapes—meant that the legal and diplomatic process between Native peoples and the European and later Euro-American policy makers would not proceed uneventfully but would be confounded by the inherent difficulties that accompanied such intercultural, interracial, and international relations. The legal traditions of Native peoples are steeped in their creation accounts, which provide for every nation a code of customs, laws, and ethics; an articulation of social values; a bounded and sacred landscape; and philosophical traditions that guide the peoples' decisions and subsequent actions. Thus, when humans, land (and the flora and fauna of those lands), values, and religious traditions are connected from ancient times, a distinctive collective identity is forged that creates a unique communal identity and a sense of responsibility and kinship to the land that distinguishes a particular Native people from all other aboriginal and nonaboriginal peoples.

The legal traditions of the Europeans who came to the Americas—the English, French, Spanish, Dutch, Russians—and the Euro-American state system that emerged as the dominant polity by the early 1800s derive from very different lands, values, and religious traditions, although for the purposes of this chapter English common law and Christianity are two features that would play a pivotal role in structuring indigenous/nonindigenous relations.

As a result, while the legal and political traditions of Native nations and the legal and political traditions of the United States developed at different historical moments, and for different historical reasons, they encountered one another early on in North America, creating, at least initially, opportunities for a synthesized indigenous/Euro-American legal and political framework, while at the same time generating a new set of legal, cultural, political, and economic concepts and traditions that would eventually elevate the Euro-American political and legal systems to a dominant position vis-à-vis Indian nations by generally denigrating the legal and political traditions of Native nations.

Thus, since the late 1800s, the Western-based legal and political traditions of the United States have been dominant, despite the fact that many Native nations continued to wield a variety of tribal governing systems—traditional systems that date back to time immemorial, hybrid models that melded traditional systems with elements of Western-style systems, or constitution-based governments that either predate the 1934 Indian Reorganization Act[7] (IRA), like those of the Cherokee, Choctaw, Chickasaw, and Creek,[8] or were created under the auspices of the IRA. It is this lack of bilateralism, the virtual absence of indigenous voices in American politics and law, that plagues the unique intergovernmental relationship between Native nations and the United States.

Traditional Indigenous Governance

As noted earlier, indigenous peoples' legal traditions, cultural identities, and governance structures and practices are intimately connected to their creation accounts and the philosophical worldviews that derive from those knowledge systems. As Champagne has noted, for many Native nations, "the world is a sacred gift and to distort it through remaking the earth and reconstructing social and political relations is to disturb the divine order of the universe and incur this-worldly disaster."[9] And while individual or personal autonomy was deeply valued in tribal societies, in contradistinction to the Western view of individual rights, native individualism was carried out within a cosmically ordered universe of purpose and balance.

Besides the clear recognition of kinship, national and individual sovereignty, extended families, bands, clans, warrior societies, and other social and political subgroups were also highly respected since they, too, were acknowledged in Native origin accounts. Thus, since indigenous social and political relations were an intimate part of each Nation's worldview, there was no discernible separation of the religious from the political.

With an estimated 5–10 million indigenous people, representing some 600 small nations prior to European arrival, governing systems ranged from simple band structures to complicated confederated governments. Many Native nations were decentralized and could be classed as direct democracies, with every individual and the various subgroups being intimately involved with matters of governance. Consensus, rather than majority rule, was the operating decision-making paradigm in most communities, although this was typically carried out at the local, rather than the national, level.

In addition, traditional governance was based on what Barsh has called the "primacy of conscience."[10] That is to say, virtually no North American nation had leadership that wielded authoritarian or coercive authority since cooperation was prized more than force. As Alfred says,

> leaders rely on their persuasive abilities to achieve a consensus that respects the autonomy of individuals, each of whom is free to dissent from and remain unaffected by the collective decision. The clan or family is the basic unit of social organization, and lesser forms of organization, from tribe through nation to confederacy, are all predicated on the political autonomy and economic independence of clan units through family-based control of lands and resources.[11]

The governing structures that embodied the physical environments and the values of consent; conscience; sacredness; decentralization; national, local, and personal sovereignty; kinship; and the merger of the sacred and secular were tremendously varied. Many Native nations were informal confederacies of linguistically related hunting groups (e.g., the Shoshone and Paiute of the Great Basin area in the western United States or the Dakota, Lakota, and Nakota who ranged widely from present-day Wisconsin to Wyoming); others were small bands and tribes that lived in villages in the Pacific Northwest along the major waterways and relied on fishing for subsistence and trade. These small nations' political systems operated only at the village or longhouse level.

A few of the larger nations developed powerful confederacies such as the Iroquois or Six Nations, the Creeks, the Miamis, and the Natchez. The Iroquois, a linkage of five related nations–Onondaga, Mohawk, Oneida, Seneca, and Cayuga (the Tuscarora would join in the early 1700s)—operated under what is considered the oldest written constitution in the world, the *Gayaneshagowa*, or Great Binding Law, that dates back to at least the 1500s. This document, originally spelled out on wampum belts made from seashells, outlined the governing structure of the confederacy; specified the powers, obligations, and restrictions of the fifty council chiefs; and specified the democratic ideals and principles of initiative, recall, referenda, equal suffrage, checks and balances, and clear delegations of war and peace responsibilities.

Some Native nations were effectively theocracies (e.g., the Pueblos of present-day New Mexico and the Hopi of Arizona) since their governing systems trace back to ancient times and the community's social, political, and economic life were organized around a religious ceremonial calendar.

For most indigenous peoples, however, there was little evidence of a formal priesthood and their governing guidelines were not written down. Rather, most tribes, say Deloria and Lytle, preferred to incorporate their political and social precedents in verbal accounts and anecdotes that described correct behavior. And they relied upon social pressures, especially the individual's fear of embarrassing his or her relatives and clan members, as their principal means of ascertaining the proper social response and penalty for any violations of native customs.[12]

In short, for the majority of Native nations, the system that enabled people to generally get along was based not on formalized governing structures per se but on the practice of kinship. Ella Deloria, a renowned Dakota anthropologist, put it bluntly:

> All peoples who live communally must first find some way to get along together harmoniously and with a measure of decency and order. . . . The Dakota people of the past found a way: it was through kinship. . . . Only those who kept the rules consistently and gladly, thus honoring all their fellows, were good Dakotas—meaning good citizens of society, meaning persons of integrity and reliability. And that was practically all the government there was. It was what men lived by.[13]

Colonial and U.S. Constitutional Impositions onto Native Nations

Various European powers had designs on North America, and while international conflicts flared, insofar as international law was concerned, each nation's claims to land were generally respected by the others. In the struggle for North America, England eventually emerged as the dominant polity, although Spain and France asserted ownership or jurisdictional authority over various portions of what became the United States, even after the conclusion of the American Revolution.

From Columbus' landing in 1492 until at least the 1763 Royal Proclamation Line, the vying European colonizers desperately needed economic, political, and military alliances with the major Native nations in order to protect their tenuous sovereignty and proprietary claims against other European states. Thus, throughout North America, European states recognized the national status of the more powerful Indian nations by negotiating a multitude of bilateral and sometimes multilateral treaty arrangements with them.

These important covenants provided clear recognition of indigenous sovereignty, some recognition of Native proprietary rights, and grudging respect for tribal military and economic power. In effect, the larger tribal nations and confederacies continued to hold the balance of power on the continent at the beginning of the American Revolution.

Following their English colonial forebears, the American leaders of the Revolutionary era and the Constitution's drafters generally adhered to three principles in their relations with Native nations. First, they fervently believed that they had gained clear legal title—notwithstanding the continuing presence of treaty-recognized Native nations—to the continent upon their successful, if unprecedented, colonial revolt. They did, however, recognize in the stronger tribal nations a lesser title of occupancy to their own lands, which had to be either purchased or forcibly taken by the Americans or would remain with the tribal nations. Second, the American founders realized the pragmatic need to continue to engage in diplomacy—treaty-making—with the larger Native nations in order to avoid additional and costly bloodshed. Third, the Americans believed that indigenous peoples were culturally and intellectually inferior to Europeans and Euro-Americans and that they would eventually need to be "civilized" in order for them to become assimilable.[14] These three interrelated tenets indicated the cultural, technological, and racial arrogance as well as the political and economic pragmatism of American policy makers. They, in fact, provided the foggy lens through which Native nations were seen by Americans.

This foggy lens equated to a schizophrenic mind-set that evidenced itself in U.S. constitutional language. When the Constitution was adopted in 1789, five of its most important clauses also implicated the indigenous/U.S. relationship: commerce, treaty-making, property, supremacy, and war and peace. These clauses affirmed that the national government, and Congress in particular, via the Commerce Clause, had exclusive authority to treat with Indian nations in regard to trade and intercourse, diplomacy (to fight or parlay), and land issues. While each of the clauses is important, treaty-making and commerce are most essential. Although the treaty-making clause (Article 6, clause 2) does not specifically mention Indian treaties, history and actual practice attest that treating with tribal nations was vigorously carried out and would continue until 1871, when formal treaty-making ended, but would immediately begin again in 1872 and continue until 1912 with the negotiation of "agreements," which were basically treaties by another name.

The Commerce Clause explicitly empowers Congress to "regulate commerce with foreign nations...states...and with the Indian tribes." It is the only express power vested to any branch of government that addresses Indian peoples. This clause, a corrective to the Articles of Confederation, which had allowed each state to regulate its own commercial relationship with tribes, should not have extended to Congress any greater power over tribal nations than it exercised over states. However, as tribal power waned during the course of the nineteenth century, the federal government, via the Supreme Court, frequently justified federal assertions of unbridled congressional and executive authority over Native nations and their lands by grounding those assertions in the Commerce Clause, by declaring Native nations to be "wards," and most problematically by developing an entirely new and wholly extraconstitutional power, *plenary power*—the theory that Congress had virtually absolute power over all things indigenous.[15]

Principles of Federal Indian Politics and Law

By the early part of the nineteenth century U.S. policy makers, particularly Supreme Court justices, had, along with the constitutional clauses, developed or modified additional principles and policies that would be continued indefinitely in their legal and political relations with Native nations.

First was the *doctrine of discovery*, which arose in the fifteenth century via Catholic papal bulls and European monarchical policies. This doctrine was issued to explorers as European states fanned out around the globe and was often linked to the *doctrine of conquest* (the acquisition of territory by a victorious state from a defeated enemy). The discovery doctrine held, in its most widely understood meaning, that European explorers' "discovery" of even inhabited lands gave the discovering state (and the United States as successor) absolute legal title and ownership of the lands, thereby reducing the native occupants to being mere tenants holding a lesser beneficial interest in the land.[16]

Conversely, "discovery" also was defined as an exclusive and preemptive right that vested in the discovering polity merely the right to be the first purchaser of any lands Native nations might choose to sell. Here, "discovery" was a colonial metaphor that gave the speediest and most efficient discovering nation the advantage in its efforts to colonize and exploit new lands. It was designed primarily to regulate competition between vying European nations; it was not intended to deny native ownership of lands.

Second, the *trust doctrine*, also known as the "trust relationship," likewise arose during the years of European discovery and settlement of the Americas and other regions. Like discovery, the trust concept also traces back to Catholic papal bulls. This doctrine holds that European nations and their representatives, as allegedly superior peoples, had a moral responsibility to civilize and Christianize the Native peoples they encountered. In a sense, "discovery" and "trust" are fundamentally related concepts, with the discoverer having the trust obligation to oversee the enlightenment and cultural development of the aboriginal peoples since Natives were not conceived as sufficiently mature to be the actual owners of their own lands.[17]

Third was the application of a doctrine of *national not state/colony/individual supremacy* regarding European/American political and commercial relations with tribal nations. In other words, it was clear that regulation of trade and the acquisition or disposition of indigenous lands needed to be managed by the national government and not left to the constituent subunits of government, land companies, or acquisitive individuals.

Finally, because of the military and political capability and territorial domain controlled by the Native nations, diplomacy in the form of treaties or comparable contractual arrangements was considered the most logical, economical, and humane method of dealing with indigenous peoples.

These important principles and policies—discovery, trust, federal (not state or local supremacy), and bilateral or multilateral diplomacy—were made evident in several early actions by U.S. lawmakers. An early instance occurred when Congress enacted the 1789 Northwest Ordinance, which defined a Northwest Territory in the Great Lakes and set up guidelines for political and economic development of the region that would eventually lead to the creation of new states.

Simultaneously, Article 3 of the ordinance contained a striking and unusual passage on the moral or trust relationship that the United States would exhibit toward Native peoples. It read, in part:

> the utmost good faith shall always be observed towards the Indians, their lands and property shall never be taken from them without their consent; and in their property, rights and liberty, they never shall be invaded or disturbed, unless in just and lawful wars authorised by Congress; but laws founded in justice and humanity shall from time to time be made, for preventing wrongs being done to them, and for preserving peace and friendship with them....[18]

This important ordinance showed that the federal government was endorsing a fundamentally contradictory policy that echoes still today. On the one hand, the United States sought to assure Indian nations that their lands and rights were to be respected, except when "just and lawful wars" were fought. On the other hand, the federal government had already essentially distributed those same lands to the present and future white settlers intent on continuing their inexorable march westward.

Native Nations and American States: The "Other" Relationship

Although the political relationship between indigenous peoples and the federal government is briefly spelled out in the Commerce Clause and is fulfilled relying on other clauses as well, the equally important relationship between Indian nations and the states is not outlined in the federal constitution, is not addressed in state or tribal constitutions, and suffers from inconsistent directives in federal statutory and case law. It is generally accepted by all three sovereigns that the primary relationship for most Indian nations remains with the federal government, with tribal peoples operating in what is popularly known as a "nation-to-nation relationship" rooted in the doctrines of inherent tribal sovereignty, congressional exclusive authority to manage the federal government's affairs with Native nations, and the treaty relationship. As one federal court noted in 1959, such historical and constitutional precedents establish that Indian nations have "a status higher than that of states."[19]

Nevertheless, over the course of that same history, tribal nations and state governments have come to stand as mutual, if different, sovereigns. Today, in the 34 states where there are federally recognized tribal nations, the two different sovereigns share some common geographic areas, with every Indian reservation or Indian community being surrounded by a state's borders, as well as some common citizens. That is, tribal citizens who live within reservations or on other Indian trust lands are both tribal and state citizens (federal as well), while non-Indian residents of Indian Country enjoy state citizenship but are not recognized as tribal citizens.

Tribal nations and states thus share some citizens and lands, but in their relations as sovereign governments each has historically sought to protect its collective rights to political power, economic and natural resources, and distinctive cultural identities. Native nations and states, in short, have rarely been friendly neighbors. As the Supreme Court said in *United States v. Kagama*, tribes "owe no allegiance to the States, and receive from them no protection. Because of the local ill-feeling, the people of the States where they are found are often their deadliest enemies."[20]

Tribal nations resent the states' frequent attempts to tax and regulate their lands, wages, and industries and are profoundly displeased that many states remain hostile to the reality of tribal sovereignty and refuse to recognize tribal competence to handle increasing amounts of regulatory and administrative duties. States resent the fact that while they have jurisdiction over all activities and persons within their borders, this does not generally extend to tribal national affairs or to Indians residing on reservations or trust lands, which are typically not subject to state jurisdiction or taxation.

The reasons explaining this tension date back to the colonial period and the debates about whether the nation or colonies/states would manage Indian affairs policies. At the Philadelphia Convention it was determined that Congress would have exclusive control over trade relations with the sovereign tribes and that the national government would continue the treaty relationship with Native peoples that other European sovereigns had established.

Later, as the American population expanded west, the enabling acts and later the constitutions admitting most states to the Union were required to contain disclaimer clauses in which the new states agreed to recognize the federal government's exclusive authority in the Indian affairs field and promised never to tax Indians or Indian trust land. These three factors—congressional plenary (exclusive) power, treaties, and state constitutional disclaimer clauses—along with tribal sovereignty effectively excluded state governments from any direct involvement in tribal affairs.

In 1832, Chief Justice John Marshall, in his often quoted opinion in *Worcester v. Georgia*, provided the first focused analysis of the tribal–state relationship. He wrote that state laws could have no force within Indian Country unless Congress authorized the action. Marshall declared that "the treaties and laws of the United States contemplate the Indian territory as completely separated from that of the states; and provide that all intercourse with them shall be carried on exclusively by the government of the Union."[21] Marshall also relied on tribal sovereignty to effectively bar states from intruding into internal tribal affairs.

Gradually, however, as more non-Indians invaded tribal lands, this led to increasing amounts of state jurisdiction being extended into Indian Country. One of the earliest cases that supported state involvement in Indian land was *United States v. McBratney*,[22] which held that states had criminal jurisdiction over non-Indians who had committed crimes against other non-Indians within reservations. The relationship between Native nations and states waxed and waned over the next century, but by the latter part of the twentieth and the early part of the twenty-first centuries, cases like *Brendale v. Confederated Tribes and Bands of Yakima Indian Nation* (1989)[23] and others[24] had dramatically shifted the relationship to favor states' rights over indigenous rights. These cases have turned the previous century and a half of federal Indian policy and judicial precedent on its head and threatened tribal sovereignty's vitality at a time when the doctrine of Indian self-determination was evolving into a permanent presence after a century and a half of direct federal assaults.

Even as the Supreme Court is challenging tribal sovereignty's force vis-à-vis states' rights, tribal nations and some states, sometimes supported by federal law and presidential directives and sometimes acting independently of federal involvement, are exercising a greater willingness to engage in constructive dialogue in an effort to avoid frequent and expensive litigation when their rights conflict. In recent years, some Native nations and their host states have entered into *sovereignty accords* (symbolic documents in which both parties acknowledge the inherent sovereignty of the other), have participated in cooperative agreements on matters such as cross-deputization, have developed comprehensive state and tribal policies on tribal–state relations, have sought to improve the educational process to ameliorate stereotypes and to educate their citizens, and have engaged in a number of negotiated settlements (e.g., water rights, Indian child welfare).[25]

But serious fault lines remain between the two sovereigns over issues like the substance and breadth of tribal sovereignty, Indian gambling revenues, hunting and fishing rights, land claims, sacred sites, and civil jurisdiction, among others. Litigation, therefore, remains the most common strategy to settle many differences, although there is little evidence that adversarial encounters lead to justice or help to promote deeper cross-cultural understanding.

The intergovernmental relationship between Native nations and states is a dynamic one. It is complicated further by the overarching presence of the federal government, which, on the one hand, has treaty and trust responsibilities to tribal nations but, on the other hand, is constitutionally connected to the states. Relations will improve, from an indigenous perspective, only if state governments recognize the fact that tribal nations are sovereign entities entitled to govern their lands and the peoples residing therein. Tribes, for their part, states contend, must be willing to consider the interests of the state if they are embarking on economic development or environmental decisions (e.g., hosting nuclear radioactive waste) that may have implications beyond the reservation boundaries.

And while jurisdictional uncertainties and economic competition will most likely persist, there is growing hope that as the two sovereigns come to recognize their respective rights to protect the health, safety, and welfare of their own citizens; to engage in cultural, political, or economic development that is appropriate for their communities; and to regulate their natural resource endowments this may lead to more amicable tribal–state relations.

Indigenous Engagement of the Political Process of Other Polities

As noted above, the treble citizenship status of individual Native citizens creates many opportunities, while at the same time creating confusion among non-indigenous governments and citizens. This is exemplified in a statement by political scientist Glenn Phelps, who observed that "claims of tribal sovereignty and immunity from state and local processes cannot in principle, coexist with the responsibilities incumbent upon citizenship and suffrage in state and local governments." Phelps went on to note that

> Indians living within Indian Country are immune from state and local taxes and are largely immune from state and local laws. Yet they claim the right to vote for representatives who can levy taxes and make rules and regulations for

non-Indians—taxes and rules from which reservation Indians themselves are immune. Not surprisingly, non-Indians find this arrangement a violation of a fundamental element of the rule of law—that the rulers also be the ruled and that they be subject to the laws they make.[26]

Native nations and their treble citizens, on the other hand, find this arrangement perfectly valid and rooted directly in their treaty relationship with the federal government and the congressional laws the United States would later unilaterally impose over Native citizens where the federal franchise was literally added onto existing tribal citizenship, with states later being required to grant the franchise to Indians as well.

In examining the various forms and patterns of indigenous political participation in the three polities they are connected to—tribal, state, and federal— we are stepping into a most complicated subject matter. It is complicated in part because of the treble citizenship status of native individuals, because of the ongoing sovereign status of Native nations, and because of the many policies, laws, and treaties that have defined indigenous–nonindigenous relations. Indian gaming revenue, overseen by a complex web of laws, rules, and policies spawned by the 1988 Indian Gaming Regulatory Act, complicates matters even more. This is because an increasing number of indigenous governments, acting, they argue, in their capacity as sovereigns, are not only actively supporting state and federal office seekers (in addition to tribal office seekers) by making significant financial contributions to political campaigns but also deeply involved in get-the-vote campaigns to benefit both their own and neighboring constituencies. In addition, some Native nations are weighing in on hot-button issues like gay marriage, tobacco legislation, and other topics that are generally unrelated to indigenous affairs.

Throughout the history of indigenous–nonindigenous affairs tribal nations have often felt compelled to lobby Washington policy makers regarding their contractual and moral obligations to protect treaty-derived native rights, but gambling wealth is providing some tribal nations with opportunities to employ lobbyist, public-relations firms and make significant campaign contributions in an effort to gain influence within state and federal political circles in a manner heretofore unknown.

This is a profound political shift and indicates a level of incorporation in American political processes for Native nations and their citizens that until recently had never been evident or sought. Such incorporation has the potential to dramatically redefine the nature of indigenous sovereignty and the historic nation-to-nation relationship originally articulated in treaties and acknowledged in the U.S. Constitution: If Native governments and their treble citizens are so actively engaged in non-Indian politics, can they still legitimately assert that they are in fact extraconstitutional sovereigns, whose treaty- and trust-based rights originally affirmed their distinctive and independent sovereignty?

Indigenous Political Participation in U.S. Politics

In the remainder of this chapter we examine some of the ways in which Native nations and individuals have and are engaged in U.S. politics, especially via voting and campaign contributions. Our emphasis, however, is primarily on indigenous participation in nontribal political affairs because there is such scant social science research available on indigenous participation in native political systems.

As noted earlier, American Indians, as individuals, were unilaterally enfranchised as U.S. citizens in 1924,[27] four years after women received the vote. The fact that American Indians secured the vote so late is ironic, given the previous decades of efforts to forcibly assimilate Native peoples into the body politic. In fact, while many racial and ethnic groups and women faced a *forced exclusion* from the American polity, American Indians since the 1850s had dealt with a *forced inclusion*, even though the franchise arrived later for Native individuals than for virtually any other ethnic group. Although federal policies were developed to coercively integrate Indians into the American social contract, many Native individuals resisted the pressure to abandon their own tribal nations, while those who embraced American citizenship were often denied voting rights in the states where they resided.

One of the earliest Supreme Court decisions denying the franchise to an otherwise eligible Native person was *Elk v. Wilkins*, handed down in 1884.[28] In this case, the Court held that despite having met all the requisite steps to vote, including having left the reservation and moved into a city where he had lived for the required amount of time in order to be eligible to vote, John Elk still maintained an allegiance to his own Native nation and could not be considered as having earned the right to vote. The Court said that Indians, like "the children of subjects of any foreign government," were not subject to the Fourteenth Amendment's provision since they belonged to "alien nations, distinct political communities, with whom the United States might and habitually did deal as they thought fit, either through treaties . . . [or] legislation."[29] In effect, the Court declared that even if individual Natives met the same basic citizenship requirements expected of other noncitizens, they still could not be enfranchised unless Congress made an affirmative declaration authorizing such a change in their standing.

Long after the Indian Citizenship Act of 1924, several states continued to deny Indians the franchise.[30] For example, Native individuals were denied the vote in Arizona until 1948 because they were deemed to be "under guardianship" and to lack the legal competence to vote. And several states, including Idaho, New Mexico, and Washington, maintained constitutional clauses that denied the franchise too because of the clause in the U.S. Constitution that refers to "Indians not taxed." Native individuals in those states could gain the right to vote only if they agreed to "sever their tribal relations and adopt the habits of civilization."[31]

Native individuals in Utah could not vote in state or federal elections until 1956. Ironically, they were denied the franchise on the grounds that they were not "residents" of Utah. The state argued that "allowing them [Indians] to vote might place substantial control of the county government and the expenditures of its funds in a group of citizens who, as a class, had an extremely limited interest in its function and very little responsibility in providing the financial support thereof."[32]

Although the Voting Rights Act of 1965 curtailed the use of many discriminatory measures, American Indians, along with African Americans, Asian Americans, Latinos, and others, still find that they are and can be discouraged or even openly denied the right to vote under so-called ballot integrity programs that are supposed to prevent fraud at polling places. As the *New York Times* noted in an editorial in April 2004, "Today, in Bennett County, S.D., Indians say they have to contend with poll workers who make fun of their names, election officials who make it hard for them to register and—most ominously—a wave of false voter fraud charges that have been made against them, which they regard as harassment."[33]

Such activities, combined with other factors discussed earlier—particularly the role of gaming revenues—however, appear to be having the opposite effect of that intended. Native individuals are registering and voting in local, state, and national elections in unprecedented numbers as they seek to protect their own nations' sovereignty, their remaining lands and treaty rights, and their fragile economic and political foothold in the larger nation's capitalist and democratic systems. As Kevin Gover, the former assistant secretary of Indian affairs, noted in the fall of 2002, just after the national elections:

> There was a lot of good news in the November 5 election results for American Indians: Indian gaming referenda were passed in Arizona and Idaho. Seven Indians were elected to the Montana State legislature. A governor very friendly to tribal interests was elected in New Mexico (former Congressman and Energy Secretary, Bill Richardson), and it appears another respecter of tribal sovereignty was elected governor in Arizona (former U.S. Attorney, Janet Napolitano). And longtime friend of the tribes, Tim Johnson, was re-elected to the Senate from South Dakota. Beneath these results, though, lies the greatest news of all—Indian votes count. And in a close election in the right state, Indian votes can be the difference between the election of a friend and the election of an adversary.[34]

There continues to be very little systematic research on the subject of indigenous voting patterns—in Native and non-Native elections—despite the ever-increasing amount of attention that Native peoples are generating in their day-to-day affairs with other polities. As Jacqueline Johnson, the executive director of the leading intertribal organization the National Congress of American Indians, recently observed: "Indian people have never been a regularly documented population in voter demographics, exit polls or in the mind of the American public as a population that can help determine election results. There has never been a nation-wide study of Native American voters."[35]

Fortunately, a few studies have been conducted in recent years that provide us with at least a modicum of Indian voter, voting behavior, and campaign contribution data. Pei-te Lien, a political scientist, collected comparative data regarding Asian Americans, Latinos, American Indians, African Americans, and whites that examined the distribution of voting and registration patterns of the members of these groups between 1990 and 1998 and found that on average 53% of American Indians were registered to vote in non-Native elections and that nearly 42% had voted in elections in the 1990s.[36]

With regard to party identification, one study of Indian voters in Wisconsin, Minnesota, North Dakota, and South Dakota from 1982 to 1992 showed a strong preference for the Democratic Party. An even stronger Democratic preference was found among the Pueblo Indians of New Mexico, who in 1994 voted for Democratic candidates by 85%. This is corroborated by the fact that a clear majority of American Indian and Alaskan Natives who have been elected to state legislatures as of 2005—thirty-six of fifty-one—identify as Democrats.[37]

It is in the area of campaign contributions where Native nations are having their greatest impact in non-Native politics. The sheer amount of money donated by tribal nations to non-Indian candidates and political parties, much of it generated by Indian gaming operations, has increased tremendously in recent years. According to one study, "in the 1994 election cycle, contributions to political parties and candidates by Indian gaming interests totaled $662,250. By the 2004 election cycle, the amount of contributions exceeded $7 million."[38]

Conclusion

Indigenous participation in nonindigenous politics does allow for greater attention to be focused on Native concerns and issues at the local, state, and national levels. And the new financial capabilities of some Native nations have not only allowed for greater direct and indirect influence but also enabled indigenous leaders to better educate and socialize the broader public and lawmakers about the distinctive status of Native rights and resources. But the complicated nature of indigenous participation in non-Indian political parties and elections promises to be a volatile and unpredictable area of study in the years to come.

It is far too early to tell whether the doctrine of tribal sovereignty, the inherent right of Native nations to exercise a considerable amount of self-governance, will ultimately be strengthened or diminished by tribal and individual Indian engagement in non-Indian politics. As the two stories that opened this essay point out, Native peoples believe, on the one hand, that they have every right to continue to function as distinctive sovereign nations when they choose to engage in international diplomacy. On the other hand, when tribal nations hire professional political lobbyists, they are drawn deeper into American politics and may run the risk of being perceived by their own citizens, the public, and Washington lawmakers as simply another well-endowed interest group, especially when their retained lobbyists turn out to be corrupt.

Nevertheless, Native nations, Native interest groups, and individual tribal citizens will no doubt continue their efforts to improve conditions affecting their people using whatever political, economic, or legal tools are available to them. Such efforts, while not guaranteed to produce success, will be in keeping with the adaptive and flexible traditions that have enabled indigenous peoples—both collectively and individually—to sustain themselves and their unique status as treble citizens despite the oppressive odds they have faced throughout history.

DISCUSSION QUESTIONS

1. Native nations and their citizens share much in common with other racial and ethnic groups—economic disadvantages, a history of discrimination, limited populations—yet their overall political, legal, territorial, and cultural status is remarkably distinct. Identify and then assess what some of these distinctions are. How do these differences affect their political rights as separate nations and as American citizens?
2. Chart the historical evolution of the concept of "treble citizenship" as applied to Native peoples. Discuss how these three layers of citizenship both strengthen and impair the rights of indigenous individuals in relation to their tribal nations and vis-à-vis the states and the federal government.
3. Explain the profound political impacts that Indian gaming revenues are producing in Indian Country and beyond. Economically and intergovernmentally, this revenue source is affecting politics on every level. Speculate on what the short-, mid-, and long-term implications of gaming revenues are for Native peoples, both internally and externally.
4. Describe and assess the similarities and differences between the indigenous–state relationship and the indigenous–federal relationship. How do these separate intergovernmental relationships affect tribal nations in their efforts to improve their citizens' lives and rights?

5. In an important 2004 U.S. Supreme Court decision involving an Indian tribe's right to prosecute Indians who were not enrolled as tribal members, *United States v. Lara*, Associate Justice Clarence Thomas noted in a concurring opinion that tribal nations, unlike states, "are not part of this [U.S.] constitutional order, and their sovereignty is not guaranteed by it." This statement affirms the extraconstitutional status of indigenous nations but also highlights the fragility of Indian nations, which lack guaranteed status within the federal and state constitutional systems. The situation is further complicated because although tribal nations lack constitutional protection, individual Indians now have a recognized constitutional status as "citizens" and the right to vote and otherwise participate in the broader American political system. This combination of radically different statuses leaves Native peoples with a bifurcated posture in regard to the broader public. Describe how this situation arose and what, if anything, can be done to create a more stable political and legal environment for Native peoples who collectively lack constitutional standing, yet individually possess the same.

Chapter 7

Linked Fates, Disconnected Realities:

The Post–Civil Rights African American Politics

Melanye T. Price
Gloria J. Hampton

On August 29, 2005, a category 4 hurricane made landfall on America's Gulf Coast. In a last-minute change of direction, the eye of Hurricane Katrina passed just east of New Orleans; and though the city was damaged, it first appeared that a great tragedy had been averted. However, initial relief was replaced with the quickly growing awareness of a massive crisis in the making. Two of the city's levees had burst, and more than 80% of New Orleans was soon under water.[1] In the days that followed, Americans were bombarded with around-the-clock televised images of mostly black residents trapped on rooftops, wading through toxic waters, stranded on overpasses, and massing on the sidewalks surrounding the city's convention center. The disturbing images included abandoned bodies, darkened corridors of hospitals without the means to adequately treat remaining patients, and male and female residents of all ages foraging for food and other necessary supplies. These images were accompanied by what would turn out to be vastly overblown accounts of looting, shootings, and other forms of lawlessness circulated as fact by authorities and reporters.[2]

The country watched in disbelief as days passed without the arrival of expected governmental assistance or efforts to evacuate remaining city residents. Even as President Bush held a news conference complimenting the efforts of his Federal Emergency Management Agency director, Michael Brown, with the now infamous "Brownie, you're doing a heck of a job,"[3] it was obvious to anyone watching at home that the government's emergency relief system had broken down and that the consequences of that breakdown would be disproportionately borne by the poor black residents of New Orleans. Speaking to a reporter for the Washington Post, a woman who spent two days with her family on the roof of her home and was "rescued" only to be deposited under a bridge for another long day and night of waiting for a way out offered a brief but heart-wrenching summary of the experience of those who lived through Hurricane Katrina in New Orleans. "It was like going to hell and back," she said.[4] The woman went on to a distinctly racialized and devastating analysis of this event. "To me," said Bernadette Washington, "it just seems like black people are marked. We have so many troubles and problems."[5]

February 10, 2007, was a much better day for African Americans as talk show host Tavis Smiley assembled leading black media, academic, business, religious, and political figures for what is known as the State of Black America Conference. Since its inception in 2000, the conference has developed into a bona fide event for African Americans. Over the past eight years, over 100,000 attendees and an additional 83 million television viewers have witnessed some portion of the conference.[6] The event has become so popular that The Covenant with Black America, a book that grew out of the 2006 conference, became the first book published by a black press to top the New York Times best-seller list. On this day in 2007, well-known African Americans like Jesse Jackson, Al Sharpton, Maya Angelou, Michael Eric Dyson, and Cornell West were joined by media entrepreneur Kathy Hughes, actor Tim Reid, Thomas Dortch of the 100 Black Men of America, Inc., and many others to consider topics like the status of the black family, the achievement gap in education, Hurricane Katrina and its aftermath, the war in Iraq, and, of course, presidential politics. Even as the panelists detailed the daunting challenges facing the African American community and debated strategies for forging ahead, their very presence in the auditorium spoke to the success that so many African Americans have found in various walks of life.

There was, however, at least one prominent African American missing from the day's events. As several panelists pointed out in their discussion of national politics, U.S. Senator Barack Obama was absent, perhaps due to the fact that he had chosen this day to make a formal announcement of his intention to run for president. Although other African Americans had challenged for the Democratic presidential nomination in the past, Senator Obama was the first African American judged by the mainstream media, political pundits, and Democratic Party leaders to be a serious contender for both the party's nomination and eventual election to the presidency.[7] Therefore, his announcement was a signal event both in the history of the country and in black efforts to assert political power.

Introduction

These disparate events—the nation's worst natural disaster, a summit of black leaders, and the announcement of the candidacy of Barack Obama—have much to offer in the way of understanding the status of black politics at the turn of the century. They illuminate the continued bonds among blacks, the growing diversity of the black community, the meaning of political representation, the role and nature of African American leaders, and the benefits and limits of electoral politics for political empowerment.

In this chapter, we will consider these issues by addressing the following questions. Is there a continuing shared "black experience" of oppression and exclusion around which African Americans can unite as they did before, during, and immediately after the 1960s civil rights movement? How have intraracial differences manifested themselves in the post–civil rights era, and what impact have these differences had on contemporary black political behavior? How has the nature and composition of black leadership changed in the post–civil rights era? What does political representation mean for black Americans? Has the focus on voting and other electoral strategies yielded the results intended in terms of a greater black presence in political and policy-making positions?

Linked Fate and an Increasingly Diverse Population

The public opinion research is replete with examples of race-based gaps in opinion on a wide range of issues including beliefs about the prevalence of racial discrimination and affirmative action,[8] the fairness of the criminal justice system,[9] antidiscrimination policies for homosexuals,[10] the use of military force to advance foreign policy,[11] and increased spending for social services.[12] These and other dramatic race-based differences in public opinion show that African Americans and whites continue to experience the world in very different ways,[13] and this truism is brought home by the differences in black and white perceptions in the wake of Katrina. For example, a 2005 Pew opinion poll found that 71% of blacks believed that the disaster showed that racial inequality is still a major problem in America, while 56% of whites did not regard this as an important lesson of Hurricane Katrina. Even more to the point, 66% of blacks believed that the government's response to the disaster was slower than it would have been if the victims were white, while only 17% of whites shared this view.[13a] When rapper Kanye West went off-script at a nationally televised fund-raising event for hurricane victims and declared "George Bush doesn't care about black people," blacks in the viewing audience were largely in agreement as post-Katrina polls showed Bush's approval rating among blacks at record lows.[14]

Blacks were also significantly more likely than whites to report personal feelings of both anger and depression as a result of the disaster. Blacks had a different view of the people who remained in the city from whites: Blacks were significantly more likely than whites to view the stranded residents of New Orleans as people who had stayed behind because they had no way out rather than as people who had freely chosen to stay, and they were also more likely than whites to characterize those who were scavenging in stores and other places as ordinary people trying to survive rather than as criminals.[15] African American attitudes surrounding Hurricane Katrina are consistent with repeated findings that African Americans across economic classes view their fate as linked to that of other blacks. Scholars have both established this sense of linked fate and shown it to be a critical component in the political attitudes and behavior of blacks.[16] As Michael Dawson defines it in *Behind the Mule*, the concept of "linked fate" moves beyond a simple racial group consciousness to the specific belief that one's own self-interests are tied inextricably to the interests of other blacks. As Dawson puts it, "the historical experiences of African Americans have resulted in a situation in which group interests have served as a useful proxy for self-interest" (p. 77). In fact, Dawson develops the idea of the "black utility heuristic" to explain how many African Americans continue to use cues about group interests provided by indigenous sources like the black media, opinion leaders, elected officials, and the black church to orient both their political attitudes and behavior. He demonstrates that those with a strong sense of linked fate are more likely to use this heuristic, or cognitive, shortcut to make sense of the political world. The cues provided by indigenous sources allow blacks to form opinions about political candidates, partisanship, and other political matters in a very efficient manner.

While African American reactions to Katrina demonstrated the continued strength of the sense of linked fate among African Americans, another story beyond the much ballyhooed black–white racial divide on perceptions of this disaster can be found by examining images from New Orleans that filled television screens in the days after the hurricane struck. The blacks who were stranded in New Orleans after the hurricane shared a critical characteristic: poverty. For the most part, those who could afford to leave did so, leaving behind those who lacked the resources to evacuate. In this way, the Hurricane Katrina experience of poor blacks was similar to the rest of their lives—an existence that is distinct and in many ways separate from the better-off parts of the African American community.

As Hurricane Katrina showed, many sectors of the black community continue to experience an all too familiar and depressing reality. Black poverty rates remain fixed at three times the rate for non-Hispanic whites, while the rate of black unemployment in the post–civil rights movement era has not moved from approximately double that of whites during both economic booms and busts. When one considers large urban centers, the statistics are even more disturbing as unemployment and poverty levels are much higher in many black inner-city communities and are tied to a cluster of troubling social conditions that include high levels of crime, absence of men in families, and drug addiction.[17]

At the same time, the post–civil rights era has brought dramatic changes to the black middle class. The proportion of African Americans in the middle class has risen to record highs. In the era of segregation better-off blacks lived and worked in the same neighborhoods as poorer ones. The black middle class was composed largely of ministers, teachers, doctors, lawyers, and others who served their black clientele. However, the current black middle class differs from the old with respect to its physical proximity to poor and working-class blacks. In the post–civil rights movement period, members of the black middle class have had new opportunities for employment and housing,[18] and these opportunities serve to distance them from their poorer counterparts. Critically, the black middle class now works primarily in the public sector and at majority white corporations rather than in the provision of services to less well-off blacks. This means that in addition to being spatially segregated from better-off blacks, poorer blacks can no longer use their patronage of businesses owned by the black middle class to assert some influence over the black agenda.

While Hurricane Katrina laid bare the growing economic chasm in black America and the singular experience of poor blacks, reactions to Barack Obama's presidential bid elucidate another reality: the increasing presence of newer immigrants from African and the Caribbean in the black community. In the days before and after his announcement, black talk radio and the Internet came alive with discussions of what Obama's candidacy would mean for black Americans. Much of that talk centered on questions of his "blackness."[19] Many of those doing the questioning pointed to Obama's mixed racial heritage and the fact that he had been raised primarily by his white mother and her parents. However, there were even more callers, bloggers, and others discussing the fact that his father was Kenyan so that Obama did not share the black American heritage of slavery and segregation. In the past, black solidarity was taken as a given in comparison to the challenges facing other minorities like Latinos and Asian Americans, who were trying to create shared identities among individuals with distinct cultures and national backgrounds. What the questioning of Obama's heritage demonstrates is that blacks increasingly will need to have the same hard conversations as other minorities about whether and how to build a solidarity that moves across lines of culture and nationality.

Indeed, both the experience of poor black residents of New Orleans during Katrina and the initial divisiveness among black Americans about Barack Obama's status as an authentically black candidate point to another thread of scholarship that explores the limits of the linked fate variable for understanding black politics. Here, scholars focus on the ways that the emphasis on linked fate has stymied necessary conversations about whose interests make it to the top of the black political agenda. Cathy Cohen points to the slow response of black leaders to the AIDS crisis as an example of the way in which some interests are downplayed in putting together the "black agenda"; the needs and interests of gay men and intravenous drug users who did not conform to middle-class black standards of propriety were simply pushed to the back burner.[20] Other works in this vein point to the struggles of black women living with HIV/AIDS to achieve political voice[21] and the growing impatience of better-off blacks with the perceived pathologies of poorer blacks.[22]

Affirmative Action and the Black Political Agenda

Conversations about diverging identities and interests in black America, while difficult, may lead to an expansion of the black agenda beyond its current emphasis. It can fairly be said that the post–civil rights movement black agenda has centered on affirmative action as a way to increase black access to higher education, government contracts for black-owned businesses, and the kinds of jobs that can build the black middle class. Affirmative action policies also stand at the center of the debate about the continuing role of racism in the lives of black Americans. Among political scientists, that debate is often undertaken by those who study public opinion.

Public opinion researchers have focused most of their efforts on developing explanations for white opposition to affirmative action, and two basic camps have crystallized. On the one side are those who see white opposition to affirmative action as driven by animosity toward blacks. Researchers in this camp argue that the racism of the pre–civil rights movement, based on notions of the biological inferiority of blacks, is no longer socially acceptable; however, the dramatic decline in the numbers of white Americans who are willing to express adherence to a biologically based racism should not be read as signaling an end to animosity toward blacks. Instead, racism has taken a new turn toward what is often referred to as "new racism" or "symbolic racism"; *symbolic racists* are those who combine adherence to traditional norms like individualism and hard work with a perception that blacks live in violation of these norms. In this view, white opposition to affirmative action is largely a socially acceptable expression of symbolic racism.

The opposing camp argues that most white opposition to affirmative action actually comes as a result of adherence to notions of color blind equality that are offended when any one racial group is privileged over another.[23] They vehemently dispute the idea that modern-day racism is somehow related to conservatism (through the centrality of traditional values to both conservatism and symbolic racism) and use experiments embedded in survey research to produce some empirical support for their argument that the chief reason that liberals are more likely than conservatives to express support for affirmative action in public opinion polls is that many liberals feel pressure to adhere to what is taken to be a cornerstone of modern liberalism rather than out of a true preference for affirmative action.[24] Some researchers in this vein even go so far as to assert that rather than serving as an *indicator* of preexisting racial animosity, white opposition to affirmative action programs actually *cause* racial resentment where none had existed previously.[25]

Even while opinion researchers debate the meaning and causes of white opposition to affirmative action, there are important facts on the ground to consider. First, researchers have begun to counter the claims that affirmative action confers unfair and unprecedented race-based advantage to blacks by focusing on the role that government played in the creation and protection of the white middle class. For example, in *When Affirmative Action Was White*, Ira Katznelson explores the way in which federal government policies of the 1930s and 1940, like the Social Security Act and the GI Bill, worked to either shield many whites from the worst consequences of the Great Depression or lift them into the middle class. In the years immediately after World War II, government programs that promoted home ownership and college attendance created the modern white middle class; unfortunately, as Katznelson demonstrates, government officials took deliberate action in both the construction and the administration of these programs to deny blacks access.[26]

Second, it is undeniable that affirmative action policies in college admissions and hiring practices have ushered many blacks into the middle class while helping to solidify the middle-class position of many others. They have served to open up many sectors, particularly in public service (e.g., police and fire departments) that had been systematically closed to African Americans. And even as we write, affirmative action policies are still an important factor in expanding and maintaining the black middle class.

However, there is another truth as well. The majority of African Americans are poor and working-class, and they largely have been left out of the benefits conferred by affirmative action policies. Affirmative action policies mostly advance the interests of those blacks most able to take advantage of the opportunities to attend college, assume management positions, etc.; indeed, while the ongoing struggle[27] to protect affirmative action programs has been instrumental for the construction of the post-1960s black middle class, it is one that virtually ignores the interests of worse-off blacks. For example, while black leaders and their white supporters vigorously fended off affirmative action challenges from the right, welfare "reform" in the mid-1990s severely reduced the welfare benefits available to poor black families. Likewise the post–civil rights era explosion in the black prison population[28] receives limited attention from black advocacy groups.

This shift from a civil rights movement that spoke to the broad concerns of blacks across income groups to the current emphasis on the interests of the burgeoning middle class is one that accompanied the demobilization of the black masses. As the civil rights movement left the streets and moved into courtrooms where civil rights cases were litigated and to a reliance on Democratic Party politics, the mass of poor blacks lost their ability to barter their active participation in return for inclusion on the agenda.[29] Instead, they and the entire black community came to rely on elected officials to represent their interests.

Representing Black Interests

One of the greatest challenges in contemporary black politics is adjudicating disputes over the meaning and measure of political representation. In *The Concept of Representation* (1967), Hanna Pitkin outlines four kinds of representation—formalistic, symbolic, descriptive, and substantive. *Formalistic representation* relates to the institutional factors that both give representatives their political standing and represent the constraints imposed by constituents. For example, members of the Congressional Black Caucus (CBC) are representatives of the African American community because they are elected by mostly black constituencies to the House of Representatives; however, if the CBC members' activities in Washington, D.C., are not congruent with the will of a majority of their constituents, they will lose their position in Congress.[30] *Descriptive representation* is, by far, the most obvious form of representation. It means that the most salient social and ascriptive characteristics that can be attributed to a group's representative should also be attributable to the group itself. Simply put, descriptive representation means that blacks will be represented by other blacks. For Pitkin, *symbolic representation* involves a kind of "standing for" in which elected leaders serve as a kind of symbol in which a group believes. However, the study of symbolic representation usually revolves around policies that "do not distribute or redistribute any public good or regulate in the standard sense, but reflect their constituents' interests and concerns."[31] Examples of symbolic policies spearheaded by black members of Congress include the creation of a federal holiday in honor of Martin Luther King, the awarding of a congressional medal to Rosa Parks, and the congressional recognition of the important contributions of African American music.[32] *Substantive representation* is often viewed by politicians and political scientists as the most important form of representation. This form assumes that a group's representative champions, initiates, and endorses the issue and policy preferences that are important to the group she or he represents.

Research suggests that African Americans fare better with some forms of representation than others. Before Lyndon Johnson signed the Voting Rights Act (VRA) of 1965, few blacks were registered to vote in the south, where they primarily lived.[33] In the first two years after the VRA, over 500,000 blacks registered to vote in the seven states the act covered; and by the 1990s 64.4% of African Americans were registered to vote.[34] With more blacks having access to voting and their numerical advantage in some jurisdictions, there was a natural assumption that there would be an increase in descriptive representation for blacks; and indeed, there has been. Today, there are more black elected officials than at any other time in American history, and nine of the ten states with the largest number of black elected officials are states that currently are or have been covered under various provisions of the VRA.[35] The success in gaining descriptive representation is reflected at the national level, where the number of members of the CBC rose to a record high of 43 after the 2006 congressional elections.

But does being represented by someone of the same race mean that individuals are substantively represented? There is some disagreement about this in the black politics literature. Carol Swain's *Black Faces, Black Interests* (1993) sparked a debate about whether or not black faces in Congress really meant that black interests were also being represented. Based on in-depth case studies of members of Congress, she ultimately concluded that whites can represent majority black districts just as well as blacks. This is good news for African Americans according to Swain for two reasons. First, as a numerical minority, blacks will only have their policy preferences transformed into national legislation through alliances with members of the numerical majority (i.e., whites). Second, because of the difficulty of getting white votes, most black representatives will come from districts with large concentrations of black voters; however, the number of new black districts that can be drawn is rapidly diminishing; therefore, the potential for continued growth in descriptive representation for blacks at the national level is decreasing.[36]

Scholars have challenged Swain's assessment from a variety of angles. For example, Jane Mansbridge argues that descriptive and substantive forms of representation are, in fact, linked for African Americans and that there are certain aspects of descriptive representation that actually enhance substantive representation.[37] Descriptive congruence between representatives and their constituencies enhances substantive representation "when party identification and campaign statements provide poor clues to representatives' future actions" and because it imbues political deliberation with "vigor" that comes with experiential knowledge.[38] Beyond substantive representation, descriptive representation is said to also provide two institutional benefits. First, descriptive representation for blacks countermanded the previously prevalent view that blacks were not suitable for governing. Second, diversity in descriptive representation provides "de facto legitimacy" to governing institutions by making blacks feel like they are part of the governing process.[39] Other researchers have established that black voters who were represented by black officials expressed increased satisfaction with their representation in Washington and electoral support,[40] while the presence of a black mayor leads to higher levels of trust among black constituents.[41]

Blacks and the Democratic Party

No matter what form of representation one considers, there is one post–civil rights movement constant: Blacks have come to rely on the Democratic Party for representation. African Americans first established a relationship with the Democratic Party during the New Deal era of the 1930s, and this relationship was solidified with the 1964 elections when the Republicans selected as their presidential candidate Barry Goldwater, who had voted against the 1964 Civil Rights Act on the grounds that it violated states' rights. Today, African Americans identify with and vote for Democrats at levels much higher than any other demographic group.[42] In the 1960s, even as blacks responded positively to the support that the Democratic Congress and President Johnson gave to major civil rights legislation, white southerners began an exodus from the party that shifted the solidly Democratic South to its current status as the electoral stronghold of the Republican Party.[43]

Shifts in white and black voting patterns and partisan identification pose a difficult dilemma for the Democratic Party as it has come to rely on black voters for electoral success[44] even as its close association with blacks has alienated white voters in the South and elsewhere who are also necessary for victory. Journalists and scholars alike have noted a primary response by the Democratic Party and its standard bearers, which is to create distance from the black base in attempts to be more appealing to white voters.[45] Subtle racial signaling often takes place during campaigns. For example, in 1992 Bill Clinton went out of his way to repudiate rapper Sistah Souljah and controversial comments she had made in the press in relation to racial unrest in Los Angeles. Clinton used a speech he was giving to Jackson's Rainbow Coalition to compare Sistah Souljah to noted white supremacist David Duke. This move received a great deal of criticism from black activists and politicians, but many believed that it served a greater purpose as a signal to white voters that he was serious about reducing the crime rate and independent of the party's black base.[46]

For African Americans this dysfunctional relationship with the Democratic Party has more serious consequences than the subtle disrespect during campaign season. In fact, the current relationship between the Democratic Party and blacks can best be understood as one of *party capture*. A group is in a state of party capture when there is no viable party alternative for that group, which allows the capturing party to virtually ignore the group's policy preferences. Put simply, Democrats know that any black threats to shift votes to the Republican Party are largely idle.[47]

However, in response to the slim margins in recent elections, Republicans (especially religious conservatives) have begun to make some overtures to black voters. Using religious and moral compatibility as an avenue for potential coalition building rather than more divisive racial and economic positions, conservatives have focused on issues such as gay marriage to appeal to African American voters. Thus far, those overtures have not translated into substantial votes. Bush's share of the black vote increased between 2000 and 2004 from 9% to 11% but not enough to sway elections.[48] Apparently, black voters have not forgotten or forgiven the open hostility that the Republican Party has shown to black interests or the implicit racial messages that became a specialty of Republican strategists in the last twenty years, like the polarizing Willie Horton ads in the 1988 Dukakis–Bush campaign and the "white hands" ad in the 1990 Helms–Gantt Senate race.[49]

At various historical moments black activists have suggested that blacks could overcome the dilemma of party capture by leveraging the black voting bloc to create bipartisan competition and real interest negotiations for black support. For example, in the 1970s there was a push to formulate a cohesive black political agenda around which the black community could coalesce and leverage political benefits from the two major parties; these efforts led to the 1972 National Black Political Convention in Gary, Indiana. This convention was composed of delegates from across the United States and included elected officials, artists, activists, and ordinary citizens. However, with respect to the goal of creating black independence from the Democratic Party, the 1972 National Political Convention and similar attempts were failures. Instead, African Americans have chosen to work within the Democratic Party for increased access to political power.

The benefits of increased electoral participation and representation seem obvious. Members of a democratic nation should have access to the institutions that govern them, and in the last few decades, we can say, at least in terms of descriptive representation, this country has become more inclusive. In terms of the political preferences and goals of African Americans being met, there is disagreement about whether the electoral strategy as a singular goal has been the right strategy. America is a two-party system, and current scholarship and media reports suggest that blacks are caught in a political conundrum: continue to support the party that tries to distance itself from one of its most loyal blocks or transfer their support to a party that took in the segregationist Dixiecrats after the civil rights movement and still employs racially polarizing electoral tactics that attract white voters with negative portrayals of blacks and their allies. There is no easy solution to this problem, but it is one that emerging black activists and politicians must address.

Blacks and Deracialized Strategies for Electoral Success

An emphasis on black politics at the national level and the struggle to gain national elected office really represents only a portion of the story as only a handful of the many blacks who have held and continue to hold elective office are at the national level; instead, the vast majority of black office holders work at the local and state levels. They are members of school boards, city councils, and state legislatures, as well as mayors. Some of these officials, particularly those in settings where blacks are not in the majority, have turned away from race-based strategies for winning office. Black political scientists began to take notice of this phenomenon beginning with the 1989 elections when there were a large number of blacks elected mayor in major urban areas and Doug Wilder became the first black to be elected governor in any American state. This electoral success was particularly important because of "the deliberate absence of familiar appeals to black voters, as well as, the absence or diminution by the winning candidates of campaign issues which could be interpreted as addressing the black agenda."[50] Many of the successful candidates in this election represented the emergence of a new black political strategy called *deracialization*, which is conducting a campaign in a stylistic fashion that defuses the polarizing effects of race by avoiding explicit reference to race-specific issues, while at the same time emphasizing those issues that are perceived as racially transcendent, thus mobilizing a broad segment of the electorate for purposes of capturing or maintaining public office.[51]

While this electoral strategy may prove to be a successful route to elective office holding, it is still unclear what it means for issues important to African Americans once deracialized candidates are called upon to actually govern. In the post–civil rights movement era, blacks have relied on black officials to voice black interests in the governing process. We also know that representatives are beholden to represent those people who voted them into office. So if a black elected official runs a deracialized campaign to win the support of white voters, then he or she has a choice: fail the people who voted him or her into office by focusing on race-specific issues or fail blacks by governing in a deracialized fashion. This could be regarded as a very rigid notion that assumes that blacks (and whites, really) only support those issues that are specific to their group. However, there is some initial support for the fact that black candidates who win using der-acialized strategies do not champion the interests of their black constituents. For example, a study of black elected officials in California found that self-identified deracialized or race-neutral candidates "were less likely to support interests that have traditionally been found to be pertinent to the black community."[52]

Assuming the Mantle of Leadership

Thus far we have discussed electoral politics with respect to representation and the kinds of strategies used by candidates to gain office. However, electoral politics are also important because elected officials have become both the primary source of leadership and de facto spokespeople for black political interests. During the civil rights era, black leadership came from sources that were able to engage in protest without retribution from white institutions that may have controlled their employment status. So, for instance, public school teachers were less likely to take on leadership roles because they were reliant on white-controlled school boards for their livelihoods; however, ministers, students, and activists in black organizations were able to act independently of the white power structure.[53] Equally important, black leaders were dependent on the support of the black masses for success, and their agenda reflected this dependence with broad initiatives designed to improve the lot of all of black America.

Initially, as blacks moved from "protest to politics," newly elected leaders came directly from the front lines of the civil rights movement. Indeed, many names that are widely celebrated for their work during the movement were ulti-mately elected to represent blacks at all levels of government. Examples would include two current members of the House, John Lewis and Eleanor Holmes Norton, who were leaders in the Student Nonviolent Coordinating Committee. Additionally, other civil rights activists, such as Julian Bond, Andrew Young, Marion Barry, and Jesse Jackson, have sought or held elective office.

Before Obama, the most successful black candidate for the presidency to date combined membership in twin strands of the black leadership tradition: the black church and the civil rights movement. In 1984 and 1988, Reverend Jesse Jackson, who had worked directly with Martin Luther King at the South-ern Christian Leadership Conference and went on to lead the Operation PUSH (People United to Save Humanity) organization, ran two significant campaigns for the Democratic presidential nomination. Running on a progressive agenda and attempting to build a "rainbow coalition," Jackson spoke directly to blacks and other disaffected members of the Democratic Party base. In the 1988 primary, the number of delegates he received was second only to frontrunner

Michael Dukakis, who refused to name Jackson as his running mate.[54] In a study of black opinions about the Jackson candidacies, Katherine Tate found that the combination of Jackson and strong anti-Reagan sentiments provided extra motivation for blacks to turn out for the primaries.[54a] However, in the 1988 general election, black turnout decreased significantly; Tate suggests that (1) blacks who overwhelmingly and fervently supported Jackson's candidacies were disappointed by a failed second attempt, (2) many thought he had been mistreated by the party in the nomination and convention process, and (3) the Democratic candidate for that year was unattractive to black voters.

In the two decades since Jackson's last campaign, several names had been put forth as black presidential hopefuls and some had even sought the nomination;[55] but none of the more recent black candidates had matched Jackson's level of success. However, the increasing heterogeneity in the black community and challenges to black solidarity are accompanied by a changing of the guard in the traditional black leadership. Here, Barack Obama's candidacy serves as an exemplar of the diverging nature of black leadership. Obama's entrance into the race for president was heralded by many who viewed him as an antidote to the continuing culture wars. Indeed, he sought to portray himself as a unifier who could move the country past the personal politics and vitriol of recent years. Many of his admirers specifically pointed to him as a fresh face who, because of his relative youth, had not been a participant in the cultural battles of the 1960s. The politics of character assassination with respect to what presidential candidates did during the Vietnam era simply would not apply to him.[56] What often went unsaid in these mainstream news accounts was that not only did he not share the heritage of slavery and segregation that has served as a central trope in unifying black Americans but he also did not come from the same civil rights tradition as previous black candidates for president. This departure from the traditional base for black leadership was reflected in the way in which Senator Obama's announcement differed from the State of Black America Conference taking place concurrently.

Both the State of Black America Conference and Barack Obama's official announcement of his presidential candidacy amassed large crowds, were televised live and in full, and were covered by both the mainstream and black press. However, there were important differences with respect to how the events fit into a discussion of black politics. First, the conference took place in the South, where the majority of African Americans still live, and was hosted by one of America's oldest historically black centers of higher education, Hampton University. All of the presenters and the vast majority of those in the audience were African Americans. This was, in short, a conversation among African Americans designed to reach some common understanding of the way forward in their continuing struggle for justice and equality. In contrast, Obama's announcement took place on the steps of the old Illinois State House surrounded by his family and a crowd largely made up of enthusiastic white supporters. The majority white makeup of the crowd was not surprising given the choice of location for the event: Obama chose to announce his candidacy in Springfield, a city in which whites make up 80% of the population, rather than in his hometown of Chicago, some 200 miles to the north and a city in which African Americans are the majority.

The differences between Obama and traditional black leadership moved beyond the choice of location for his speech. At least early on in his campaign, it appeared that he would rely on both a deracialized agenda and style. Indeed, many of his white supporters pointed to the contrast between him and other black leaders by asserting that he seemed less "angry" than other blacks and black politicians. Perhaps this is what fellow senator and Democratic candidate Joe Biden meant when he referred to Obama as the first black presidential candidate "who is articulate and bright and clean and a nice-looking guy."[57]

Writing on the website of the black newspaper the *Pittsburgh Courier*, black political scientist Ron Walters pointed out that the very qualities that made Obama attractive to white audiences raised questions for many African American observers.

> His novelty has meant that he presents a view of racial diversity that is attractive to Americans, the non-threatening variety. One variety of diversity comes with a compensatory edge, where blacks are demanding compensation for the past of slavery and post-slavery racism has been rejected by the Supreme Court, by the states of California, Washington, and more recently Michigan. There is another kind of diversity that is based on the simple proposition of the positive desire to include all people of whatever stripe in the American experiment. The latter is where Barrack [sic] Obama wins his appeal from America. This is suggested by his parental background and his upbringing and now become an out-front aspect of his persona.[58]

Walters went on to argue that Obama should be made to earn the support of black voters rather than receiving it merely on the basis of his ability to provide descriptive representation.[59] This same sentiment was voiced by several of the prominent speakers at the State of Black America Conference, who wondered aloud why Obama had chosen to make his candidacy announcement on the day of their conference instead of joining the conveners for an intraracial discussion of the needs and goals of black America.

Perhaps this skepticism signals a growing realization that in this post–civil rights era black citizens will need to be more vigilant in holding their leaders accountable. More responsive leadership will only result from a black population that recognizes that reflexive support for black politicians, even those who would achieve historical firsts, cannot solve the problems of black America. As Walters concluded, blacks must be more active in choosing their champions:

Barrack [sic] Obama should run. But he should also be held accountable by the black community. If he truly does not want to be held accountable on that score, he should be judged accordingly. And if he does, then he should really run and perhaps try to use his campaign to bring the rest of America along. He can't win that way, you say. Then, of what value is a black president of the United States?[60]

Conclusion

During the course of the State of Black America Conference, Tavis Smiley announced a first step in efforts to hold all of the presidential candidates accountable for their positions on issues of interest to black America. For the first time, both Democratic and Republican candidates were invited to attend separate nationally televised forums at which they would outline their positions on the issues presented in the *Covenant with Black America*. At the same time, many states were moving to reduce the undue influence of the disproportionately white electorates in New Hampshire and Iowa in the primary process by moving their own primaries up in the election season. Optimally, earlier primaries in states like California, Missouri, New York, New Jersey, and Illinois allow African American voters to play an enhanced role in picking the candidate of the Democratic Party. If black voters can use the candidate forums and other sources to inform themselves about positions that the candidates are taking on issues of import to the black community, then they may be able to translate their numbers into real influence in the selection of the Democratic Party nominee. This could for the first time offer black voters an effective way to address the dilemma of party capture.

At this writing, Democrats have regained the majority in both chambers of Congress, and several of the forty-three members of the CBC have translated their seniority into chairs of key congressional committees, including the Ways and Means Committee and the Judiciary Committee.[61] Members of the CBC also form a critical voting bloc within a slim Democratic majority; however, this newfound political power will be challenged by the determination of many Democratic leaders and strategists to advance a timid agenda so as not to alienate the moderate voters that they see as key to future victories. Yet even a cursory examination of the statistics for black high school graduation, college attendance, incarceration, poverty, and health inequities, among others, leads to the inexorable conclusion that timidity is not a strategy that will make a difference for those who live their lives on the short end of those statistics.

Quite simply, the color line that DuBois identified as the chief problem of the last century continues to challenge us.[62] Another familiar part of our racial landscape is that African Americans still look to government as one of the sources for remedies for social and economic inequality. The stakes with regard to black political empowerment are high; therefore, it is not surprising that the effectiveness of various strategies for black political empowerment continue to be the subject of enormous interest, disagreement, and importance for those who study the politics of race. As we make our way through this new century, blacks will need to come to grips with the ramifications of increased intraracial diversity, the meaning of black representation, the dilemmas of party politics and strategies for building influence, and the challenge of identifying leaders of the black community and holding them accountable for their positions and actions.

DISCUSSION QUESTIONS

1. Is there such a thing as "black interests"? Should blacks continue to organize on the basis of racial solidarity? What are the benefits and potential pitfalls of race-based solidarity?

2. Do black faces equal black interests? Do you agree with Carol Swain's argument that blacks can be represented just as well by liberal whites as they are by blacks? If yes, how would whites who represent blacks differentiate themselves from whites who represent whites in terms of policy and legislation? If no, how can black representation be increased to secure increased representation for the African American community?

3. Suppose African Americans, as a voting bloc, decided to leverage their votes in the next election. If African Americans announced that they would not vote for either party in the next election unless they were offered policy or legislative guarantees, how would this change the relationship between blacks and both political parties? What would be the benefits of this? What would be the drawbacks? Do you see this as a viable strategy?

4. How has the movement from protest to politics changed the nature of black politics? How has it affected the nature of black leadership? What about the issues on the black agenda? What, if any, alternatives are there to electoral politics for the pursuit of black interests?

5. Was it inevitable that an African American candidate would make a successful run for the White House? Was Obama forced to run a deracialized campaign, or could he maintain close connections to the black community and still win? What issues did Obama have to avoid/address? What kinds of appeals were necessary for whites to support his candidacy? How were they different from black expectations?

Chapter 8

The Influence of Context and History on the Policy Positions and Partisanship of Hispanics in the United States[1]

Jessica Lavariega Monforti
Lisa García Bedolla

In April 1961, a group of about 1,500 U.S.-based Cuban exiles, who were armed and trained by the U.S. government, landed in the Bay of Pigs. Their intention was to overthrow the revolutionary government of Fidel Castro, which had taken power in Cuba in January 1959. As early as March 1960, Republican President Dwight D. Eisenhower was concerned about Castro's potentially communist leaning, so the CIA had begun to plan for a possible invasion of the island to overthrow him. The plan was ultimately carried out by Eisenhower's Democratic successor, President John F. Kennedy. The basic premise of the plan was that, as Cubans on the island learned about the exiles' arrival, they would simultaneously rise up against the Castro regime. Additionally, the exiles' success was seen as dependent upon U.S. air strikes that would destroy Castro's air force and therefore hamper his regime's ability to respond to the invasion. Kennedy, however, was uncomfortable with a military plan he "inherited" and therefore had little say about and was also concerned about how the United States' direct intervention in Cuba might be viewed by the international community. Therefore, he chose to continue to fund and supply the exile group but refused to provide the air support. The invasion ended up being a dismal failure. Sixty-eight of the exiles died, and the remainder were captured. The Castro regime remained firmly in place.

For Cubans opposed to the Castro regime, many of whom had already fled the island, the Bay of Pigs debacle was a deep disappointment. Accustomed to significant U.S. intervention in the island's politics (e.g., the United States intervened directly in

Cuban politics in 1906, 1912, 1920, and 1933), they expected the United States to get rid of a government many of them perceived to be communist. Manuel, a Cuban American currently living in California, is a good example of this. Manuel was newly married and living in Havana in 1959 when Castro first came to power. By 1961 he already had deep misgivings about the new Castro regime. When rumors began to swirl that the United States was going to intervene in Cuba, Manuel hoped that he would not have to flee his homeland. The failure of the Bay of Pigs, in his mind due to the failure of President Kennedy to commit U.S. air forces to the fight as promised, is what finalized his decision to leave Cuba. Manuel migrated to the United States and, a few years later, naturalized as a U.S. citizen and registered to vote. When deciding which party to register with, he chose to register as a Democrat. By this time, President Kennedy was already dead, having been assassinated in 1963; but Manuel became a Democrat so that he could vote against any Kennedy who decided to run for political office. A feeling of personal betrayal is what drove his party registration, and Manuel's antipathy toward President Kennedy extended to his entire family.

Introduction

This story of party identification and political behavior is very different from what we often hear in political discourse in the United States. This was not a decision based on moral values or economic self-interest but, rather, a personal, visceral reaction to a life-changing experience. Further, this example illustrates the importance of contextual differences among U.S.-based Hispanic communities such as homeland history, U.S. foreign policy toward the homeland, and migration experience. Mexican-, Cuban-, Puerto Rican–, and Central and South American–origin populations have not had uniform experiences in the United States across these factors. Each country-of-origin group has had its own unique history, immigration, and settlement patterns; and the diversity of these experiences affects their political behavior and partisan choices today. While panethnic terms such as "Latino" and "Hispanic" are used by the media and politicians and in pop culture, these conceptualizations of group identity gloss over important, substantive differences among the various Latin-origin populations in the United States today.[2] A brief overview of the historical and migratory experiences among these populations helps us to understand the diversity of opinion, priorities, and behavioral patterns that mark their political experiences in the United States.

Hispanics, Past and Present

Despite popular conceptions about the Hispanic community, it is important to note that not all Hispanics trace their ancestry to sojourners who voluntarily (legally or without documentation) migrated to the United States. For example, at the time of the ratification of the Treaty of Guadalupe Hidalgo in 1848,[3] approximately 100,000 former Mexican nationals resided in the United States. The descendants of these Hispanics with a territorial connection to what is today the southwestern United States are an exception to the idea that all Hispanics are immigrants or the children thereof.[4] A similar case can be made for Puerto Rico and Cuba. In 1898, as a result of the Spanish–American War and the Treaty of Paris, Puerto Rico came under U.S. control and continues to be a commonwealth of the United States today. Therefore, many have argued that Puerto Ricans are not immigrants because Puerto Rico has been colonized (taken without the consent of the Puerto Rican people and government) by the United States for more than 100 years. The status of the island of Puerto Rico and Puerto Ricans in the U.S. political system continues to be a major issue today. As a result, in March 2007 HR 900, entitled the Puerto Rico Democracy Act, was introduced to Congress. The purpose of this legislation is "To provide for a federally sanctioned self-determination process for the people of Puerto Rico."[4a]

History also plays an essential role in understanding the Cuban case. After the Spanish–American War, the United States occupied Cuba until 1902. At that time, the United States recognized Cuba as an independent state. Yet, before ending the occupation, the United States required that the new Cuban constitution include the Platt Amendment, which allowed the United States to intervene in Cuban affairs whenever the U.S. government deemed such action necessary. That was the justification underlying the multiple U.S. interventions in Cuban politics prior to 1934, when the amendment was rescinded. This history serves as a backdrop for Fidel Castro's rise to power in 1959. In the political, social, and economic unrest that ensued, many Cubans felt they needed to leave their homeland and live abroad. Because of the long-term ties many Cubans already had with the United States, the vast majority chose to settle there. Yet, they do not consider themselves voluntary immigrants; rather, they consider themselves exiles. But their presence in the United States cannot be understood outside the geopolitical context that characterized U.S.–Cuban relations during the twentieth century.

Similarly, the United States was deeply involved in the politics and economics of most countries in Central America, particularly Nicaragua, Honduras, and Panama. The U.S. military invaded Nicaragua in 1894, 1896, and 1910 and occupied the country from 1912 to 1933. U.S. troops entered Honduras in 1903, 1907, 1911, 1912, 1919, and 1924, in most cases in response to conflictual elections. The United States was instrumental in making Panama a separate country from Colombia so that the United States could build the Panama Canal and was heavily involved in the country's politics in order to ensure its function and defense. U.S. companies were also heavily invested in many Central American countries, particularly the United Fruit Company (now Chiquita Banana). United Fruit developed an integrated production plan, not only producing bananas but also building and controlling the infrastructure necessary to get them to market, such as roads, railroads, utilities, and ports. In many Central American countries, United Fruit owned the majority of the infrastructure that existed, making it a key player in the countries' politics and economics.

This deep relationship among the U.S. government, its companies, and Central American regimes had an important impact on the political stability and development in the region, which in turn affected the area's migration patterns. For example, in 1954 a progressive, democratically elected government in Guatemala attempted to expropriate some uncultivated United Fruit land as part of a national agrarian reform program. United Fruit, unhappy with these developments, complained to the Eisenhower administration. The U.S. government, citing cold war concerns, invaded Guatemala and overthrew the government of Jacobo Árbenz. Two of the ships used in the invasion were lent to the U.S. government by United Fruit. Many analysts cite this action as the underlying cause of the Guatemalan civil war, which left an estimated 250,000 people dead and 1 million displaced as refugees. Many of those refugees ended up migrating to the United States.

Thus, Latin American migrants come to the United States for very different reasons. Those reasons are often related in important ways to U.S. foreign and economic policies toward their countries of origin. This broader, global context is important to keep in mind when considering migration flows and patterns. It also has important effects, as we saw with the case of Manuel above, on how Hispanics incorporate themselves into the U.S. political system.

The political and economic upheaval that has characterized many Latin American countries during the twentieth century led to a significant growth in the Latin American–origin population in the United States. During the 1970s, Hispanics comprised only 4% of the total U.S. population, and by 1980 the population had grown to 6%. However, according to a report from the U.S. Census Bureau, entitled "The Hispanic Population in the United States: March 2002," there were 37.4 million Hispanics in the civilian noninstitutional population and more than one in eight people in the United States were of Hispanic origin.[5] Between 1980 and 2000 the rate of growth among Hispanics was nearly four times higher than that of the general population. Estimates of population growth in the United States posit that this trend will continue at least until 2030.

Not only has the population increased in size over time but also the different country-of-origin groups have grown at different rates. This, again, supports the idea that there are many, rather than one unified, Hispanic populations in the United States and that various factors are related to these growth rates. The patterns of increased immigration from Latin America are related to the push factors discussed above, such as civil war, economic crisis, and/or political and social instability in each of the countries in the region, as well as pull factors, such as family reunification and employment opportunities in the United States. For example, increases in immigration from Mexico in the early 1900s and 1940s–1960s, El Salvador in the 1980s, and Colombia and Venezuela in more contemporary times were all linked to civil war and/or political unrest or change in each location. The Mexican Revolution started in 1910 and lasted almost ten years. As is often the case with war, the revolution had created a state of turmoil; and more than 890,000 legal Mexican immigrants came to the United States for refuge between 1910 and 1920. The railroads hired a bulk of these Mexican migrants for employment in the construction and maintenance sectors. Similarly, a weak economy and the twelve-year civil war in El Salvador (1980–1992) led to increased immigration to the United States. From 1982 to 1990, the United States received 45,000 asylum applications from Salvadorans, which is more than double the number of applications from previous periods; just less than 3% were granted.

In terms of pull factors, in 1942, as the United States was experiencing labor shortages linked to World War II, the governments of the United States and Mexico signed the Bracero Treaty, which allowed for the recruitment and legal migration of temporary agricultural workers from Mexico. The word *bracero*, loosely translated, means "laborer." Between 1942 and 1964, more than 4 million Mexicans were recruited and imported into the United States as laborers under the Bracero Program to work temporarily under contract for U.S. growers and ranchers in the fields. Under this program, the braceros were allowed to return to Mexico only in cases of emergency and then required written permission from the employer. However, when the temporary work contracts expired, the braceros were mandated to relinquish their permits and return to Mexico. At the end of World War II, workers coming out of wartime industries and returning servicemen ousted Mexican workers from their jobs. By 1947 the Emergency Farm Labor Service was working on decreasing the amount of Mexican labor that was imported, and by the 1960s an overflow of undocumented agricultural workers had eroded the appeal of the Bracero Program. These events, added to the gross humanitarian violations of bracero employers, brought the program to an end in 1964. Nevertheless, there has been a long history of recruitment of laborers from Latin America by U.S. industries.

In the last decade or so, large-scale immigration has marked Colombian society, with roughly one of every ten Colombians now living abroad. Political, social, and economic problems coupled with widespread insecurity have fueled both voluntary and forced migration after forty years of armed conflict and a persistent drug trade.[6] According to the Ministry of Foreign Affairs, there were about 770,000 Colombians officially registered in consulates worldwide in 2003; but it is estimated that as many as 4.2 million Colombians live abroad. Among these, about half have migrated to the United States. More recently, political unrest linked to Hugo Chávez's rise to power in Venezuela has resulted in increased immigration to the United States as well. In 2005, over 10,000 Venezuelans sought permanent residence in the United States, more than twice as many as who sought admission in 1999, when Chávez first took office. Of these, about one-tenth were people fleeing political persecution and requesting asylum. Venezuelan immigration to the United States, both legal and undocumented, has gone up more than 5,000% since 2000. Consequently, in March 2007 five representatives of the U.S. Congress (Ileana Ros-Lehtinen, Connie Mack, Lincoln Díaz-Balart and Mario Díaz-Balart, all Republicans from the state of Florida, and Jerry Weller, Republican from Illinois) made a formal request to President George W. Bush to give temporary legal status to undocumented Venezuelan immigrants in the country, claiming "there exists a dictatorship in Venezuela."[6a]

As a result of the political, economic, and social upheavals that have occurred in the more than twenty Latin American countries over time, there has been uneven growth across these communities. For example, certain segments of the population, such as Puerto Ricans and Cuban Americans, are now relatively smaller than they have been in the past, while others such as those of Mexican origin and "other Hispanics" have grown substantially.[7] At this writing, the Mexican-origin population comprises the largest of all Hispanic subgroups (about 60%), followed by Puerto Ricans (about 10%), the Cuban-origin population (about 4%), the Dominican-origin population (about 2%), and then Central (about 5%) and South (about 4%) Americans.[8] Therefore, because different Hispanic communities have arrived in the United States at different periods of time and in response to different factors such as war, unrest in the home country, family reunification, and jobs and have had myriad experiences in terms of settling into U.S. society, each constitutes a unique subgroup. Therefore, while country-of-origin groups certainly share some similarities as Hispanics, such as speaking Spanish and a tradition of Catholicism, it is important to acknowledge the realities of their disparate experiences. The example provided by Manuel's narrative at the beginning of the chapter may not be so unique insofar as party identification among Mexican- and Cuban-origin Hispanics does not always seem to follow traditional paths of earlier waves of European immigrants, precisely because of the historical and political differences that have been highlighted above.

Campaigns, Party Politics, and Hispanics

For at least the past three presidential election cycles, it has been understood that the electorate in the United States is almost evenly split. The popular vote in presidential elections has been closer than the historic norm, and the margin of seats held by the majority party in Congress has been smaller than during any period since the New Deal. This political stalemate has led the two major political parties to try to identify new constituencies they can convince to support their party. One of the main groups to become the focus of this kind of political targeting is the U.S. Hispanic population. The tremendous increase in the size of this population, discussed above, makes it a growing and important part of the American electorate. But there are a couple of caveats to that demographic story. First, about half of the Hispanic population in the United States is foreign-born, and a full 40% are noncitizens, making them ineligible to participate formally in electoral politics. Second, Hispanics are, on average, significantly younger than the rest of the U.S. population. That means the proportion of individuals aged over 18, and therefore eligible to vote, is lower as well. Third, Hispanics have, on average, lower income levels and levels of educational attainment than non-Hispanic whites. Income and education are two of the variables most highly correlated with voter turnout: Those with higher levels of both are more likely to vote. These three factors—citizenship status, youth, and socioeconomic status—make the Hispanic proportion of the voting age population in any locality much lower than their overall numbers in the population. For example, Hispanics make up over one-third of the California state population yet only about 12% of the statewide electorate. This limits Hispanics' ability to have a political voice in keeping with the size of their demographic presence.

Yet, despite the fact that Hispanics are not adequately represented within the electorate, the sheer size of the population makes it potentially important within the context of a hotly contested election. For that reason, both political parties have begun targeting the Hispanic vote in presidential campaigns. The Democratic Party has been mobilizing Hispanics during presidential races since the 1960s. For example, President Kennedy's 1960 campaign organized "Viva Kennedy" clubs around the country. Many believed that the clubs gave Kennedy the margin of victory in this close election, particularly in Texas, which Kennedy carried by just 30,000 votes. In some predominantly Mexican American south Texas voting precincts, Kennedy won up to 98% of the total vote.[9] Yet, this kind of mobilization often has been sporadic, depending on the preferences of the particular candidate, and focused only on high-concentration Hispanic states, such as California, Texas, New York, and Illinois. However, since the 2000 presidential campaign, this kind of outreach has become much more systematic within both political parties, with candidates making bilingual appeals in stump speeches and a more significant investment in Spanish-language advertising. In 2000, Republicans strongly courted the Hispanic vote for the first time and, also for the first time, actually outspent Democrats in Spanish-language advertising.[10] After the 2004 election, many analysts argued that this strategy paid off, citing increased Hispanic support for candidate George W. Bush and contending that the Hispanic vote was now "up for grabs."[11] This increased sense of competition between the parties may explain why, for the first time, the major presidential candidates vying for the 2008 Democratic nomination participated in a bilingual debate on Spanish-language television—a historic first.

Yet, this raises the question of what exactly party identification is and why it is important. *Party identification* refers to an individual's stated attachment to a particular political party. If you are a registered Democrat or Republican, then that is your party identification. Even those voters who consider themselves to be independent often "lean" toward one party or another, often in relation to their political ideology. *Political ideology* refers to where an individual places him- or herself on the liberal–conservative scale. In general, individuals who report themselves to be more conservative lean toward the Republicans and those who consider themselves liberal often lean toward the Democrats. Those attachments are important because studies have shown that people usually vote their party identification. Those who are Democrats, for example, tend to see Democratic candidates more favorably and are much more likely to support them. This clearly held true in the 2004 presidential election, where 91% of Hispanic Democrats supported Kerry and 87% of Hispanic Republicans supported Bush. Scholars have found that, once established, party identification remains relatively stable over the course of one's lifetime.[12] Thus, the political parties are betting that if they bring new Hispanic voters into their partisan fold, those voters will become long-term supporters of that party. Given the demographic trends discussed above, the potential political payoff is quite high.

But what really drives people's party identification? Most of the research to date has focused on party identification within the Anglo population. These studies have shown that Democratic identifiers tend to have lower incomes and less education than those identifying as Republicans.[13] Republican identification among Anglos is related to conservative ideology. But it is unclear whether this holds true among Hispanics. The Republican Party is betting that it does not and has begun to invest resources in appealing to Hispanic voters based on the presumption that conservative candidates can win Hispanic votes because of the social conservatism found among Hispanics, especially Mexican Americans. In particular, they point to Mexican Americans' general opposition to abortion and their high levels of religiosity and identification with Catholicism.[14] Republican strategists believe that, by appealing to these voters, they will be able to show them that the Republican Party is more in line with their social values than the Democratic Party. This approach is built primarily on the assumption that Hispanic voters will base their votes on their social values, rather than, say, their economic interests. Yet, Alvarez and García Bedolla[15] found that Hispanic party identification is much more likely to be based on Hispanic economic values and attitudes toward government than on abortion attitudes. In this study, Hispanics' opposition to abortion had a negligible effect on their partisan attachments. This and other works suggest that historic support for the Democratic Party by Mexican Americans and Puerto Ricans was based on support for redistributive government economic policies rather than on social issues, which has been found to be the case among Anglos.[16]

The same seems to hold true for the only Hispanic national-origin group that is strongly identified with the Republican Party—Hispanics of Cuban origin. Unlike Mexican Americans and Puerto Ricans, public opinion polls have consistently shown Cuban Americans to be pro-choice and to support government programs for the poor and the elderly. Yet, it is estimated that over 80% of Cuban Americans vote in favor of Republican presidential, gubernatorial, and local candidates. The experiences of Mexican Americans, on the one hand, and Cubans and Cuban Americans, on the other, suggest that the relationship between political ideology and party affiliation is different among Hispanics than it is among Anglos, likely due to the historic differences discussed above. Thus, Hispanic partisanship does not necessarily fall neatly along the left–right ideological continuum that exists in U.S. politics.

We also should not assume that socioeconomic status (e.g., educational level) has the same effect for members of different racial/ethnic groups. Given the important differences that exist among groups in terms of their social, economic, and political opportunities, it is only reasonable to think that socioeconomic status, social context, and other demographic variables will have different effects for different groups with regard to their partisanship.[17]

To better understand the connections between ideology, we used a national survey to explore the party identification and policy attitudes of Mexican- and Cuban-origin Hispanics. We chose these two groups because they are often discussed as the "bookends" of partisanship among Hispanics in the United States. Mexicans and Mexican Americans historically have been strongly identified with the Democratic Party. It was Mexican American political organizations, in fact, that largely were responsible for the organization of the Viva Kennedy campaigns across the Southwest.[17a] Cubans and Cuban Americans, on the other hand, are the Hispanic national-origin group most strongly identified with the Republican Party. It was Cubans working for the party, in fact, who were credited with organizing the protests that helped to bring an end to the recount after the 2000 presidential election in Florida.[17b] Thus, if the previous work on

TABLE 8.1. Party Identification by National Origin

	Mexican Origin	Cuban Origin
Democrat	34.6%	18.8%
Republican	13.5	47
Independent	26.4	17.3
Something else	11.9	5.9
Don't know	11.9	7.4

partisanship holds true, then we should expect to see Mexicans and Cubans holding very different policy attitudes. Cubans, in line with Republican ideology, should favor small government and fewer social programs and should be very concerned with social issues such as abortion and gay marriage. Mexican attitudes, conversely, should play out in the opposite fashion.

Table 8.1 summarizes the self-reported party identification of the respondents to this nationally representative survey. As would be expected, the party identification of each group looks very different, with Mexican-origin respondents being almost twice as likely as those of Cuban origin to report a Democratic affiliation. The same holds true with Republican identification: Cuban-origin respondents are more than five times as likely to say that they identify as Republicans. But what does this mean, concretely? The partisanship literature would lead us to believe that this means that individuals of Mexican and Cuban origin would have very different policy attitudes and preferences. Yet, looking at Table 8.2 this does not seem to be the case. Table 8.2 shows the respondents' answers to a number of questions related to their policy preferences. We focused on the areas most related to party ideology—the role of government and social issues. Given Cubans' strong Republican identity, we would assume that they are in favor of smaller government and fewer social services and that they would be antiabortion and anti-gay marriage. The opposite should be true for those of Mexican origin.

Looking at Table 8.2, we see that this is not the case. Those percentages marked with an asterisk indicate responses where there were statistically significant differences between the two groups. In other words, if the percentages are not marked with an asterisk, there is no discernable difference in attitude between respondents of Mexican and Cuban origin. Looking at attitudes toward government and services, we see there is only one area of disagreement between the two groups: Cubans are less willing than Mexicans to say that they would pay more taxes in order to provide more government services. But the majority of Cuban-origin respondents still said that they would pay more taxes for more services—not what would traditionally be considered a "Republican" position. In terms of the importance of other social programs, like education and Social

TABLE 8.2. A Comparison of Mexican and Cuban-Origin Policy Attitudes

	Mexican Origin	Cuban Origin
Attitudes toward role of government		
Prefers to pay more taxes to have more government services	58.2*	51*
Education very important issue	94.7	93.6
Social Security very important issue	83.5	87.2
Health care and Medicare very important issues	88.8	89.5
Government should provide health care	83.2	86
Social/moral attitudes		
Moral values very important issue	74.2**	84.6**
Pro-choice	41.4**	54.6**
Pro–gay marriage	45.1	39.4*
Religion important in my daily life	61	57
Issues and vote choice		
Must agree with candidate on abortion	18.4	21.1
Must agree with candidate on gay marriage	20.6**	25.4**
Must agree with candidate on Iraq	16.7**	24*

*Significant at the 0.05 level, **significant at the 0.01 level.

Security, the two groups agree overwhelmingly, with more than 80% stating that they care deeply about these issues. Given that taxes and the role of government are two of the issues that divide the parties most fundamentally, it is surprising to find this level of agreement between the two groups, given that they identify with the parties so differently.

Moving to social issues, again we see the respondents' answers moving in a different direction from what we would expect. There is more disagreement between the two groups on these issues but not in ways that are consistent with each group's party affiliation. As has been found in previous studies, Cuban Americans are much more pro-choice than Mexican Americans. They are, in fact, the only Hispanic national-origin group that has consistently reported being pro-choice. On our other social issue, however, Cubans are significantly more against gay marriage than Mexicans. That said, both groups are over-whelmingly against gay marriage; here, the differences should be interpreted as being more a question of degree. On the religious side, while Cuban-origin respondents are more likely to say that moral values are important to them, Cuban- and Mexican-origin respondents were equally likely to say that religion is important to their daily lives. Thus, similar to the respondents' attitudes about government services, the social/moral concerns of these Hispanic respondents do not coincide neatly with those of their chosen party.

In the end, the reason policy attitudes and party identification matter is because of the effects they have on which candidate a voter chooses. Individuals make voting decisions based on a range of issues, but usually there are one or two key issues that most strongly influence how they choose to vote. In order to get at this question, the survey asked individuals to say how important it was to them that a particular presidential candidate agreed with them on a particular issue in order for them to feel comfortable voting for that candidate. The questions asked, "If you were to disagree with a presidential candidate on issue___, could you vote for him anyway?" The respondents were asked this question in reference to three issues: abortion, gay marriage, and the Iraq War. Their responses may be found at the bottom of Table 8.2. Looking first at abortion, Mexican- and Cuban-origin respondents agree that it is not an important factor in their vote choice. Only about 20% of each group said that this was an important factor in their voting; that means about 80% do not think it is important, which is similar to previous findings.[18] Cuban-origin respondents do seem to think gay marriage is more important than Mexican-origin respondents do, yet the proportion is small—only about one-fourth of Cuban-origin respondents. The two groups also disagree about the importance of Iraq to their vote, but again the magnitude is not great, with only about one-fourth of Cubans stating this position. Thus, the issues that mainstream political discourse tells us drive much of the differences between the parties—moral values and foreign policy—do not seem to be driving vote choice among Mexican- and Cuban-origin Hispanics. These two groups disagree about party identification but seem to agree quite a bit about many political issues.

The examples from this survey highlight the degree to which common wisdom about American politics does not necessarily explain partisanship and vote choice among Hispanics. But if demographics and policy attitudes cannot explain Hispanic politics, what does? History and social context are key factors. As we saw above, the Mexican-origin population in the United States began with those populations that were present in the Southwest when the United States annexed half of Mexico's northern territory at the end of the Mexican–American war. These populations were offered a second-class citizenship in these areas, subject to segregation, discrimination, and political exclusion. That history made this population especially sympathetic to appeals from the Democratic Party, starting particularly during the period of the New Deal.[19] Like African Americans, many Mexican Americans supported the social programs and economic opportunities that typified New Deal politics. That relationship solidified with the Viva Kennedy campaigns and the pro–civil rights position taken by the Democratic Party during the 1960s. Because Mexican Americans still experience significant residential segregation, newly arrived Mexican immigrants often settle in areas where native-born Mexican Americans live.

That commingling ensures that new generations of Mexican-origin populations living in the United States tend to be socialized into having an affiliation with the Democratic Party.

Similarly, history and local context played an important role in the development of party identification among Cubans and Cuban Americans in Florida. Cubans have been migrating to Florida since the late nineteenth century, and the Cuban American community in Florida had always been strongly Democratic. When large numbers of Cubans began arriving in Miami after the 1959 Cuban Revolution, they followed in their compatriots' footsteps and joined the Democratic Party. In the early 1970s, a majority of Cubans in Florida were Democrats. Miami at this time was a machine city, controlled by the Democratic Party. When Cubans began to approach the party leadership in order to run for political office, the Democrats shut them out. They would not allow Cubans to run on the Democratic ticket. The Republican Party, however, figuring it was likely to lose the elections in such a Democratic Party–dominated city, allowed Cuban Americans on the ballot as Republicans. The Cubans won, and this has helped to cement their loyalty to the Republican Party to the present day.[20] These local-level issues, combined with the general hostility Cuban exiles felt toward Democrat John F. Kennedy because of his role in the Bay of Pigs debacle and the strong anticommunist feelings they held, has led many Cubans and Cuban Americans to identify strongly with the Republican Party. But the election of Democrats Bob Menéndez in New Jersey and Alex Penelas in Dade County, Florida, illustrate that Cuban Americans are willing to cross party lines in order to vote for Cuban-origin candidates. Thus, partisanship among Cuban Americans seems to be driven by both history and the exile experience, rather than the issue-based factors we would otherwise expect.

Conclusion

In sum, the literature on partisanship in the United States leads us to think that there are clear patterns, in terms of demography, group identity, and policy positions, that are associated with party identification. In other words, if a person wants more government services and is supportive of abortion and/or gay rights, she or he will be a Democrat. If a person is less in favor of government provision of services, concerned about tax rates, and against abortion rights and/or gay marriage, she or he will be a Republican. Generally speaking, in U.S. politics voters who are older, more educated, and wealthier tend to identify as Republican and those who are younger, less wealthy, and less educated tend to be Democrats. Women are also much more likely to identify as Democrats than men.[21]

Yet, looking solely at these individual-level factors suggests that these political attachments are disconnected from voters' issue positions or group-level political socialization experiences. However, it stands to reason that opinions about issues and policy *should* be a part of this process and that group-level differences in historical and social contexts and the way in which partisan identification relates to group-level identification have an important impact.[22] Our study reveals that when examining Hispanic national-origin populations in the United States, many of the expectations built up by past research and conventional political wisdom are not met. When looking at issue areas, we see that Mexican- and Cuban-origin Hispanics seem to agree on quite a few areas of policy, despite their divergent party affiliations. In both cases abortion does not seem to be a key issue, and both groups agree about a strong role for government in providing social services. The only areas of disagreement are in moral values, with Cuban Americans being somewhat less conservative than Mexicans on abortion but more conservative on gay marriage. Yet, neither group sees moral values or foreign policy concerns as critical to the choice of a presidential candidate. Overall, this is not the picture that one would have expected, given the findings of research on other populations within American politics.

This analysis suggests that Hispanic and Anglo partisanship may be based on different factors, as is the partisanship of different Hispanic national-origin groups. This is likely related to the fact that these groups vary in how they have been socialized into the U.S. political system. The party identification literature has consistently emphasized the importance of socialization, and this is likely what is driving the differences we find here. As we saw above, Mexican Americans and Cuban Americans have had very different migration experiences, which in turn have led them to develop distinct relationships with the political parties. Even though we know less about the experiences of other national-origin Hispanic groups, it follows that their reasons for migrating and their relationship to the U.S. government will affect how they see the political parties. For example, Nicaraguan immigrants to the United States during the 1980s were fleeing the communist Sandinista regime. Much like Cuban exiles, they received refugee status upon arrival and have received preferential treatment (compared with other Central Americans) in terms of immigration policy. One would expect that these experiences would affect their ideological attitudes in the United States and their attitudes toward the U.S. government. Thus, why migrants come, when they arrive, and the political context they encounter upon arrival, both nationally and locally, have an impact on their political socialization and resulting political attitudes.

For Hispanic political incorporation, then, context and history matter. Each Hispanic national-origin group has had particular experiences with the political parties, and those experiences affect how these groups relate to the parties. This is likely to also be true for Anglo partisanship. But it is important to keep in mind that the majority of Hispanics in the United States have arrived within the past fifty years, have come to the United States for a wide variety of reasons, and have had different migration and settlement experiences. As a result, they are still in the process of establishing their relationships with the political parties and developing their political attitudes. This chapter provides an important snapshot of the current state of Hispanic partisan socialization. It will be interesting to see whether, with time, Hispanic populations' relationships to the parties remain distinct, if the different national-origin groups begin to converge, or if their partisanship begins to look more like that of Anglos. At the very least, we cannot expect Hispanic partisanship, or the resulting political behavior, to remain static. Future research will be needed to track this process within this growing population.

DISCUSSION QUESTIONS

1. Some people argue that Hispanics are an immigrant population, while others point out that some Hispanic populations do not consider themselves part of the immigrant community. What is your position on this issue? Explain.
2. Explain why there are many Hispanic communities, as opposed to one unified community, in the United States.
3. Why have Mexican Americans traditionally aligned themselves with the Democratic Party and Cuban Americans with the Republican Party?
4. In this chapter, it was demonstrated that conventional explanations for partisanship do not apply to Mexican and Cuban Americans. Why? How can we be better informed about these populations?
5. Debate whether Republicans can gain Mexican American votes or Democrats can gain Cuban American votes.

believe

Chapter 9

Model Minority or Perpetual Foreigner?

The Political Experience of Asian Americans[1]

Morrison G. Wong

*In 1982, 27-year-old Chinese American Vincent Chin was celebrating his
upcoming wedding with some friends at a bar in Detroit, Michigan. A
confrontation broke out between Chin and his friends and two individuals—
Ronald Ebens (an auto plant supervisor) and Michael Nitz (his unemployed
stepson). They accused Chin, who they thought was Japanese, of causing the
problems of the U.S. economy. America was in a recession, and the American
automobile industry was hit hard with competition from Japan. They all were
asked to leave the premises. Ebens and Nitz went to their car, opened its trunk,
and took out a baseball bat. In the interim, Chin had just said goodbye to his
friends in front of the bar. When Ebens and Nitz returned to the bar, Chin saw
them and started to run away. Ebens and Nitz gave chase. Catching up with
Chin at the parking lot of a McDonald's, Nitz held Chin while Ebens swung
the baseball bat four times at Chin's skull. Chin collapsed to the ground with
blood coming out of his cracked skull. He died four days later. Nine months
later, Ebens and Nitz pleaded guilty to manslaughter, but the Michigan judge
sentenced them each to just three years probation and a fine of $3,780! This
lenient sentencing outraged the Asian American community. American Citizens
for Justice (ACJ) was formed to seek justice for Vincent Chin. They placed
considerable pressure on the Department of Justice to reopen the case and appeal
the verdict on grounds that Ebens and Nitz violated Chin's civil rights. Two years
later, a second trial was convened and Ebens was found guilty and sentenced to
25 years; Nitz was acquitted. This verdict was later thrown out on a technicality.
The case was retried in Cincinnati because of the tremendous amount of
publicity Chin's killing received in Detroit. Ebens was acquitted in April 1987.*

ACJ was one of the first grassroots panethnic advocacy organizations to deal with Asian American issues. Although it lost its first legal case, it galvanized the Asian American community to deal with racism against Asian Americans at all levels. It provided a model for future grassroots Asian American advocacy organizations, demonstrating that by being politically active, they may be able to enact change.

Introduction

The political landscape of Asian America has changed rapidly over the past ten to twenty years. While seemingly invisible in the political arena during most of the twentieth century, Asians in America have continually and dramatically increased their political presence, especially in cities such as San Francisco, Los Angeles, New York, Boston, Chicago, and Houston and on the West and East Coasts. The metamorphosis from an insignificant group with little or no political input to one having the potential of being the swing or winning vote in significant electoral contests is due to numerous social, political, and economic factors. Nonetheless, Asian Americans still encounter numerous barriers that may hinder or limit their participation in the American political arena as voters and candidates.

In this chapter I hope to shed some light on the complex political experience of Asian Americans in the United States. First, a brief description of the social, demographic, and residential patterns of Asian Americans will be presented. Second, two major stereotypes of Asian Americans—model minorities and perpetual foreigner—and their implications on political participation will be analyzed in depth. Third, the seemingly contradictory political affiliations of Asians will be described. Barriers that affect Asian Americans' access to the voting polls and candidacy will be documented. The state of Asian American political office holding, including Asian American candidacy and campaign contribution holdings, will be discussed. Lastly, speculations regarding the future of Asian American politics in the first part of the twenty-first century will be presented.

Who Are Asian Americans?

Asian Americans are the fastest-growing racial group in the United States. Between 1980 and 1990, the Asian American population of 3.7 million (1.6% of the U.S. population) increased by about 85% to 6.9 million (2.8%). The growth rate for the total U.S. population for this period was 10%. In the next decade, the Asian American population growth rate declined slightly, ranging 52%–74%, but was still much higher than the 13% for the general population. The 1990 and 2000 figures are not directly comparable as 2000 marked the first time that the U.S. Census allowed respondents to check more than one racial category. The category "Race Alone" is for those respondents who checked only one Asian category. The "Race in Combination" category is for those respondents who checked one Asian category and another racial category. Hence, the "Race Alone" category can be looked upon as the minimum or lowest limit of who were Asian Americans, and the "Race in Combination" category can be viewed as the upper limit of all who considered themselves, in some shape or form, as Asian American. In sum, there were from 10.1 million (3.6%) to 11.6 million (4.1%) Asian Americans residing in the United States in 2000.

The 2000 U.S. Census lists 24 different Asian groups. This discussion of the political participation of Asian Americans will be limited to peoples of Chinese, Japanese, Filipino, Korean, and Asian Indian ancestries, as well as Southeast Asian refugees-turned-immigrants, consisting of Vietnamese, Cambodian, Laotian, and Hmong Americans in the continental United States. Asian Americans are the majority population in Hawaii and their social, political, and economic experiences are quite different from those of other Asian Americans on the mainland. Despite the obvious ethnic and language differences within this broadly defined group, the term "Asian American" is significant and meaningful. These groups have been shaped by similar historical experiences in the United States and today confront a myriad common issues.

The residential concentration of Asian Americans in certain states and cities has resulted in political influence greater than their population size. In 2000, over half of Asian Americans lived in just three states. The largest number of Asian Americans, about 4.1 million, resided in California, where they comprised about 12% of the state's population and over one-third of the Asian population in the United States. New York had the second largest number of Asian Americans, 1.2 million, comprising about 6% of the state's population and 10% of the Asians in the United States. Hawaii, the only state with a majority of its population being Asian American, was the residence of the third largest number of Asian Americans, about 703,000.

New York City had the largest Asian population, with about 873,000 Asian residents. Los Angeles came in a distant second, with less than half the New York Asian population, about 407,000. Other cities with at least 200,000 Asian Americans included San Jose, San Francisco, and Honolulu. Cities with at least 100,000 Asian Americans included San Diego, Chicago, Houston, Seattle, and Fremont (California).

Model Minority or Perpetual Foreigner?

Stereotypes regarding Asian Americans, both positive and negative, abound. On the negative side, they are seen as clannish, unassimilable, isolated, and disloyal. On the positive side, they are seen as highly educated, occupying high status positions, having high income, and being prodigies on the piano and violin. Remarkably, these stereotypes, some originating almost 150 years ago, persist to the present day. Their persistence may be because there is a "kernel of truth" to them. If they were devoid of reality, then they would not exist. Two contrasting stereotypes that will be discussed are Asian Americans as model minorities and Asian Americans as perpetual foreigners.

ASIAN AMERICANS AS MODEL MINORITIES

One of the most persistent stereotypes of Asian Americans during the past forty years is that they are model minorities. The emergence of the stereotype began in 1966 when two articles[2] in national magazines praised the exemplary academic and occupational achievements of the Japanese and Chinese.

The model minority stereotype is based on several interrelated arguments. Asian Americans, because of the value they place on education, have attained exceptionally high educational achievements, have joined the ranks of the occupationally prestigious (such as professionals, doctors, and engineers), and have been rewarded with high family incomes. Without complaining, Asian Americans have overcome the harsh racial antagonisms by the dominant society and have successfully entered into the American mainstream—the educational, economic, and political arenas. Moreover, Asian Americans no longer need public services such as bilingual education, government documents in Asian languages, help in translation of ballots, or bilingual interpreters at the polling booth. The success of Asian Americans is used as an example (or model) for other racial/ethnic minorities (e.g., blacks and Hispanics) to emulate in their quest to overcome barriers in their way to achieving the American Dream. After all, if Asian Americans can do it, why can't they? Given the political and public policy attention that surrounds the model minority stereotype, let us look at the statistics or facts that "prove" that Asian Americans are "successful."

Asian Americans are a highly educated group. In 2000, about 43% of Asian Americans compared to 25% of the general population had four or more years of college. Asian Americans also had a higher proportion of advanced degrees than other racial groups, include non-Hispanic whites. They had a greater proportion involved in highly skilled occupations (professional and technical positions) and enjoying a higher median household income compared to all other racial groups, including whites. The median household income for Asian Americans in 2000 was about $51,000 compared to $45,400 for whites, $29,500 for blacks, and $33,700 for Hispanics.

Looking at these socioeconomic indicators, it is hard not to conclude that Asian Americans are model minorities, that they have become accepted into the American mainstream, that they no longer experience any discrimination, and that they have "made it" in American society. While there may be some merit to such an interpretation, it is a rather deceptive overstatement for all Asian American groups. Many have argued that the socioeconomic success of Asian Americans can be understood only within the context of a high percentage of urbanization, more wage earners per family, and per capita income compared to median family income.[3] In so doing, a different picture of the Asian American model minority stereotype emerges. Although most Asian Americans may be advantaged relative to blacks and Hispanics, they are still disadvantaged relative to whites.[4]

First of all, national statistics of median family incomes are a very poor indicator of relative Asian American success. They compare the family income of Asian Americans who tend to be residentially concentrated in urbanized areas (San Francisco Bay Area, Los Angeles, New York, Boston, and Honolulu) that have a much higher cost of living and, hence, higher wages with whites who live not only in the same areas but also in lower–cost of living regions across the country. A much better and more accurate comparison would be between the family incomes of Asian Americans and whites in the same city. When such comparisons are made in cities such as Chicago, Houston, Los Angeles, New York, and San Francisco, the median family income for Asian Americans was $7,000–$12,000 less than that of their white counterparts.[5]

Second, the, relatively high household incomes among Asian Americans are very much due to Asian American families having more workers in the household compared to whites.

Third, it would be more accurate to look at per capita income instead of median family income to test Asian American success. With their high educational achievements and their concentration in the professional ranks, Asian Americans should have a much higher per capita income than their white counterparts. However, this was not the case. The per capita income for whites ($24,819) was about $4,100 more than that of Asian Americans ($20,719). Other studies found that Asian males with four or more years of college education or working full time had a median per capita income that was $2,000 lower than that of white males.[6] In dollars and cents, even though Asian Americans invest in education in hopes of achieving a higher standard of living, this strategy appears to have only limited financial return.

Belief in the model minority diverts attention from very real and very serious social and economic problems that plague many segments of the Asian American population, problems that begin to materialize when one looks at a more detailed analysis of the socioeconomic status of Asian Americans. For example:

- Only 53% of Asian Americans compared to 72% of whites own their homes.[7]
- Asian Americans (20%) are ten times more likely to live in crowded housing conditions than whites (2%).[8]
- Asian Americans are more likely to be in poverty or at 200% of the poverty level than the white population.[9]
- Asian Americans, especially Southeast Asians, are more likely to receive public assistance than whites.[10]
- Only 11% of the general population and 4% of the white population are foreign-born compared to over 63% of the Asian population.[11]
- About 36% of Asian Americans have limited English proficiency compared to 2% of the white population.[12]
- Only 1% of the white population compared to about one-quarter of the Asian population feels linguistically isolated.[13]

Statistics don't lie. It just depends on which statistics you use to support your position. Chan[14] noted, for example, the persistence of the model minority stereotype despite the seemingly economically disadvantaged position of Asian Americans. In California, about half of the Vietnamese remain on public assistance, yet some still apply the model minority stereotype to them. However, instead of focusing on median family income or per capita income as measures, they may focus on the relatively high labor force participation rates or on how rapid these refugee families have moved out of poverty or on the extraordinary educational achievement of their children. Hence, the model minority concept persists despite contradictory evidence.

Many Asian American activists look upon this model minority stereotype, despite its positive take, as more of a burden than a breakthrough. They argue that the model minority stereotype distracts public attention away from continued, often overt, racial discrimination faced by Asian Americans, such as racial profiling, glass ceilings, sweatshop conditions, or voting harassment. It also serves to fuel competition and resentment between groups, particularly among other racial minorities who are told if Asian Americans can succeed, why can't they? As Pei-te Lien points out,

> The perceived advantage of Asians in the socioeconomic sphere may have also convinced many members in the community to accept the "model minority" labeling and fantasize about the group's fictional ability to "make it" by themselves and enjoy an equal political status with whites.[15]

ASIAN AMERICANS AS PERPETUAL OR FOREVER FOREIGNERS

A second persistent stereotype of Asian Americans is that they are perpetual foreigners, strangers from different shores or forever foreigners;[16] that is, Asian

Americans are viewed not quite as Americans, with all the rights and privileges thereof. Unlike the more "positive" model minority stereotype, this stereotype is negative. Regardless of how many generations their families may have resided in the United States, Asian Americans are still viewed as foreigners. On occasion, such stereotyping may be benign. Third- and fourth-generation Asian Americans may be complimented on their fluency or mastery of the English language, despite the fact that English is the only language they know. They will be asked where they are from, with the expected response being some exotic Asian country. If the response given is not the one that is expected, such as "San Francisco" or "Fort Worth, Texas," the person may persist in asking where his or her parents, grandparents, or great grandparents were from until the desired response (insert Asian country here) is evoked.

At other times, the perpetual foreigner stereotype may be more hostile. For example, in 1996, a Los Angeles radio talk show host complained about Asian American dominance in women's figure skating.

> "You know, I'm tired of the Kristi Yamaguchis and the Michelle Kwans!" stormed Bill Handel of station KFI-AM. "They're not American....When I look at a box of Wheaties, I don't want to see eyes that are slanted and Oriental and almond shaped. I want to see American eyes looking at me.[17]

The fact that both Yamaguchi and Kwan are not recognized as U.S.-born citizens is evidence of Asian Americans being perceived as perpetual foreigners.

The persistence of Asian Americans as perpetual foreigners implies that Asian Americans, regardless of their generational status, are not really quite Americans. As foreigners (or of foreign ancestry), they are accorded second-class status and are treated as an inferior group. In other words, discrimination against Asian Americans is justified.

These two stereotypes, Asian Americans as model minorities and as perpetual foreigners, have serious implications for their political participation. These stereotypes may raise or lower the barriers that they face and influence their decisions to run for political office.

Asian Americans: Democrats, Republicans, or Independents?

In 1996, the Voter News Service conducted a poll and found that Asian Americans were more likely to be Republican than Democrat (48% vs. 32%).[18] However, a Los Angeles Times poll came to a different conclusion. It found that Asian Americans were more likely to be Democrats than Republicans (44% vs. 33%).[19] How can these two scientific polls come up with such contradictory findings? Part of the answer lies in the methodological procedures that were used to ascertain the opinions of the Asian American populace and whether such procedures were sensitive to sample size, residential restrictions, and the use or lack of use of a foreign language during the interviews.

The model minority thesis suggests that due to Asian Americans' high education, occupational status, income, and "acceptance" by the dominant society, they would most likely be registered and vote Republican. The perpetual or forever foreigner thesis would argue that because Asian Americans are still considered a minority in American society and still face prejudice and discrimination, they would have more in common with other minorities. This argument would predict that Asian Americans would more likely register and vote Democrat. So which argument is supported by empirical research?

Looking at more recent, and methodologically sophisticated, studies that have been conducted on the voting behavior of Asian Americans, several interesting findings are noted. First, the proportion of registered Asian American voters for a particular political party usually does not form the majority in their political jurisdictions.[20] This is due to the extremely high proportion of Asian Americans who were not affiliated with either the Democratic or Republican Party but who classified themselves as Independents (or who did not want to be classified). This figure ranged from 20% to 36% of Asian Americans. Second, despite the lack of a majority of Asian Americans registered as Democrats or Republicans, when it came to actual voting, Asian Americans tended to vote Democrat. In all the presidential election surveys, Democrats Gore and Kerry received the majority of Asian American votes, ranging 50%–74% of the total votes. What this suggests is that there is considerable crossover voting on the part of Asian Americans. Many Asian Americans may be registered as Republicans but vote for Democratic candidates.[21]

Asian Americans' political affiliation and voting behavior tend to defy political logic or traditional minority voting patterns. Some argue that the attitudes and voting behavior of Asian Americans lie squarely between those of whites and ethnic/racial minorities and that Asian Americans and whites are most likely to form a voting bloc for the same political party in any partisan election.[22] This view is most in line with the model minority thesis. Others argue that there is evidence that Asian Americans are more issue-oriented than political party–oriented.[23] For example, although California passed Proposition 209 in 1996 that prohibited affirmative action in public education and employment, the majority of Asian Americans (as well as Hispanics and blacks) in California voted against this proposition. In June 1998, California passed Proposition 227, which banned bilingual instruction and permitted only English instruction in public schools. About 43% of Asian Americans voted against the proposition, a percentage that was larger than that of whites but smaller than that of Hispanics and blacks.

In 2004, considerable crossover voting was noted by Asian American Republicans to support Proposition 72, which would have increased health insurance coverage in California, a proposition that was opposed by California's Republican Party. Lastly, their voting behavior in presidential elections suggests that their status as perpetual foreigners influences their voting patterns, that Asian Americans tend to vote on issues that lean toward the voting patterns of other minorities.

Barriers to Asian American Political Participation

That barriers have been erected to hinder the participation of Asian Americans in the American political process is beyond dispute. All one needs to remember is that during the course of the history of Asians in the United States, federal laws were passed that denied Asian Americans the right to vote. In 1870, the Chinese in the United States were expressly prohibited from being naturalized as citizens. In 1922, the Supreme Court, in *Ozawa v. the United States*, declared that Japanese were ineligible to acquire U.S. citizenship; and in 1923, Asian Indians were ruled to be aliens ineligible for citizenship. In 1934, although Filipinos were nationals of the United States, the Tydings-McDuffie Act denied them the right to vote. It was not until 1952, with the passage of the McCarran Walter Act, that the law was changed to allow Asians the right to U.S. citizenship, which then allowed them to vote. Hence, Asian Americans lost at least three generations of political development because of federal laws that barred them from citizenship and full political participation. While much has been done to rectify past discriminatory practices that prevented Asian Americans from being active participants in the United States, the evidence suggests that Asian Americans continue to face barriers in their pursuit of equality of participation in the political process.

LINGUISTIC NEEDS AND RESOURCES

One of the major barriers that affect Asian Americans' participation in voting is their lack of facility with the English language, which is further complicated by the lack of bilingual voting materials and scarcity of interpreters.[24] Although some facility with the English language is necessary in order to become a citizen and have the right to vote, it should be noted that in 1990 about 65% of Asians Americans spoke an Asian language at home, 56% indicated that they did not speak English very well, and 35% stated that they were linguistically isolated.[25] The monolingual ballot-casting system in most states excluded a high percentage of Asians from registering and voting.

More recent surveys suggest that the situation has not changed drastically. In 2004, a survey of 11,000 Asian Americans revealed that 85% of Southeast Asian voters were naturalized citizens and about half (46%) were voting for the first time. About half (48%) of these voters had limited proficiency with the English language. About 60%–66% of the Vietnamese and Cambodians in Boston needed interpreter assistance and translated written materials. Linguistic needs and resources are in dire need for the growing Asian American voting population.[26]

A study of the voting needs of Asian Americans in southern California in 2004 found similar findings. From 37% to 40% of Asian American voters in Orange County and Los Angeles County had limited proficiency and trouble reading English and, hence, used some form of language assistance when voting.[27]

Some argue that the cost of bilingual ballots or voting materials or having interpreters at voting polls is too high. However, such arguments are not based on hard evidence. Several in-depth analyses found that the cost of providing bilingual ballots is only about 3% of the total election costs.[28] Many community organizations provide free interpreter services for those in need. About 59% of jurisdictions surveyed incurred no additional costs by providing oral language assistance, and 54% incurred no additional costs by providing bilingual written materials. Overall, 40% of jurisdictions reported no extra costs for providing oral and written language assistance. Financial considerations aside, the most compelling reason for bilingual ballots or voting materials and having interpreters at voting polls is because it is the law! Section 203 of the Voting Rights Act of 1992 makes Asian Americans, along with other language minorities, eligible to receive bilingual voting assistance if they reside in an area where at least 5% of the voting-age citizens belong to the same language minority or where at least 10,000 voting-age citizens from the minority group had limited English abilities.

Laws are only as good as they are enforced. Asian Americans face a wide range of unlawful barriers in trying to exercise their right to vote. Listed below are some descriptions of these barriers that Asian Americans faced during the recent 2004 and 2006 elections:[29]

- Incidents of ballot translations that had faulty transliterations of candidates' names and/or were too small to read[30]
- Shortages of interpreters, resulting in some Asian Americans being turned away[31]
- Poll workers blocking Asian language interpreters from assisting voters[32]
- Translated voting materials being hidden from Asian American voters[33]
- Although telephone hotlines were available, they could not provide assistance in the required foreign language[34]
- Poor, or in some cases no, notification of election district and/or poll changes (In 2004, a first-time South Asian voter in New Jersey had to go to six different poll sites to vote. She eventually voted but by provisional ballot.)[35]

- Poorly trained or unqualified interpreters who were unable to assist voters (A survey of 113 poll sites in 2004 found that 73% fell short of the required Chinese and Korean interpreters. In 2005, 61% of 18 poll sites in Manhattan and 53% of 19 poll sites in Queens fell short of the assigned number of interpreters.)[36]

INADEQUATE SOURCES OF INFORMATION

Much of what most native-born Americans learn about the candidates for political office or political issues they learn from mainstream English-language media, such as television and newspapers. But such traditional sources are not easily accessible to Asian Americans. Since many Asian Americans are not that proficient in English, they must seek information about politics as well as local and community affairs from alternative sources. One study found that more than 56% of Asian American voters received their information from ethnic media sources, ranging from native-language and bilingual newspapers to radio and cable television programming and Internet sites. About 42% of Asian American voters received their news from ethnic media sources in Asian languages.[37]

IMMIGRANT STATUS, SOJOURNING, AND HOMELAND POLITICS

Immigrant status is a great barrier to political involvement. Numerous studies have found that immigration-related characteristics like country of origin, naturalization processes, length of stay in the United States, and the sojourner's attitude have a strong impact on the political behavior of Asian Americans.[38] Portes and Rumbaut argue that immigrants keep alive the identification and loyalties into which they were socialized and, accordingly, regard politics in the host society with relative indifference.[39] Xu further argues that due to initial economic hardship upon their arrival to the United States, their focus on the well-being of their family, and their intent on sojourning, Asian immigrants focus most of their energy on economic activities involving income generation, while dismissing political involvement.[40]

A related issue is whether or not the Asian immigrants came from a country with a democratic tradition. Asian immigrants from countries where there was a tradition of democracy may be more likely to take on the responsibility of political participation and realize the importance of voting compared to those who come from less democratic societies.

REDISTRICTING

Another barrier to Asian American political participation is *redistricting*, a political process where legislative boundaries are redrawn following the reapportionment of legislative seats to reflect population changes found in each decennial census. Asian Americans have complained that their political power has been diluted by redistricting plans that split the Asian American population in an area into several districts. For instance, following the 1981–1982 redistricting, Koreatown in Los Angeles was divided into three congressional, four state senatorial, 32 state assembly, and two city council districts, effectively diluting any political influence that Koreans may have had in city, state, or congressional district politics.[41] Filipinotown and Chinatown in Los Angeles and in many other areas of Asian American concentration in the mainland have experienced similar cases of fragmentation.[42]

HARASSMENT, DISCRIMINATION, AND RACISM AT THE POLLS

Many Asian Americans, although foreign-born, are U.S. citizens. Nonetheless, many are denied equal access to the ballot box. Examples of the lack of enforcement of the Voter Rights Act of 1992 have been discussed above. Recent surveys and polls have documented outright harassment, discrimination, and racism against persons of Asian ancestry trying to exercise their right to vote by the very people who were supposed to ensure that they were granted equal and just access—election officials.[43]

- During the 2004 election, a Cook County (Illinois) election judge commented that an Asian American voter whom he was unable to understand should "learn to speak English." Similarly, in a precinct in Cook County with a very high concentration of Chinese Americans, there was only one Chinese ballot booth. No sign indicated that the booth was for Chinese speakers. When asked about this concern, the election judge replied, "They don't need them anyway. They just use a piece of paper and punch numbers. They don't read the names anyway, so it doesn't matter."[44]
- A poll worker in Boulder, Colorado, after making racist comments to an Asian American voter, told her she was not registered and then turned her away after she had waited in line for over an hour. The voter watched as others completed provisional ballots. When she asked if she could do so as well, she was told that her circumstances were different. The voter continued to watch as another Asian American was also turned away. A call to the election hotline revealed that she indeed was properly registered to vote at that location. She returned and eventually was allowed to vote.[45]
- In West Palm Beach, Florida, an election poll worker told a voter that they were not handling Asian American voters at that particular polling place.[46]

- In Jackson Heights, Queens, one poll worker said, "You Oriental guys are taking too long to vote." Other poll workers commented that there were too many language assistance materials on the tables, saying, "If they [Asian American voters] need it, they can ask for it." At another site in Queens, when a poll worker was asked about the availability of translated materials, he replied, "Where are we, in China? It's ridiculous."[47]
- In 2004, 51%–69% of Asian American voters in New York, New Jersey, and Massachusetts reported that poll workers improperly required them to provide identification to vote, even when no identification was required.[48]
- In 2004, in Queens County, New York, a poll worker commented, "I'll talk to [Asian voters] the way they talk to me when I call to order Chinese food," and then said random English phrases in a mock Chinese accent.[49]
- In 2004, at a voting poll in Queens County, New York, several whites screamed at Asian American voters, "You all are turning this country into a third world waste dump!" And "You should prepare and learn English at home before you come out to vote."[50]
- In 2002, in Queens County, New York, a pool worker referred to South Asian voters as "terrorists."[51]
- In 2004, a poll worker in Edison, New Jersey, directed comments toward Asian American voters for several minutes, stating, "If you are an American, you better lose the rest of the [Asian] crap."[52]

These forms of harassment and discriminatory acts by election officials toward Asian American voters convey the message that they continue to be perpetual foreigners, not quite citizens even though they are, and that the opportunity to voice an opinion in the political process is going to be met with additional hurdles.

HARASSMENT AND DISCRIMINATION OF ASIAN AMERICAN POLITICAL CANDIDATES

Voting represents one form of political participation. Running for elected office represents another. Even in this situation, there have been incidents of harassment and discrimination against Asian American political candidates.

In 1999, the mayor of Palisades Park, New Jersey, attacked a Korean American candidate for city council, writing, "Now we are faced with a new problem—one that threatens to wipe out our history and our heritage....Our quality of life will be brought to an abrupt and chaotic end."[53]

In 2005, Trenton, New Jersey, radio hosts denigrated Asian Americans by using racial slurs and speaking in mock Asian gibberish during an on-air radio show. The hosts demeaned a Korean American mayoral candidate and made various other derogatory remarks. They urged their listeners to "Vote American." One of the hosts, Craig Carton, made the following remarks:

> Would you really vote for someone named Jun Choi (said in fast-paced, high-pitched, squeaky voice)?...And here's the bottom line...no specific minority group or foreign group should ever dictate the outcome of an American election. I don't care if the Chinese population in Edison has quadrupled in the last year, Chinese should never dictate the outcome of an election, Americans should....And it's offensive to me...not that I have anything against uh Asians...I really don't...I don't like the fact that they crowd the goddamn black jack tables in Atlantic City with their little chain smoking and little pocket protectors.[54]

Jun Choi eventually won the election.

Although the barriers that prevented Asians from becoming citizens, and hence eligible to vote in U.S. elections, have been struck down and laws have been passed to help Asians gain access to the voting polls, many barriers continue to block their pursuit of equal participation in the various political arenas. The stereotype of Asian Americans as perpetual foreigners "justifies" the continued harassment and discrimination they encounter by voting poll officials and by the general public. The passage of laws to protect Asian Americans' rights to the voting polls is but one piece of the puzzle of political equality. Enforcement is the other piece.

Asian Americans and Political Office

Naming five Asian American politicians would be a hard task for the vast majority of Americans. It seems that there is a dearth of Asian American elected officials at the local, state, and national levels. Scholars on the Asian American political experience have come up with various explanations for the lack of Asian Americans' political representation, ranging from cultural docility, a lack of a democratic tradition, and an emphasis on socioeconomic rather than civic success to political complacency and a sojourner's attitude (perpetual foreigner).[55] However, Lien argues that such a depiction of Asian American political participation is not true. Asian Americans have been running for political office since the mid-1970s, and the numbers have been increasing.[56]

Before one can hold office, one must run for office. We will discuss the patterns and trends of Asian Americans running for political office. Then, we will look at the role campaign contributions play in the success of Asian American candidacies. Lastly, we will look at the status of Asian American political office holders.

ASIAN AMERICAN CANDIDATES

Although Asian Americans have been running for office for the past thirty years, it was not until very recently that we have seen a dramatic increase in the number of Asian American political candidates. In 2002, about 190 Asian American candidates ran for office at the local, state, and national levels. Two years later, more than 230 Asian American candidates ran for elected office (that number increases to 300 if losing primary candidates are counted). This reflects an increase of approximately an astonishing 21% every two years.[57] Despite this increase, Asian Americans are still underrepresented in the political arena compared to their proportion in the population.

It is commonly assumed that, like black and Hispanic candidates who tend to run in districts with a high concentration of blacks or Hispanics, Asian Americans tend to run for political office in districts where there is a high concentration of Asian Americans. However, the data do not support such an assumption. While districts with a higher proportion of Asian Americans may attract some Asian American candidates, all districts in which 10% or more of the population were Asian American were represented by non-Asians. Interestingly, in districts where Asian Americans ran for political office, the average proportion of Asian Americans was relatively small.[58]

Because of their small population size, substantial crossover support from members of the dominant group or from a coalition of minority groups is necessary in order for Asian American political candidates to be victorious. Asian American politicians cannot win by relying on strictly the Asian American vote.

CAMPAIGN CONTRIBUTIONS

In order to be a successful candidate, contributions are necessary. From whom and to what extent do Asian American political candidates receive contributions? Asian Americans are more likely to make contributions to political campaigns and contribute more than most other racial groups. This should make them a desirable group for politicians to woo. However, because of their small population size, language barriers, and a lack of integrative leadership, as well as their methods of contributing, the benefits that they might receive for their campaign contributions are negligible.[59] Most presidential and congressional candidates tend not to champion issues related to Asian Americans in their political platforms, nor are they interested in the Asian American vote. The message that is transmitted to the general public is that the political participation of Asian Americans is of little significance.

Asian Americans do not fit the classic image of a political campaign contributor. They are basically bad, "irrational investors" in the political arena, not seeking much in return. The motives that guide their contributions to political candidates are different from those of other groups. They seek to symbolically (via finance) support and express ethnic solidarity to the Asian American candidate rather than the winner. As a consequence, Asian Americans may not contribute much to their own representatives but may instead contribute to the campaigns of other Asian Americans in other districts or other states from whom they will receive little in return. Cho found that of the total number and amount of contributions that Asian American candidates received, the percentage that came from Asian American contributors was extremely high: About 60% of contributors to Asian American candidates were Asian Americans. Elimination of the contributions of the Japanese raised this to an astonishing 79%. A case in point is the political campaign of S. B. Woo, who ran for lieutenant governor of the state of Delaware. It is reported that 93% of his contributions came from Asian Americans throughout the United States.[60]

The image of Asian Americans being deep-pocketed donors who seek influence within the American political system is more myth than fact. As the 1996 presidential campaign approached, many Asian American activists felt that the time was right for them to make a statement on the American political landscape. Instead, however, they found themselves embroiled in a campaign contribution controversy after allegations surfaced late in the year that the Clinton campaign had accepted illegal contributions from Asian sources. It was found that John Huang, a Democratic National Committee fund-raiser, served as a conduit for money from foreign Asian sources. Foreign countries are forbidden from contributing to U.S. political campaigns. Over the next year, the media was filled with stories about Asian contributors and Asian American intermediaries. Then, additional allegations were made that China was the source of some of the donations and that Chinese nationals had sought to gain access to government secrets in exchange for their contributions. Although only a few Asian Americans were involved, reports began to surface that all Asian Americans were being treated with suspicion, singled out for heightened scrutiny, and asked if they were citizens. Even if they were native-born U.S. citizens, many were questioned by the FBI about their "questionable" contributions. The stereotype of Asian Americans as perpetual foreigners reared its ugly head again. The distinction between "Chinese" and "Chinese American" was never made. They were all perpetual foreigners.

ASIAN AMERICAN POLITICAL OFFICE HOLDERS

Over the past thirty years, we have witnessed a dramatic increase in the number of Asian American office holders, especially at the local and state levels.

In 1978, when comprehensive records were first compiled, there were only 120 Asian American elected officials in key local, state, and federal offices.[61] In 1996, there were only about 300 Asian American elected officials nationwide. This list included forty-one state representatives, eighty-three city council members, and twenty-six mayors. In 2005, that number had nearly doubled to 555, including sixty-four state senators, ninety-seven state representatives, three state governors, nineteen mayors, 123 city or county council members or other elected municipal elected officials, and 236 judges. The number of Asian American city council members increased by more than half, and the number of Asian American state representatives more than doubled.[62]

Lien found similar and additional trends regarding Asian American political office holders at the local and state levels. She noted the following trends since the 1970s when Asian Americans began to run for office:

- There has been a dramatic increase in Asian Americans elected and appointed officials to over 1,200 in 1998.
- There was an increased frequency of Asian Americans occupying higher or more prominent offices and an increase in the acceptance by the mainstream electorate of officials with Asian faces. S. B. Woo was elected lieutenant governor of Delaware in 1988, and Gary Locke was elected governor of the state of Washington in 1996.
- There has been greater ethnic representation among elected officials beyond persons of Japanese or Chinese descent. We are now seeing office holders of Filipino, Korean, Asian Indian, and Vietnamese descent.
- Whereas Asian Americans are less likely to hold political office where they comprise a large proportion of the voting population, more recent trends suggest the establishment of more equitable political representation of Asians in localities with high concentration of Asians.
- Lastly, there is a persistent gap between Asian Americans running for office and Asian Americans winning political office.[63]

At the state level, Asian Americans have been successful in campaigning and electing their own candidates despite the lack of a single Asian majority congressional district by galvanizing voting and by running as mainstream, crossover candidates.[64]

Asian Americans are also gaining a greater political presence at the national level. In 2000, President Clinton named the first ever Asian American cabinet secretary, Norman Mineta, to head the Department of Commerce; and Gary Locke (the nation's first Chinese American governor) was reelected to a second term in the state of Washington. President Bush retained Mineta as secretary of transportation and appointed another Asian American, Elaine Chao, as secretary of labor. In 2000, Asian Americans represented about 4% of the population in the United States, but in Congress they had 1.3% of the representation, the lowest of all racial groups in the House. Although Asian Americans had a greater ratio of representation in the Senate than other nonwhite groups (two senators from Hawai'i), this ratio is still below their national population share. In the 2006 Congress, there were nine Asian American legislators in Congress—six representatives and one delegate in the House (1.6%) and two senators.

In conclusion, this survey of Asian Americans running for and holding political office at all levels of government paints a rather bleak picture of their acceptance to participate as equals in democratic governing and jurisprudence. In recent years, there has been a dramatic increase of Asian Americans running for and holding political office. The model minority stereotype may be partly responsible for the gradual acceptance of Asian Americans in politics—that their high educational and socioeconomic attainment and their emphasis on family values made Asian Americans acceptable, if not ideal, political candidates. However, Asian Americans remain woefully underrepresented at all levels of government. Discrimination persists at all levels of the political process. The image of the Asian American as perpetual foreigner may persist, even for Asian American political office holders. A case in point is that U.S. Congressman David Wu (D-Oregon) was denied entrance to the U.S. Energy Department, where he was scheduled to give a speech. The guards refused to believe that he was an American citizen, even after he produced his congressional identification![65]

Conclusions

Asian Americans have begun to change the social and political landscape of America. One of the major reasons for the dramatic increase in the political participation of Asian Americans is the change in a racist immigration policy. Previous to 1965, Asian immigration to the United States was restricted to a small trickle, with quotas placed on the number of Asians allowed to immigrate to the United States. For example, a quota of 105 Chinese was enforced. Japanese were also restricted.[66] However, passage of the 1965 Immigration and Naturalization Act allowed Asians to immigrate to the United States on a more or less equal basis with those from other countries. Instead of an inequitable and restrictive quota system, each country, whether European or Asian, was given an annual quota of 10,000 immigrants. The racist immigration policies of the United States were overturned. As a consequence, the influx of Asian immigrants arriving to the shores of the United States increased dramatically, swelling the size of the Asian American population already in the United States. Currently, about one-third of the 800,000 legal immigrants to arrive to the United States each year are from Asian countries.

The increased immigration from Asia has three important implications for the political participation of Asian Americans. First, more important than just the number of Asian immigrants arriving to these shores is the high naturalization rate for U.S. citizenship of the Asian immigrant population, rates higher than for other immigrant groups in the United States. Despite the fact that the majority of Asian Americans are foreign-born, about 70% of Asian American adults were U.S citizens by birth or naturalization in 2006. This translates into a growing number of Asian Americans who are eligible to vote and to be involved in the political process. Second, the dramatic influx of Asian immigrants since the late 1960s has led to an emergence of a significant second-generation Asian American population as well as the emergence of those who arrived as children coming of age to vote in the late 1990s. Third, this increased number of Asian Americans combined with their concentration in states such as California and New York provides them with potentially disproportionate political influence as critical swing votes.

Despite having a large proportion of their population claiming Independent as a political affiliation, Asian Americans vote Democratic and most Asian American elected political officials are Democrats. Asian American voters continue to face barriers in their access to the voting polls such as the lack of bilingual resources, translators, redistricting, and discrimination. Asian American candidates, relying on campaign contributions from other Asian Americans and crossover voting from members of the dominant group or from other minority groups, have become increasingly more successful in winning elections, despite still facing prejudice. The model minority stereotype and the perpetual foreigner stereotype persist, sometimes hindering and sometimes aiding Asian American political participation.

As the twenty-first century unfolds, the political future of Asian Americans remains unclear. It is still very much a work in progress, and the next decade or two could see considerable changes. The growing number of Asian Americans in local and state office is creating an expanding pool of veteran candidates who are likely to be able to mount effective campaigns for office. Their experience at coalition building and crossover voters is valuable for higher political offices.

Although the increase in the Asian American population means a potential increase in Asian American voters, it also means an increase in diversity within the Asian population, with many different political agendas and orientations, degrees of affluence, and social views. If they are able to put aside these differences, then Asian Americans will be a political force to be reckoned with. But this may be a difficult task to accomplish. Asian Americans of different ancestries can come together much more easily over common domestic issues such as bilingual ballots, anti-Asian violence, discrimination, or immigration reform than over issues such as political corruption in South Korea or civil tensions in the Philippines.

This chapter began with a description of the Vincent Chin case, an incident that galvanized the Asian American community to speak up against racial injustice. This effort would not have occurred if not for a grassroots organization that advocated on behalf of the Asian American community. Over the past twenty years, Asian American interest groups have proliferated. Long-established Asian American groups such as the Japanese American Citizens League (1929) and the Organization of Chinese Americans (1973) witnessed the founding of numerous additional Asian American groups, such as the Southeast Asian Resource Action Center (founded in 1979 as the Indochina Refugee Action Center), the Korean American Coalition (1983), the Asian Pacific American Legal Center (1983), the Asian and Pacific Islander American Health Forum (1986), the National Asian Pacific American Legal Consortium (1991), and the Asian Pacific American Institute for Congressional Studies (1995). It is these and hundreds of other advocacy, educational, legal, professional, and student groups that have helped create a massive Asian American political infrastructure that provides a training ground for new and aspiring Asian American politicians. Organized interests are critical in wielding political influence in America. Asian influence in Washington, D.C., and elsewhere is greatly enhanced by the growth of this political infrastructure. Attacks on Asian Americans, once met with silence, are now met with swift responses that are only possible from organized groups with sufficient resources. This was the case for Wen Ho Lee.

In the late 1990s, there was considerable diplomatic tension between China and the United States. A prevalent belief among many Americans was that nuclear secrets were being passed to China. In 1999, a scientist at the Los Alamos Nuclear Laboratory by the name of Wen Ho Lee was arrested and charged with 59 felony counts of transferring secret nuclear weapons data to unsecured computer terminals and computer tapes. He was denied bail, kept in solitary confinement, and forced to wear leg shackles and chains for nine months. Lee was never charged with espionage—just mishandling classified documents—something that many others, including his superiors, did at Los Alamos. Lee's arrest prompted nationwide attention and political action among numerous Asian American groups and the Asian American community. On June 8, 2000, hundreds of Asian Americans gathered at Day of Outrage rallies held in cities across the nation, protesting Lee's treatment, calling for due process, and urging government officials to free him on bail. Charges of racial profiling were hurled at the FBI and U.S. Attorney General Janet Reno's offices. In September 2000, just two days before the government was forced to produce documents to support their case against him, they dropped all but one of those 59 charges. It was found that FBI agents provided false testimony in the initial investigation. In an unprecedented move, the judge of the case apologized to Lee for this travesty of justice. The *New York Times* also apologized to Lee, admitting that they did not do the proper research and fact finding when they first investigated the story and that they were wrong in presuming that Dr. Lee was guilty and wrong for helping to convict him in the court of media sensationalism and public opinion. The vindication of Dr. Wen Ho Lee would not have occurred without the support of the various Asian American advocacy groups.[67]

These groups provide ready-made avenues for political involvement, greatly reducing the difficulty of making one's voice heard. It may be that the future of what is called "Asian American politics" may not lie so much in the Asian American politicians who are elected or appointed to various offices at the local, county, state, and federal levels—for these individuals are beholden to those who elect them, of whom only a small proportion are Asian Americans—but in the growing influence of the numerous small grassroots, panethnic Asian American advocacy organizations that have sprung up over the past twenty years that are committed and will take up issues of importance to the Asian American community. Asian American politics will only be able to mature if millions of individuals see themselves as sharing a common Asian American heritage and a common destiny.

DISCUSSION QUESTIONS

1. Discuss the demographic characteristics and residential patterns of Asian Americans in the United States. What are the consequences of such patterns on the political participation and experience of Asian Americans?

2. Asian Americans can be stereotyped positively as model minorities and/or negatively as perpetual foreigners. What are the bases of these stereotypes? What counterarguments can you provide to these stereotypes? What impacts do these stereotypes have on the political participation of Asian Americans?

3. What are some of the barriers that Asian Americans face in terms of their access to voting polls and political office? What recommendations would you suggest to ensure that Asian Americans receive fair and equal access and treatment?

4. Some argue that there are Asian American politicians. Others argue that there are politicians who happen to be Asian Americans. What are the implications of these two arguments? What argument do you think holds the greatest weight? Why?

5. A conclusion of the chapter is that the political future of Asian Americans remains unclear. It is argued that in the future Asian American advocacy groups may play a greater role in Asian American politics, a greater role than even Asian American politicians. What are the strengths as well as the weaknesses of this argument? What do you think is the political future of Asian America?

Chapter 10

Anti-Semitism and the Jewish American Political Experience

Paul Mendes-Flohr

In the wake of the Six Day War of 1967 and the euphoric outburst of Jewish pride engendered by Israel's startling victory, the American Jewish comedian Jerry Lewis quipped, "Now we could get our noses back." He was referring to the practice of many Jews who undergo cosmetic surgery in the hope that "non-Jewish" facial features may pave the way to social and professional acceptance. Indeed, as the cultural historian Sander Gilman has shown, cosmetic surgery was developed in late nineteenth-century Germany by Jewish surgeons for virtually an exclusively Jewish clientele.[1] The desire to "pass" by surgically erasing one's allegedly "Jewish" appearance became a nigh obsession of upward-bound, assimilating Jews. I well remember that most of the Jewish girls in my high school in the late 1950s had "nose jobs" before their senior year and their departure for the big world beyond the confines of our secure Jewish enclave in Brooklyn.

At the time, I sympathized with my female classmates and shared their hopes that the surgical removal of the stigma of a blatant Jewish appearance would pave their way to a happy future. I now realize that it was a psychologically unhealthy response to the challenge of resisting the "tyranny of the majority" and of accepting that one is different. A classmate of my sister, who is a year younger than I, seems to have at least intuitively understood the challenge and refused to follow the pack. With proud defiance, she retained her Jewish nose. Her name was Barbra Streisand. Going on to have a sterling career as an actress and entertainer, she sought to neither erase her Jewish countenance nor dissimulate her Jewish affiliation. By so doing, she helped

174

replace the regnant myth of America as a homogenizing "melting pot" with a new self-image as a multiethnic society, composed of individuals with diverse physiognomies and religious and cultural heritages.

Introduction: The Ideological Claims and Origins of Modern Anti-Semitism

As an ideology, anti-Semitism[2] developed in Europe as a by-product, as it were, of the protracted debates regarding the *emancipation*, the name given to the process of liberating the Jews from the legal disabilities associated with their centuries-long confinement to ghettos. In contrast to Europe, the Jews of the United States were never "emancipated"; for one, there were no legal ghettos in America and, more importantly, the right of the Jews to citizenship was not questioned, at least on legal grounds. All Jews born in the United States were granted citizenship without question, and others could seek naturalization according to the procedures set for all foreign-born individuals. The Jews of America were never legally discriminated. The situation in Europe was utterly different. The contrast between the Jewish experience in Europe and that in the United States is crucial if we are to appreciate the eventual failure of ideological anti-Semitism to take deep roots in the American political and social fabric. This is not to say that anti-Semitism did not find its way into America. It did. In the discussion that follows, we shall endeavor to explain why the American political and legal ethos ultimately did not allow anti-Semitism to take on the virulent expression it did in Europe.

Jewishness as an Incorrigible Moral Deformation

The obsessive attempt to rid oneself of the last vestiges of one's Jewish provenance—symbolized by the "Jewish nose"—which cultural assimilation failed to, indeed could not, remove, reflected an internalization of anti-Semitic stereotypes. Analogies could be found among other minorities eager to remove the physiognomic stigma attached to their ethnic origin. What the Jews often discovered is that their Jewishness was deemed incorrigible; even conversion to Christianity and cosmetic surgery could not—so the anti-Semites argued—eliminate the insidious traces of their intrinsically corrupt culture and ethnic makeup. As one anti-Semite remarked,

> A Jewish question would still exist, even if every Jew were to turn his back on his religion and join one of our major churches. Yes, I maintain that in that case, the struggle between us and the Jews would make itself felt as ever more urgent.... It is precisely the baptized Jews who infiltrate furthest, unhindered in all sectors

of society and political life. It is as though they have provided themselves with an unrestricted passport, advancing their stock to those places where members of the Jewish religion are unable to follow.[3]

Yet another anti-Semite observed, "Whether, after conversion, they cease to be Jews in the deeper sense, we do not know, and have no way of finding out. I believe that the ancient Jewish influences continue to operate. Jewishness is like a concentrated dye: a minute quantity suffices to give a specific character— or, at least some traces of it—to an incomparably greater mass."[4] With a more ominous tone, the German philosopher Johann Gottlieb Fichte exclaimed, "I see of no way of giving [the Jews] civil rights, except, perhaps, one night we chop off their heads and replace them with new ones, in which there would not be one single Jewish idea."[5]

Assimilation and conversion could not help. The Jew, alas, would remain a Jew by ethnic disposition. The claim that Jewishness was a deep-seated, irredeemable character deformation was at the very heart of modern anti-Semitism. By arguing that although the Jews may be emancipated from Judaism they would nonetheless remain beholden to inborn Jewish traits, the anti-Semites, in effect, challenged the founding principle of liberal democracy, that a common humanity constitutes the intrinsic dignity of all human beings and their right to civic equality. In philosophical terms, anti-Semitism—as all racist theories and ethnic stereotyping—rejects the ontological and humanistic premise of the liberal ethos.

The European Origins of Modern Anti-Semitism

In nineteenth-century Europe, anti-Semitism developed into a full-blown racial theory grounded in pseudoscientific theory based on evidence drawn purportedly from somatic and anatomical measurements, particularly, of course, of the nose. Disregarding the fact that the Jewish people, from their biblical origins, were comprised of a mixture of races, as they continue to be, the racial anti-Semites declared the Jews to be a distinct race, whose peculiarly ugly physical deformities reflect their inner twisted moral disposition. Indeed, the term "anti-Semitism" was coined in 1879 by one Wilhelm Marr as a plea to recognize the Jews as an innately evil breed of human beings bent on destroying by devious means Christian European civilization. Hence, Marr issued an urgent call, in his case to his fellow Germans, to mobilize before it was too late and resolutely rebuff the Jewish "Semites" and their baneful influence on contemporary society, economy, culture, and politics:

The Jews were late in their assault on Germany, but once they started there was no stopping them.... Dear reader, while you are allowing Germany to be skinned alive I bow my head in admiration and amazement before this Semitic people, which has us under heel. Resigned to subjugation to Jewry, I am marshalling my last remaining strength in order to die peacefully, as one who will not surrender and who will not ask forgiveness.[6]

As a last-minute, desperate attempt to stop the evil march of Jewry, Marr founded the League of Anti-Semites, which was the first effort at creating a popular political movement based on anti-Semitism. Many similar efforts throughout Europe and elsewhere were to follow, culminating in the parliamentary electoral victory of the German National Socialist Party, led by Adolf Hitler, in 1933. The crazed scheme of the Nazis to eliminate the scourge of "world Jewry" was not born in a vacuum. *The Protocols of the Elders of Zion,* for instance, a concocted document from about 1902 purportedly recording the minutes of a secret meeting of the leading representatives of all sectors of the Jewish people, bore on its title page words that foreshadowed Hitler's "final solution" to the so-called Jewish question: "Gentiles, Beware! The Jews are an alien bacillus that must be urgently contained and isolated." An English translation of *The Protocols,* originally written in Russian, was, incidentally, distributed in the United States, under the foreboding title *The Jewish Menace,* by the American automobile manufacturer Henry Ford. An avowed anti-Semite, Ford had his daily newspaper, *The Dearborn Independent,* cite liberally from *The Protocols* and, indeed, serve as an organ in the struggle against the "Jewish menace."

The Failure of Anti-Semitism to Take Root in the United States

Eventually, a libel suit was brought against Ford's newspaper and he was obliged by the court to apologize and publicly repudiate anti-Semitism.[7] What is significant, however, is not the success of the suit but the fact that Ford did not achieve his objective of organizing in the United States anti-Semitism as a political force. To be sure, anti-Semitism abounded in the United States in the social sphere—where many institutions, such as country clubs and hotels, were closed to Jews and leading academic institutions sought to limit the number of Jewish students and faculty. Nonetheless, the United States did not provide a fertile soil for political anti-Semitism.

In a volume, provocatively entitled *Why Blacks, Women, and Jews Are not Mentioned in the Constitution and Other Unorthodox Views,* Robert A. Goldwin points to the wisdom of the makers of the Constitution of the United States for referring only to individuals and not corporate entities, such as blacks, women, and Jews. Hence, Goldwin argues, the constitution implicitly transcends prevailing prejudices toward national, religious, and sexual groups. To be sure, for many decades blacks were excluded from citizenship and women did not enjoy suffrage until the twentieth century—but by social consensus, not by law. When in time the consensus was challenged, the Constitution did not present an obstacle to the recognition of blacks and women as citizens.[8] In contrast to blacks and women (and Native Americans), Jews were granted citizenship from the very founding of the American Republic. And in striking contrast to Europe, no debates were ever held in the halls of Congress questioning the Jews' eligibility to what the Declaration of Independence of July 4, 1776, called the "inalienable right [to] life, liberty, and the pursuit of happiness." Their right to citizenship, according to another key phrase from this founding document of American democracy, was "self-evident." No special legislation was ever enacted granting the Jews citizenship. Even in the most enlightened states of Europe the right of Jews to citizenship was not self-evident. On the contrary, the constitutional struggle to accord them citizenship—a process called "emancipation," for it entailed the removal of centuries-old restrictions that confided the Jews to ghettos and the margins of society—lasted for more than a century. Legislation entitling the Jews to civic equality was enacted, only to be later repealed or qualified.

The emancipation of the Jews of the Austrian-Hungarian Empire was only first firmly established in 1869 and in Prussia a bit later and only fully with the founding of the Weimar Republic in 1918. Poland waited to grant the Jews civic equality until it was obliged to do so by the terms of the Treaty of Versailles in 1919, and it took another fifteen years to implement its treaty obligations fully. The millions of Jews of Russia had also to wait until the upheavals wrought by World War I, which brought the Bolsheviks to power. The Baltic states—Finland, Estonia, Latvia, and Lithuania—also deferred granting the Jews civic rights until after World War I. Full emancipation was achieved in Denmark in 1849, Sweden in 1870, and Norway only in 1891. The drawn-out process was accompanied by ramified debates that took place in the legislatures and in the public squares of Europe. Thus was born the "Jewish question"—to which Hitler offered a "final solution"—engaging both the rabble and some of the best minds of Europe.[9] The explanation for Europe's reluctance to regard Jewish civil rights as "self-evident" that scholars often proffer is that prejudice against the Jews and Judaism remained endemic to European civilization. It is pointed out that the age-old contempt of the Jews—with deep roots in Christianity—proved to be doggedly resilient and adjusted itself to the temper of the modern era by quickly donning the attire of secular arguments against the Jews and their emancipation.

The inadequacy of this explanation is immediately highlighted by the fact that the founding fathers of the United States were not utterly free of bias toward the Jews and their ancient faith. It was the constitution that prevailed over prejudice. Moreover, the eventual absence of one dominant ethnic community in the United States and the ever multiplying minority communities have also played a decisive role in preventing anti-Semitism from gaining a firm hold in the political landscape of the United States. By *force majeure* the United States became a pluralistic society, in which cultural, religious, and ethnic distinctions do not disqualify one from membership. The white Protestant America of the founding fathers gradually emerged as a multiethnic and multicultural society. The inclusion of Jews within the evolving civil society was thus, indeed, "self-evident." This is poignantly illustrated by an exchange between the Jewish congregation of Newport, Rhode Island, and George Washington, shortly after his inauguration as the first president of the republic. In a message dispatched to President Washington on August 17, 1790, greeting him upon his visit to Newport, the elders of the congregation noted

> Deprived as we have hitherto been of the invaluable rights of free citizens, we now, with a deep sense of gratitude to the Almighty Disposer of all events, behold a government, erected by the majesty of the people, a government which to bigotry gives no sanction, to persecution no assistance, but generously affording to all liberty of conscience and immunities of citizenship, deeming every one, of whatever nation, tongue, or language, equal parts of the great governmental machine.[10]

In reply, Washington gratefully acknowledged the salutations extended to him and remarked

> The citizens of the United States of America have a right to applaud themselves for having given to mankind examples of an enlarged and liberal policy, a policy worthy of imitation. All possess alike liberty of conscience and immunities of citizenship. It is now no more that tolerance is spoken of, as if it was the indulgence of one class of people that another enjoyed the exercise of their inherent natural rights. For happily the government of the United States, which gives to bigotry no sanction, to persecution no assistance, requires only that they who live under its protection should demean themselves good citizens, in giving it on all occasions their effectual support.... May the children of the stock of Abraham who dwell in this land continue to merit and enjoy the good will of the other inhabitants, while every one shall sit in safety under his own vine and fig-tree, and there shall be none to make him afraid.[11]

This eloquent exchange between the Hebrew congregation of Newport and the first president of the United States served to articulate the young republic's unfolding conception of what is now called "civil society" as an inclusive, multiethnic social fabric—deeming everyone, of whatever "nation, tongue, or language, equal parts of the great governmental machine," in which each individual will be allowed to dwell "in safety under his own vine and fig-tree." There were—as there still are—of course many rough edges in American civil society. Old and new prejudices infected not only intercommunal attitudes but also at times legislation, for instance, the acts of Congress in the 1920s restricting the mass immigration, particularly of Jews from eastern Europe, who, according to a report to the Department of State submitted to the House of Representatives, "are of the usual ghetto type. . . . They are filthy, un-American and often dangerous in their habits."[12] But once Jews—and other minority peoples—reached the shores of America, they were, despite the prevailing antipathies toward them, naturalized in accordance with the Constitution and given legal protections. Therefore, unlike their counterparts in Europe, the Jews of the United States did not have to mount a drawn-out struggle for emancipation. This is not to say there was not a need to combat anti-Semitic defamation and discrimination, but their constitutional rights were secure. The nation's inclusive conception of civil society, which in principle remained neutral with regard to ethnicity, national original, and religious affiliation, perforce embraced Jews. Their right to citizenship was, as George Washington pointedly underscored, beyond a question of tolerance. Or as the first native-born American rabbi, Gershon Mendes Seixas of New York City's Sephardic congregation, joyfully declared in 1811, "The United States is, perhaps, the only place where the Jews have not suffered persecution, but have, on the contrary, been encouraged and indulged in every right of citizens."[13] Significantly, Rabbi Seixas was invited to serve as one of the four officiating clergy at the inauguration of President Washington in 1789. Hence, from the very beginning of the republic, Judaism was recognized as part and parcel of the nation's spiritual tapestry.

The commitment of the founding fathers of the nation to religious pluralism was a blessing to Jewry. The refusal to establish an official state religion, which might have encouraged discrimination against other faiths, allowed for the flourishing of religious diversity. This process was undoubtedly abetted by the need for immigration, especially of those with proven economic enterprise, which, in turn, led to the ever-growing ethnic and religious diversity that has come to characterize the United States. As a result, unlike in many nation-states of Europe, the Jews were not the most conspicuous ethnic and religious minority; moreover, their status in the United States was not under the shadow of the legacy of ghettos or legally restricted residential areas governed by a separate juridical system. The remaining remnants of legal restrictions from the colonial period that limited the rights of Jews to vote and hold office in some of the states of the Union were all removed by the beginning of the nineteenth century.

Nonetheless, anti-Jewish prejudices continued to ripple throughout the history of the United States, occasionally erupting into virulent, even violent expressions of outright anti-Semitism. But a sustained manifestation of anti-Semitic sentiments was not marked until the twentieth century. One must recall that at the founding of the republic the Jews were a very small minority, numbering in 1776 no more than 2,500, or less than one-tenth of 1% of the entire population. In the 1840s and 1850s immigration from Germany increased the Jewish population to about 200,000, while the entire population of the United States reached some 30,000,000. The Jews were hardly noticed. Social and economic frustrations were vent on other, more prominent minorities. In the pre–Civil War era Catholics were the principal subject of religious discrimination and prejudice, not Jews. Further, the question of slavery then dominated the interethnic discourse. It was not until the Civil War that anti-Semitism poisoned public life. Voices on both sides of the divide accused Jews of constituting a fifth column clandestinely aiding the enemy and of war profiteering. The most infamous expression of these sentiments was voiced by General Ulysses S. Grant. On December 17, 1862, he issued an order calling for the expulsion of all Jews, whom he accused of illegal trade, within twenty-four hours from the areas under his control. When this order was brought to the attention of President Lincoln, he immediately had it revoked. He sternly chided his general for branding a whole group of citizens for the alleged misdeeds of a few of its members. Indeed, he underscored the principal opposition to governmental or official discrimination against not only the Jews but all minorities.

At the beginning of the 1870s there was a notable recrudescence of social anti-Semitism. In these years America was experiencing profound social changes attendant to the post–Civil War industrial boom and the rise of a new vibrant middle class, which numbered among its ranks Jewish entrepreneurs, who challenged the older elite of white Anglo-Saxon Protestants. The latter sought to secure their social position by systematic discrimination against the "upstart" Jews. Private schools, social clubs, and resorts—institutions of the upper classes—were closed to Jews. In an interview he gave to the *New York Herald* in July 1879, Austin Corbin, the owner of the Long Island Railroad and the Manhattan Beach Club, explained why he wished to ban Jews from Coney Island, Brooklyn, which he was developing as a fashionable resort:

> Personally I am opposed to Jews. They are a pretentious class, who expect three times as much for their money as other people. They give us more trouble on our railroad and in our hotel than we can stand. Another thing is, that they are driving away the class of people who are beginning to make Coney Island the most fashionable and magnificent watering place in the world.... [They] are hurting us in every way, and we do not want them. We cannot bring the highest social element to Manhattan Beach if the Jews persist in coming. They will not associate with Jews, and that's all there is about it.[14]

Antagonism toward the Jews intensified with the mass immigration of east European Jews initially sparked by the pogroms in czarist Russia in the early 1880s. By 1925 there were close to 4,500,000 Jews in the United States. Driven by anti-Semitism and poverty, the immigrants were drawn to the larger cities, especially of the East Coast and of the Midwest, which had become centers of rapid industrial expansion and economic opportunity. The concomitant depression of the agricultural economy and the impoverishment of small town, rural communities led to a growing resentment of the immigrants. To be sure, the Jews were not the only immigrants who rushed to the shores of America, but they came to symbolize in the eyes of many "native" Americans the underside of the demographic and economic changes that were transforming the face of the country in these years.

The xenophobia and isolationism that gripped many Americans thus often focused on the Jews. The violent potential of the ever intensifying hatred of the "alien" Jews was tragically manifest in the lynching of Leo Frank in 1915. An American-born engineer, Frank had come from New York City to work in his uncle's pencil factory in Atlanta, Georgia. When in April 1913 a young employee of the factory was found murdered, Frank was accused of the crime. During the trial a leading local newspaper demanded the execution of "the filthy, perverted Jew of New York." On the basis of dubious evidence, Frank was convicted by the Atlanta court; his subsequent appeal to the Supreme Court, which rendered the case a national *cause célébre*, was turned down. When the governor of Georgia, who was convinced of Frank's innocence, commuted his scheduled execution to a life term, a mob rushed the prison, dragged Frank out, and hung him. More than seventy years later, Frank was vindicated when an elderly man, Alonzo Mann, came forth and filed an affidavit testifying that as a child of thirteen he saw one John Conley dragging the body of the murdered child. Threatened to keep silent lest he too be murdered, Mann guarded his secret until 1983. Encouraged by his testimony, the Anti-Defamation League, which was born in the wake of the Frank affair (see following section), successfully petitioned the state of Georgia's Board of Pardons to grant Frank a posthumous pardon. In March 1986 the governor of Georgia signed the pardon but without clearing him of the crime.

Organizational Response to Anti-Semitism

The lynching of Frank pointed to the upsurge of anti-Semitic feelings sweeping America, especially in the southern and western states where Jews were identified with the eastern financial establishment and the oppressors of farmers and small business owners. Numerous organizations were founded to combat the Jews and other putatively pernicious alien elements. Shortly after World War I, the post–Civil War secret order of the Ku Klux Klan was reestablished and by 1924 reached a nationwide membership of over 4,000,000. Although the Klan's primary enemies were Catholics and African Americans, it also targeted Jews as threatening the American ethos and ethnic integrity. Among the other organizations that promoted anti-Semitism, the Christian Front led by Father Charles E. Coughlin was perhaps the most threatening. In the midst of the Depression of the 1930s, Father Coughlin, a Roman Catholic priest from Detroit, employed his exceedingly popular radio program with an audience of millions to launch a virulent anti-Semitic campaign. His journal, *Social Justice*, which identified the Jews as the root cause of the world's economic woes, was widely distributed throughout the large cities of America.

The organized Jewish community did not sit idle and came to the defense of their compatriots. In response to the anti-Semitic agitation surrounding the trial of Leo Frank, the Jewish fraternal order B'nai Brith in 1913 founded the Anti-Defamation League (ADL) "to end the defamation of the Jewish people ... [and] to secure justice and fair treatment for all citizens alike." Through legal action and principally education, the ADL counters anti-Semitic stereotypes and calumnies. Earlier, in 1906, the American Jewish Committee (AJC) was established "to prevent the infraction of the civil and religious rights of Jews, in any part of the world." As this statement of purpose indicates, the AJC sought to combat anti-Semitism everywhere, including the United States. The ADL is not a membership organization but a "commission" of professionals from various disciplines specializing in such areas of communal life as religion, law, education, labor relations, politics, and government. From the very beginning, the ADL adopted a pragmatic approach to combating anti-Semitism, responding to specific incidents and developments perceived as threatening the rights and security of Jews as individuals and as a community. Initially, the ADL focused its efforts on countering hateful agitation against Jews, job discrimination, and restrictions on Jews residing in certain neighborhoods and towns, attending certain schools (until the 1950s many of the leading universities in the United States had a *numerus clausus*, limiting the number of Jews they would admit), and joining certain country clubs and fraternal orders. Although it occasionally engaged in legal action to eliminate these obstacles to full equality of Jews, the ADL tended to favor educational means to combat the defamation of the Jews. The commission, thus, for instance, published a series of articles, pamphlets, and books challenging vulgar stereotypes and caricatures on the stage and in the media. Similarly, the ADL sponsors studies on the sources of ethnic, racial, and religious prejudice.

In the early 1960s, the ADL departed from its general policy of preferring anti-defamation activity and constructive programs to engender intercommunity understanding and tolerance. Joining a coalition of Jewish and non-Jewish organizations, the ADL played a prominent role in promoting the passage of the Civil Rights Act of 1964 and the subsequent fair housing and voting rights laws. Although these legislative procedures did not bear directly on anti-Semitism, they reflected the ADL's conviction that safeguarding the human and civic rights of the Jews required the strengthening of America as a democratic, pluralistic society.

As it name suggests, the American Jewish Committee was literally a committee, initially of 60 prominent communal leaders (expanded by 1931 to 350), to check the scourge of worldwide anti-Semitism, particularly as it bore on the situation of American Jewry. Hence, the initial impulse to the founding of the organization was anti-Jewish riots — the so-called Kishinev pogrom of 1905 — in czarist Russia. Indeed, the plight of Russian Jewry preoccupied the AJC for much of the early decades of its existence. Accordingly, the AJC pursued various activities to secure liberal American immigration policies. The committee largely concentrated its efforts on quiet diplomacy and "discreet" lobbying. It rejected the confrontational policies of other organizations. It was feared that such policies would only serve to reinforce the anti-Semitic charge that Jewish interests were at odds with those of other Americans. The rise of the Nazis led the AJC to lobby for the rescue of German Jews and their immigration to the United States and other possible havens. At the time, the committee joined with the ADL in the struggle against the alarming rise of organized anti-Semitism in the United States. Abandoning its preference for quiet diplomacy, it devised educational programs and supported the investigation of hate groups and their subversive connections to the Nazi regime. With the defeat of Hitler, the committee assumed a ramified program to rehabilitate the survivors of the Holocaust and to help reconstruct Jewish cultural life in Europe. After World War II, the AJC became a membership organization and expanded its ranks by 2005 to 150,000 individuals organized in thirty-three chapters throughout the United States. It maintains a vigilant program of combating the recrudescence of anti-Semitism, especially in Muslim countries and South America. With respect to internal American affairs, the AJC seeks to strengthen the country's foundations as a pluralistic democratic society, and to this end it takes an active interest in fostering the rights and liberties of non-Jews as well as of Jews.

Dissatisfied with what was regarded as a paternalistic approach of the AJC, a group of individuals founded the American Jewish Congress in 1918 as an umbrella organization of Jewish groups that represented diverse Jewish interests, religious and ethnic — hence the name "congress." Regarding itself as a "grassroots" organization, the American Jewish Congress did not regard itself as merely a defense and community-relations agency. It would not confine its activities to quiet diplomacy and anti-defamation education. The congress thus adopted a vigorous program of legal advocacy. Moreover, in contrast to the ADL and AJC, the congress unabashedly affirmed the Jews to be both an ethnic and a religious community, a people with a distinct cultural history who should not fear to advocate openly their collective interests. The congress, which in 2005 had a membership of some 40,000, was thus at the forefront of aggressive legal and social action to combat prejudice and discrimination. Similar to the ADL and AJC, the American Jewish Congress seeks to strengthen the institutions of American democracy. It, therefore, joins forces with non-Jewish organizations such as the National Association for the Advancement of Colored People (NAACP) and the American Civil Liberties Union (ACLU) in pursuing legal action against discrimination in all areas of American life. In viewing itself as the "lawyer" of American Jewry, the congress has paved a distinctive path in the continuing struggle against anti-Semitism.

The strategies of these and similar organizations converge in their firm commitment to interfaith dialogue, especially as inspired by the irenic spirit of Pope John XXIII and the Second Ecumenical Council of the early 1960s. Vatican II spoke of a universal reaffirmation of human rights, as enshrined in the Charter of the United Nations of 1945, and the resolve to eliminate the scourge of racism and bigotry that blighted Europe and Asia in the Second World War. The conscience of civilized humanity was especially touched by the horrific genocide against European Jewry, now known as the Holocaust.

Conclusions

The lingering anti-Semitism in the United States and elsewhere in the world was discredited, leading eventually to the removal of all vestiges of informal discrimination, such as quotas for the number of Jews admitted to elite universities and their faculties. Both public and private expressions of anti-Semitism were now considered scandalous. To be sure, the greatest triumph of the new spirit was the dismantling of segregation and other disabilities suffered by African Americans, an effort in which many Jews took part. Nonetheless, Jews have often found themselves in conflict with African Americans, particularly in the large urban communities where they live in mutual proximity. Although Jews have been for decades at the forefront of the civil rights movement, some—and certainly not all—African American leaders have employed anti-Semitic rhetoric to voice their community's understandable grievances about continuing social and economic inequality. In recent years, opposition to the policies of the state of Israel, whose founding in 1948 was strongly supported by the United States, especially with respect to the Palestinians, has led some to bolster their criticism with stereotypes borrowed from the arsenal of anti-Semites.

In the extreme, the medieval claim that the Jews use the blood of Gentiles for ritual purposes is evoked, usually as an emotion-laden metaphor, to characterize Israeli "oppression" of the Palestinians. Occasionally, even the ancient charge of deicide, which indicts the entire Jewish people throughout the ages for the crucifixion of Jesus, resurfaces in the rhetorical battle against the state of Israel. More often, this battle is waged by comparing the policies of the Jewish state to the anti-Semitic crimes of the Nazis, a deliberately hyperbolic comparison meant to morally embarrass the state of Israel by insidiously suggesting that the victims of the Holocaust act no better than those who slaughtered millions of their number in the gas chambers. Some critics of the state of Israel go so far as to claim that Zionists exaggerate the extent of the Holocaust in order to mobilize world sympathy for the state of Israel in its struggle against the Palestinians. The common denominator of these and similar accusations is that the Jewish people are collectively responsible for the actions of the state of Israel. The tarring of an entire community for the conduct and views of some of its members is, of course, typical of racism.

A critical appraisal of the policies of the state of Israel—as that of any other government—is legitimate and, indeed, the responsibility of any thoughtful human being. But political and ethical judgments should not be articulated with an appeal, explicit or otherwise, to cultural and ethnic stereotypes. Once laced with anti-Semitic imagery, criticism of the state of Israel becomes in effect an *ad hominem* argument and, thus, ultimately undermines the political and ethical efficacy of the criticism.

On the positive side of the ledger, it should be noted that throughout the world governments and other official agencies have promoted public acknowledgment of the Holocaust through commemoration, museums, and educational programs designed to raise consciousness of the scandal of anti-Semitism and all forms of racism. The heightened awareness of the lethal potential of anti-Semitism, as noted, has led to the delegitimization of open contempt of the Jews and Judaism, certainly in the United States; it is no longer *salonfähig*, that is, proper and respectable, except perhaps when clothed in criticism of the state of Israel and its supporters. Consequently, violent expressions of anti-Semitism have decreased. In its annual report monitoring anti-Semitic attacks in the United States, the ADL notes that in 2006 there was for the second year running a discernable decrease in incidents of harassment, threats, and assaults against Jews; on the other hand, in 2006 there was a rise in anti-Semitic vandalism of Jewish institutions.[15] Many of these crimes are, sadly, perpetrated by Muslims who construe the Israeli–Palestinian conflict as an interfaith dispute between Islam and world Jewry.

In July 2006, Naveed Afzal Haq, a U.S. citizen of Pakistani descent, forced his way past security guards at the offices of the Jewish Federation of Seattle and, brandishing a gun, declared, "I am a Muslim American, angry at Israel."[16] Thereupon he opened fire, killing the assistant director of the federation and wounding five others.[17] Equally troubling, as the report of the ADL comments, the reason for the decline of anti-Semitic incidents is apparently the fact that illegal immigrants drew the wrath of hate groups.[18] The national debate on immigration seems to have refocused the energies of extremists away from their traditional target to other minorities, particularly Hispanics and, especially since 9/11, individuals from Muslim countries.

Although anti-Semitism has its distinct origins and character, ethnic and religious hatred thrive on similar emotional mechanisms. Hence, all who honor the founding principles of the American Republic, so powerfully articulated by George Washington, to give "bigotry no sanction, to persecution no assistance" should be ever vigilant to guard against the politics of hate against whomever it may be directed.

DISCUSSION QUESTIONS

1. List and discuss four characteristic themes of modern anti-Semitism.
2. Define political anti-Semitism and discuss why it failed to take root in the United States.
3. Distinguish between legitimate criticism of the policies of the state of Israel and an anti-Semitic characterization of those policies.
4. How has the memory of the Holocaust served to strengthen the struggle against anti-Semitism and, indeed, all forms of racism and intercommunal intolerance?
5. Describe and evaluate the contrasting strategies adopted by various Jewish defense organizations in combating anti-Semitism.

Chapter 11

Islamophobia, the Muslim Stereotype, and the Muslim American Political Experience

Manochehr Dorraj

"My parents have asked me to invite you over to our house for Christmas holidays. Would you like to go?" asked his roommate. He thought, It beats staying in the dorms all alone for a month, and said, "Sure, why not." They took the bus to Perryville, Missouri, a small town in the southern part of the state. He was very warmly received by all of his roommate's family members. They were very generous and kind and he felt so welcome. This was the first time he was seeing an American family environment close up, and it was so interesting for him to observe the similarities as well as the differences with his own family. Just about every other night they were invited to a different Christmas party. At the parties he was an object of friendly curiosity and interest. When they visited his roommate's former high school, he was even asked to speak to one of the classes. The next day the high school paper wrote a feature article about the views he had expressed to the class about the Vietnam War. He liked all the attention he was receiving. He felt good about being considered both different and interesting. He was impressed with the openness of the American society. He also thought the United States was a great country and was filled with anticipation for all the adventures that awaited him as the stranger from the exotic and distant lands of the Middle East.

One day she came and told him, "I cannot see you anymore." He asked, "Why? What have I done?" She said, "You haven't done anything. My head nurse has threatened me that if I don't stop dating 'the sand nigger' (you), she will fire me. I want to keep my job." "A sand nigger, what is that?" he asked. She explained. He said, "A sand nigger,

188

huh?" looking at himself in the mirror with bewilderment. As a well-read 18-year-old foreign student who came from a good middle-class Muslim family and was featured as an exemplary high school student in the national newspaper of his home country, he suddenly had to cope with his new diminished social status as a foreigner and come to terms with this dehumanization. A range of emotions overtook him, including confusion, self-doubt, alienation, resentment, and anger. More than anything else he felt like an unwelcome guest who did not belong. As an immigrant to the United States, the rest of his life became a struggle to belong and come to terms with the realities of his new identity in his adopted home that he loved in many ways.

Introduction

Many American Muslims, in contrast to their European counterparts, are better integrated, better educated, and financially better off. Some are even regarded as "success stories." Nevertheless, many, especially those from the ranks of the first generation of immigrants, are often the target of prejudices that are unique to their existential experience as Muslim Americans.

Muslim Americans are estimated to number about 7.5 million and are roughly 0.02% of the U.S. population. In the first major survey of U.S. Muslims, undertaken by the Pew Research Center, the portrait that emerges is that of a well-assimilated group. The survey reveals that, despite the fact that 65% of U.S. Muslims are for-eign-born, 80% are U.S. citizens and African Americans constitute only 20% of U.S. Muslims. Muslim Americans "mirror the U.S. population in both education and income."[1] Most report that the largest proportion of their friends are non-Muslim. Thus, most U.S. Muslims are "much like the middle class mainstream."[2] However, the majority of U.S. Muslims surveyed also report that it is increasingly difficult to be a Muslim in post-9/11 America. A case in point is that when it was announced in September of 2007 that New York City would open the nation's first public school dedicated to teaching Arabic and Arab culture, it created a major stir. While it is only "one of 65 specialty dual-language schools in New York, it is the only one that has sparked controversy."[3] While supporters see it as playing a vital role in dispelling the popular myths and misperceptions about Muslims and Arabs, critics fear that it may be used to teach political extremism.[4] This stark paradox, the reality of Muslim lives versus their pervasive negative perceptions, begs explanation.

This chapter sets out to explain the historical, social, and political roots of anti- Muslim prejudices in Western societies in general and in the United States in particular. It delineates the causes of negative stereotypes about Muslims, stereotypes that would be regarded as unacceptable in regard to other minority groups. The chapter concludes with the argument that the tenacity and resil-ience of anti-Muslim sentiments is not a matter of mere misunderstanding and ignorance but has a functional value in so far as it serves the political agenda of power politics in general and U.S. foreign policy in particular. It also serves the needs of some unscrupulous politicians to control and manipulate public opinion, especially in times of war and conflict with the Muslim world, which in recent history has been abundant.

As the Western world has gone out of its way to acknowledge and repent for all sins of anti-Semitism toward the Jewish people since the Second World War, the pervasiveness of anti-Muslim prejudices, which for the most part rage without impunity, raises a legitimate question as to why, in this age of political correctness, such examples of anti-Muslim bias persist. What are the factors that animate and inform this prejudice and are responsible for its intensity and resilience?

The Historical Context

The historical competition and conflict between the Muslim world and the Christian West are long-standing. The Islamic conquests and incursions into the Christian lands in the eighth century, which reached as far as Spain and lasted until the sixteenth century, were followed by the crusaders' invasion and conquest of the Middle East from the eleventh to the thirteenth centuries. This in turn was followed by the Ottoman conquest of eastern and central Europe from the fourteenth to the seventeenth centuries. However, with the decline of the Ottomans at the end of the eighteenth century and the ascendance of Europe, the West enjoyed an unprecedented dominance and hegemony over the Muslim world.[5] With the dawn of the colonial era in the late eighteenth century, this was no longer an even competition between two rival civilizations. The relationship transformed to that of the colonizer and the colonized. One side held all the power, and the other side was powerless. This dominance was not confined to the realm of finance, military, and technology but also extended to the realm of recreating the image of the colonized.

To justify the exploitation and dehumanization that accompanied colonization, the colonized were often projected to be wicked, immoral, and barbaric. The colonizers saw themselves as good, virtuous, righteous, and benevolent. Middle Eastern scholar Albert Hourani summarizes the general perception of Islam and Muslims in the Christian West in the following way: "Islam is a false religion, Allah is not God, Muhammad was not a prophet, Islam was invented by men whose motives and character were to be deplored, and propagated by the sword."[6]

Since they entered the political scene as a force, Muslims have been perceived by the Christian West with a mixture of bewilderment and fear.

Menacing, abhorrent, and evil were the pervasive images, never completely human or ordinary. Not having a history of colonial presence in the Muslim world until the Second World War, Americans for the most part inherited their negative perceptions of Muslims from Christian Europe.

According to some scholars, "Americans have used the Muslim world as a reference point to highlight their exceptionalism."[7] By the time the United States replaced Great Britain and France as the major Western power in the Middle East and as a nation that used public relations more effectively than most in its foreign relations, the leaders of the United States deployed the mass media extensively in order to recreate and recast the image of Muslims, thus hoping to better serve their interests.[8]

As the nationalist aspirations of some of the Muslim nations proved to be at odds with U.S. policy interests and the conflict between Muslim nationalists and the U.S. government escalated into wars, the Muslim image took a decidedly negative turn among the American public. As the cultural industry in the United States came into its own and television became the major source of news from the 1950s onward, its control and manipulation played a key role in the production and reproduction of Muslim "reality." Thus, the image of Muslims was recast to serve the project of power politics. A scholar of orientalism, the late Edward Said, observed that the West could only know Islamic civilization through the prism of imperial dominance, conflict, and hostility.[9]

According to Ahmed, one of the keen observers of the contemporary Muslim world, the roots of more recent Western antipathy toward Muslims lie in multiple factors that are both historical and contemporary. The list includes

> Blame for the oil crisis, atavistic memory of the Crusades, anti-Semitism (Muslims now take the place of the Jews as alien, repugnant Orientals), plain Western jingoism, the collapse of the Communist states and the revival of Christian heritage, the ire of those who dislike the holier-than-thou attitude of Muslims and the incapacity of Muslims to explain themselves effectively, have all helped to focus on Islam as the new enemy.[10]

One can add to this list the persistence of the Arab–Israeli conflict, the United States' and other Western countries' support of Israel, and the pro-Palestinian sympathies of most in the Muslim world. Specific political events, such as the U.S. invasions of Lebanon in 1958 and 1982, the U.S. bombing of Libya in 1986, the U.S. military confrontation with Iran in 1987, the U.S. invasion of Afghanistan in 1991and the U.S. wars with Iraq in 1991 and 2003, all contributed to the acrimonious relationship between the region and the United States.

One of the earliest policies of targeting Arabs in the United States in response to events abroad occurred during the Nixon administration after the

Palestinian terrorist attack on Israeli athletes at the 1972 Olympics in Munich. Under "Operation Boulder," politically active Arab Americans were targeted for special investigations and surveillance.[11] The two major catalytic events, however, that ushered in dramatic changes in government policy and public opinion in the United States regarding Muslims were the Iranian Revolution of 1979 and the terrorist attack of September 11, 2001.

The Iranian Revolution of 1979

The Iranian Revolution of 1979 that established the first Islamic theocracy in the modern Middle East was a major watershed in U.S.–Iranian relations. During the 1960s and 1970s as many as 50,000 Americans lived and worked in Iran and a large number of Iranian students studied in the United States. Iran was a major political partner and a pillar of U.S. policy in the region. There were extensive cultural exchanges between the two countries, and Iranians felt welcome in the United States, as were Americans in Iran. Indeed, some Americans jokingly referred to Iran as the fifty-first state. A few months after the revolution, however, Iran transformed from one of the closest allies of the United States in the region to a pariah on the global stage. The ensuing hostage crisis of 1980, in which fifty-two American embassy personnel were taken as hostages for 444 days, led to the breaking up of diplomatic relations between the two countries. The reckless rhetoric on both sides, whereby Ayatollah Khomeini would refer to the United States as "the Great Satan" and President Jimmy Carter characterized Iranian leaders as a "barbaric and crazy group," contributed further to the deterioration of their prior relationship.[12]

After the Iranian Revolution of 1979, a national poll of Americans revealed that close to 50% regarded Muslims as "barbaric," "cruel," "treacherous," "cunning," "war-like," and "bloodthirsty."[13] The Islamic revolution and the populist policies of the regime in Tehran came to be identified in the American popular imagination with terrorism and extremism. The prerevolutionary image of Iranians as "friendly," "charming," and "exotic" was now replaced with the "Muslim fundamentalist terrorist." The U.S. strategy of isolating the Iranian Revolution and containing its further expansion required the mobilization of American and global public opinion. The achievement of this goal necessitated a campaign of demonization and vilification of Islamic culture and values.

The Iranian Revolution and the hostage crisis took place under the Carter administration and, because of President Carter's inability to free the hostages, proved to be decisive in his inability to get reelected. Thus, Democrats particularly disdained the Iranian regime. For example, some foreign diplomats reported that when discussing Iran "the otherwise reserved, subtle, and judicious manner of Warren Christopher, the Secretary of State, vanished and his eyes flashed."[14] He regarded the Iranian government as the foremost promoter of terrorism and political violence and recommended a policy of "relentless pursuit."[15] Anti-Islamic sentiments, however, crossed party lines and partisan politics. For example, after his 1980 election, in an interview with *Time* magazine, President Ronald Reagan proclaimed that "Muslims were reverting to their belief that unless they killed a Christian or a Jew, they would not go to heaven."[16]

This type of negative projection of Muslims in general made them particularly vulnerable to discrimination in public life in the United States. Hostilities toward Muslims would increase exponentially during times of war and conflict. Indeed, a steady reoccurrence of wars and conflicts with the Muslim world in the last four decades has fostered jingoism and intolerance, thus ensuring a continuous anti-Islamic campaign in some mainstream media outlets. This campaign has served the dual function of simultaneously towing the political agendas of the different respective administrations and garnering public support for war. For example, during the Persian Gulf War of 1991, to oust Saddam Hussein from Kuwait, "hate crimes against Muslims and Arabs reached an all time high."[17]

The 1992 terrorist attack on the World Trade Center in New York City by Muslim extremists, unfortunately, provided further fuel for anti-Muslim sentiments. Muslims are not the only group who engage in violence or terrorist activities against the United States inside the country or abroad, but they seem to be particularly targeted for retaliation and hate crimes. For example, the FBI recorded the following number of terrorist attacks within the United States during the period 1982–1992 by the following groups: Puerto Ricans, seventy-two attacks; left-wing groups, twenty-three attacks; Jewish groups, sixteen attacks; anti-Castro Cubans, twelve attacks; right-wing groups, six attacks. A similar pattern of anti-U.S. terrorist attacks were committed abroad. In 1994, forty-four took place in Latin America, eight in the Middle East, five in Asia, five in western Europe, and four in Africa.[18]

In the aftermath of the Oklahoma City bombing of 1995 by Timothy McVeigh, some "terrorism experts" in the United States were pointing fingers at Muslims as the culprits. In just three days, "more than 200 violent attacks against Muslim-Americans were recorded."[19] According to the *New York Times*, the nature of these attacks ranged from "burning mosques, to spitting on women who wore shawls to death threats to shots fired at Mosques to a fake bomb thrown at a Muslim day care center."[20]

The anti-Muslim passion that arose after the terrorist attack of September 11, 2001, however, made what had previously surfaced seem tame and benign. September 11 was a major turning point that ushered in a sea change in the perception of Muslims in the Western world in general and in the United States in particular.

The Terrorist Attack of September 11, 2001

The terrorist attack of 9/11 ushered in an emotional avalanche of outrage, anger, shock, grief, hurt, and fear. Justifiably, most American citizens felt violated. Many people lost their loved ones. Because innocent civilians were randomly targeted for annihilation, it made the violence that much more horrific. The killing of more than 3,000 defenseless people on American soil had no precedent in American history. The Japanese attack on Pearl Harbor in 1941 was against military personnel and naval targets. The fact that all the perpetrators of this heinous crime were Muslim Arabs and people of Middle Eastern origin, using religion to justify their action, paved the way for the outpouring of anti-Islamic sentiments that was to follow. In such an emotionally charged atmosphere, many innocent Muslims and Arabs became the target of public anger. Despite the fact that President Bush visited a mosque in Washington, D.C., a week after the attack and stated that our enemies were terrorists, not Islam or Muslims, his admonition was to no avail. As illustrated below, guilt by association became a widespread phenomenon. Even a (non-Muslim) Sikh, because of his turban, was mistaken for a Muslim and killed. Numerous mosques were torched; thousands were beaten, harassed, and humiliated. Islamophobia reached an all-time high.

President Bush's slogan "You are either with us or you are with the terrorists" left very little room for nuanced discussion of the root causes of terrorism. The tragedy of September 11 was separated from the context of U.S. foreign policy in the Middle East. The social, political, and psychological dynamics responsible for creating terrorists were seldom discussed in much of the mainstream media. The antiterrorism strategy first and foremost was reduced to a military response.

A gathering of foreign ministers from fifty-six Muslim countries in Qatar on October 10, 2001, denounced the terrorist attack against the United States in the strongest terms. Some Muslim leaders came to the United States for an interfaith dialogue and expression of solidarity with the American people in their hour of tragedy. Muslims in several Middle Eastern nations held candlelight vigils for the victims of 9/11. Polls taken among the Arab American community in the aftermath of 9/11 revealed that 69% fully supported an all-out war against the countries that harbor or aid terrorists and 65% felt embarrassed about the fact that the attack was initiated by people from Arab countries.[21] However, none of these actions seems to have helped much to decisively modify the negative media blitz targeting Muslims and Arabs in the aftermath of 9/11. For example, in the *National Review*, the conservative columnist Ann Coulter wrote, "We should invade their countries, kill their leaders and convert them to

Christianity.... We carpet-bombed German cities; we killed civilians. That was war. And this is war."[22] The editor of the *National Review*, Rich Lowry, had a similar recommendation: "If we flatten part of Damascus or Tehran or whatever it takes, that is part of the solution."[23]

As a partial consequence of this type of reckless anti-Arab and anti-Muslim rhetoric on the part of the media, the Washington, D.C.–based American-Arab Anti-Discrimination Committee reported that in the first nine weeks following 9/11 there were more than 700 violent incidents against Muslims and Arabs and more than 800 cases of employment discrimination.[24]

Government Action Toward Arabs and Muslims After 9/11

In the aftermath of 9/11, some 1,200 people from Arab and Muslim origins were apprehended on the basis of "secret evidence." Those taken into custody were deprived of their constitutional rights to confront and cross-examine the evidence against them. Their status and the outcome of their cases remained undisclosed. The Justice Department's inspector general reported that "many cases were unjustified and many individuals were harshly treated, something heretofore deemed shocking by our legal standards."[25] Other Muslims and Arabs were targeted for "special registration." Several Muslim charity groups were shut down, and the FBI began frequently visiting mosques. The FBI directive of January 27, 2003, instructed that "all field supervisors should count the number of mosques and Muslims in their areas and use this information to establish the number of terrorism investigations they are expected to carry out."[26] As Akram and Johnson observed, should the government "target white Irish Catholics or Jews or another racial/ethnic minority in such a sustained manner, they would doubtless face significant and vociferous challenge for racial or religious profiling."[27]

These violations, according to Akram and Johnson, were ultimately perceived as justified because Arabs and Muslims have been "raced" as " terrorist": "Foreign, disloyal and imminently threatening." They refer to this phenomenon as "racialization," which is socially, not biologically, constructed.[28] According to Professor Nabeel Abraham, Arabs and Muslims have been racialized in three distinct ways: first, "through political violence by extremist groups based on the Arab–Israeli conflict in the Middle East," second "by xenophobic violence targeting Arabs and Muslims at the local levels," and third, "through the hostility arising from international crisis affecting the United States and its citizens."[29] This racialization simultaneously reinforces and justifies racist images and conduct, thus legitimizing the violation of rights of Muslims and Arabs.

Sexual Stereotypes and Dehumanization

The vilification of Muslims is not confined to the political domain; it extends into the cultural realm as well. In fact, the negative perception in one context reinforces and feeds that in the other. If the racist stereotype of African American men is that "they are all a bunch of criminals and rapists," according to media scholar Jack Shaheen, the racist stereotype of Muslim men is that "they are all anti-women and a bunch of marauding sexual predators."[30] Muslim men are frequently depicted by the mainstream Hollywood film industry, in popular TV shows, and in literature either as terrorists, sinister villains, or sex maniacs.[31] They are portrayed as individuals who are incapable of genuine human feelings of warmth, friendship, and respect toward their female counterparts. Hence, their sexuality is seen as perverted and degenerate.

Professor Shaheen, for example, chronicles hundreds of Hollywood movies that depict Muslims with negative images. He claims that such images are particularly summoned and crudely cultivated in times of national crisis, wars, or conflict that involves the Muslim world or the Middle East. The complacency of the mainstream mass media and the crucial role that it plays in forging these negative images has become particularly distinct in the last two decades as the role of the media has transformed from being a "watch dog" to a "lap dog." Much of the mainstream media and the entertainment industry are increasingly willing and conscious participants in the biased representation of Muslim people.

In the aftermath of the hostage crisis with Iran in 1980 and on the eve of the U.S.–Iraqi war of 1991, the Hollywood film industry produced and distributed a movie entitled *Not Without My Daughter*. The film, based on a true story and narrated from the point of view of the American mother/wife (Betty Mahmoody), is an account of an Iranian man (her husband) who returns to Iran with his family after the revolution, undergoes a religious conversion, and no longer wants his family to live in the United States. He is portrayed as a brutal fanatic who wants to keep his daughter in Iran against the wishes of his wife. He attempts to hold his wife and daughter as hostages. The wife manages to escape the country with her daughter with the help of a well-meaning Westernized Iranian man. Upon her return to the United States, Mahmoody became an instant celebrity. She frequented several TV talk shows and was sought after on the lecture circuit. She even became a consultant to the U.S. State Department, and her book about her experience became a best-seller.[32] Many Iranians, on the other hand, viewed the movie as a distasteful propaganda piece, designed to project them and their culture in a negative light.

Before and during the two Persian Gulf Wars of 1991 and 2003 against the Iraqi regime, there were several television talk shows or news stories that featured American women who were formerly married to Middle Eastern men, telling the viewers tales of their mistreatment at the hands of "brutal Arab men." Needless to say, the stories of thousands of happy marriages between American women and Muslim Middle Eastern men never made it to the small screen.

It is not much of an exaggeration to state that after the U.S. war against the Taliban regime in Afghanistan in 2001, as Western audiences became exposed to the Taliban's brutal treatment of Afghan women, the image of Muslim men underwent a thorough "Talibanization." In the popular imagination, the immense diversity within the Muslim world—the different interpretations of Islam, class and cultural divisions, and the individuality in Muslim societies—were now overlooked. Similarly, the fact that the Muslim world has already had female prime ministers in Pakistan, Turkey, Bangladesh, and Indonesia in the last two decades has been overlooked by much of the mainstream media. Whitewashed also was the fact that by choosing women to be the leaders of men and women alike, these countries displayed their collective respect for women as equal partners. To be sure, as less developed societies, the individual rights of women in the Muslim world are not as advanced as they are in the West. Patriarchal domination remains ascendant in many Muslim societies, as is the case in many other parts of the third world. This, however, does not justify the projection of an entire culture or people as antiwoman.

The dehumanization and degradation of Muslims is perhaps most egregious when it comes to sexuality. The image of the "lecherous oily sheikh" abounds in American movies, television comedies, cartoons, and fiction. Hence, Muslim and Arab women are invariably depicted as submissive, weak, and mute or as empty-headed belly dancers intent on seducing Western men.[33]

The Politics of Anti-Muslim Bias

Professor Shaheen's scrutiny of Hollywood movies reveals that racial epithets against Arabs as "assholes," "bastards," "camel-dicks," "pigs," "devil-worshippers," "jackals," "rats," "rag-heads," "towel-heads," "scum-buckets," "son-of-dogs," "buzzards of the jungles," "son-of-whores," etc. abound.[34] According to Shaheen, it took the Hollywood film industry some eighty years to stop projecting African Americans in negative terms in the movies. Only in the last three decades, as the long struggle of African Americans for equality culminating in the civil rights movement of the 1950s and 1960s began to bear fruit, has the negative, stereotypical cultural representation of African Americans changed.

This, however, with a few recent exceptions,[35] is not true for Muslim Americans. Unfortunately, the continuation of war and conflict with parts of the Muslim world feeds the negative perceptions and stereotypes to the extent that much of the American public has become desensitized toward this dehumanizing monolithic image of Muslims and Arabs. The significance of this continuing negative image is found in the results of recent public opinion surveys. According to an ABC news poll in March 9, 2006, some 46% of the American public have an unfavorable view of Islam and 58% regard Islam as a violent religion. Often, such public sentiments manifest themselves politically and in specific policies.

The congressional uproar, encompassing both Democrats and Republicans, when a Dubai-based company operated by the United Arab Emirates government attempted to buy the contract of operation for six ports in the United States from a British company, is another indication of the pervasive anti-Arab and anti-Muslim bias. When it became clear that the security of the ports would be under the management of the U.S. Coast Guard and Customs and that the overwhelming majority of the staff of the company would be British and American citizens and only the ownership of the company would be with the Dubai Ports World company, still opposition to the deal continued. Even when it became clear that with the exception of the port facilities in Seattle, Washington, which are operated by an American company, all the other ports in the United States were operated by foreign companies, the opposition to this particular deal continued. The opposition did not subside when it became clear that only 5% of the incoming cargo to the ports of the United States gets inspected. Therefore, it really does not matter who operates the ports as long as this procedure remains intact. The opposition continued when it was revealed that Dubai World Ports has served thousands of American ships, including naval ships, for almost a decade with no incident. Finally, under relentless congressional opposition and public pressure, Dubai Ports World on March 9, 2006, withdrew its bid and transferred the operations of the six ports to an American-owned company.

The uproar over Keith Ellison, the first black Muslim American member of Congress, a Democrat from Minnesota, and his desire to use a Quran in his swearing-in ceremony in January 4, 2007, is another indication of anti-Muslim bias. Ellison received numerous angry e-mails and was the subject of harsh criticism on several conservative blogs after his intentions were made public. While the U.S. Constitution clearly indicates that "no religious test shall ever be required as a qualification to any office...under the United States," this did not prevent some commentators and opinion molders to portray Congressman Ellison's desire to swear his oath on the Quran as "un-American." For example, the conservative pundit Dennis Prager called it "an act of hubris...that undermines American civilization. In so far as a member of Congress taking an oath to serve America and uphold its values is concerned, America is interested in only one book, the Bible. If you are incapable of taking an oath on the book, don't serve in Congress."[36]

The nuclear standoff with Iran, the imposition of economic sanctions, and the threat of bombardment of Iran's nuclear facilities—though according to a U.S. national intelligence estimate (a collective analysis of some 16 U.S. security agencies) released on December 3, 2007, Iran has halted the pursuit of a nuclear weapons program since 2003[37]—stand in sharp contrast with the U.S. treatment of Israel and India, two powers that possess nuclear capability and large stockpiles of nuclear weapons. The Bush administration insisted on imposing additional economic sanctions on Iran and maintained its acrimonious political posture even after the report was published. While Iran, a signatory to the Nuclear Non-Proliferation Treaty (NPT), has been the target of one of the most intrusive inspections by the International Atomic Energy Agency (IAEA), both Israel and India, which developed their nuclear programs in secrecy and are not members of the NPT, are protected from IAEA scrutiny and enjoy close relations with the United States. In fact, the March 2, 2006, nuclear cooperation agreement, which would allow the transfer of U.S. nuclear technology to India, would exponentially increase the ability of India to build many more lethal nuclear weapons. Such double standards are not lost on most in the Muslim world in general and Iranians in particular.

The attitude of some politicians on this issue reflects the fear-mongering that is reminiscent of the "Red Scare" of the 1950s. For example, during the Republican presidential debate in June 2007, when the issue of Iran's nuclear challenge came up, with the exception of Representative Ron Paul of Texas, who stood out in saying "Iran has done no harm to us directly and is no threat to our national security," the rest of the panelists unanimously agreed that "all options are on the table" and if chosen as president, they would engage in a preemptive strike against Iran's nuclear power facilities by using either tactical nuclear weapons or conventional weapons.[38] Hence, the hype and spin surrounding the alleged Iranian eminent military threat has gone beyond the pale and is representative of the pervasive Islamophobia in the post-9/11 American political culture. In the words of one commentator,

> the American discussion about Iran has lost all connections to reality. Iran has an economy the size of Finland's and an annual defense budget of around $4.8 billion. It has not invaded a country since the late 18th century. The United States has a GDP that is 68 times larger and defense expenditures that are 110 times greater. Israel and every Arab country (except Syria and Iraq) are quietly and actively allied against Iran. And yet we are to believe that Tehran is about to overturn the international system and replace it with an Islamo-fascist order? What planet are we on?[39]

Instead of an insidious portrayal of Muslims that is designed to serve the agenda of power politics and pretending that the violent reaction of the extremists has nothing to do with our foreign policy, we would be better served if we evaluated our foreign policy options critically and tried to understand Muslims in their own terms, that is, see them as they see themselves and once in a while see ourselves as they see us. This intellectual exercise may prove to be very educational indeed. This type of understanding is the first necessary step toward overcoming our own prejudices and helping them to see theirs. As John Esposito, one of the premier American scholars of Islam, has noted, "to understand the love–hate relationship, the attraction–repulsion toward America that exist in many parts of the world, and is widespread in the Muslim world, we must not only know who we think we are and how we view others but try to understand how others might see us."[40]

Given these ambivalent feelings of love and hate discussed by Esposito, the pertinent question is whether it is what America is or what America does that conjures up the morbid feelings of hate on the part of some in the Muslim world. Since there are many attributes of American culture, civilization, and achievements that are admired by a large number of people throughout the Muslim world, a strong case can be made that it is what America does, rather than what America is, that is the source of conflict. It is instructive to imagine ourselves at the receiving end of U.S. government policies. As the American historian Paul Kennedy has poignantly observed, a few of us ask

> How do we appear to *them*, and what would it be like were our places in the world reversed.... Suppose that there existed today a powerful, unified Arab-Muslim state that stretched from Algeria to Turkey and Arabia—as there was 400 years ago, the Ottoman Empire. Suppose this unified Arab-Muslim state had the biggest economy in the World, and the most effective military. Suppose in contrast this United States of ours had split into 12 or 15 countries, with different regimes, some conservative and corrupt. Suppose that the great Arab-Muslim power had its aircraft carriers cruising off our shores, its aircrafts flying over our lands, its satellites watching us every day. Suppose that its multinational corporations had reached into North America to extract oil, and paid the corrupt, conservative governments big royalties for that. Suppose that it dominated all international institutions like the Security Council and the IMF. Suppose that there was a special state set up in North America fifty years ago, of a different religion and language to ours, and the giant Arab-Muslim power always gave it support. Suppose the colossus state was bombarding us with cultural messages, about the status of women, about sexuality, that we found offensive. Suppose it was always urging us to change, to modernize, to go global, to follow its example. Hmm...in those conditions, would not many Americans steadily grow to loath the colossus, wish it harm? And perhaps try to harm it? I think so.[41]

Conclusions

While there are many well-meaning and enlightened Americans who abhor any manifestation of anti-Muslim prejudice, the Islamophobic images of Muslims chronicled in this chapter have long gone mainstream and are "the reality" for the majority. This is in large part due to the complacent role of the mass media and the deliberate policies of the U.S. government, especially in times of war and conflict. There is something perverse about a political culture that uses the pretext of "national security interests" as a justification to denigrate and dehumanize an entire culture and people. This raises the legitimate question of why in this age of political correctness such pervasive negative stereotypes of Muslims persist and are tolerated. In other words, why is the prejudice permissible?

In addition to the power politics agenda of the U.S. government, its ambitions for power and conquest, and the need to mobilize public opinion in times of war and conflict as discussed above, there are several other important factors that explain the resilience of anti-Muslim prejudices.

First, not being of the Judeo-Christian tradition and coming from a part of the world in which America has a continuing history of war and conflict, Muslims can become easily targeted for guilt by association. Thus, in "the land of migrants," they are often perceived or treated by some "as the enemy within," "the unwelcome guests," and "the undesirable others."

Second, because of their cultural and religious differences, many Muslim Americans are not well accepted in American society. They are more likely to stand out as "alien" and, thus, to be set up for discriminatory conduct.

Third, slightly more than half of American Muslims are foreign-born; while they are eager to fit in, they suffer from linguistic, cultural, and political isolation. Moreover, they are not as yet a part of the American collective history, culture, and consciousness. For example, most Americans have a distinct sense of collective guilt toward their inhuman treatment of African Americans under the system of slavery and the segregated society that existed prior to the 1950s. This, however, as yet is not the case with Muslim Americans. The conflict with the Muslim world, with the exception of 9/11, for most Americans has been a distant issue, fought on foreign lands with "smart bombs" and "against a hateful enemy." Most Americans are not witness to the carnage and suffering on the ground caused by U.S. military incursions in the Muslim lands. Perhaps more importantly, very few Muslim Americans are represented in the power structure, government, popular culture, sports, and the entertainment industry. Thus, their "collective faces" are not humanized. They are faceless aliens. The lack of representation makes them more vulnerable to the negative perceptions chronicled above.

Fourth, unlike blacks and Hispanics, who constitute a significant voting block, and unlike Jewish Americans, who possess significant financial, political, cultural, and intellectual influence, Muslims for the most part lack such powers. They neither are a significant political constituency (although their number exceeds that of the Jewish population in the United States) nor possess the political leverage of other minority groups. They are the weakest link. Thus, they can be easily targeted for discrimination and abuse.

Fifth, Muslim Americans are not well organized and until recently did not use the electoral process effectively to empower themselves politically. Furthermore, the acquiescence and passivity of many Muslim intellectuals has been an obstacle to educating the American public about the pervasive negative Muslim stereotypes.

Sixth, the lack of any viable political movement that can raise consciousness and change public opinion is another factor. Muslims are fragmented by ideological, sectarian, and national differences. This makes their political mobilization an arduous task.

Seventh, the inability or unwillingness of secular Muslims and Muslim modernists to effectively denounce the criminal terrorist activities of groups such as Al-Qaeda in no uncertain terms has created some moral ambiguity regarding their loyalty and stand on this issue.

Eighth, Muslims have not yet learned to use the American legal system effectively to punish those who violate their civil rights and degrade and dehumanize them. Therefore, they are not feared. Those who engage in racist conduct do so because they think they can get away with it. In fact, this lack of impunity may partially explain why even some "liberals," who may otherwise go out of their way to display their "sensitivity" on issues pertaining to race and gender, are unabashed when it comes to harboring anti-Muslim prejudices.

As Weiner and Wilcox in Chapter 5 of this book observe, increasing contact among different religious groups often leads to increasing tolerance. Let us hope that, as the contact between those Americans who come from the Judeo-Christian tradition and Muslim Americans increases, some of the widely held prejudices against Muslims will subside and Muslim Americans can fully participate in pursuing their American dream.

DISCUSSION QUESTIONS

1. What are the causes of the continuation and resilience of negative Muslim stereotypes? Why is the prejudice permissible?
2. To what extent can the negative Muslim stereotypes be attributed to religion and the fact that Muslims are not part of the Judeo-Christian tradition?
3. Are Muslim Americans less likely to assimilate in American society compared to other minorities?

4. Is it likely that if the U.S. governments' wars and conflict with the countries in the Muslim world should escalate, then anti-Muslim prejudices in the United States would escalate as well, even though Muslim Americans have nothing to do with the cause of the conflict?
5. What are some of the social and political initiatives that can help to overcome anti-Muslim biases?

Chapter 12

Concluding Thoughts on a Changing America

Valerie Martinez-Ebers
Manochehr Dorraj

The "American Dream" is a popular term used throughout the United States. It is a subjective expression that means different things to different people but usually implies achieving a successful and satisfying life as a result of hard work.[1] While many people measure their achievements in material terms, such as earning a high income or owning a house, others' perceptions of "living the American Dream" are more abstract and typically described in terms of having personal freedom, enjoying equal rights, and ensuring safety or security for one's self and family.[2] The allure of the dream explains the motivation of countless immigrants across the years who come to the United States to escape the lack of opportunity and poor quality of life or political repression in their home countries. The unfulfilled promise of the dream is a source of frustration for many individuals, especially minorities, and a source of conflict between groups in the United States.

In a way, the story of America—its foundation, history, development, and success—is the story of various groups who left their familiar homelands (sometimes involuntarily) and ventured into the unknown. Their trials, sufferings, struggles, and triumphs made America, its culture, and society what it is today. To be sure, many such groups, if they were different from the majority Anglo-Saxon protestant culture, commonly experienced initial prejudice and discrimination. However, through assimilation, acculturation, resistance, or collective action to change the system, as well as a good amount of hard work, each group carved a place for itself in the cultural mosaic of America.

The story of America is also the narrative of individuals, especially those who managed to survive and thrive as a minority in the majority culture. Sometimes it takes a rebel, someone who refuses to accept the status quo, to leave the familiarity and the security of one's native culture and venture into the unknown. And it takes a dreamer to envision and believe in a brighter future. In this sense, multicultural America is the land of rebels and dreamers.

As the different migrant groups have come to America, they have brought their culture and values with them; and in the process, they have changed America, as America has changed them. However, American minorities are not monolithic. While there are some universal experiences that all minorities have in common, there are also distinct differences that set them apart. The minorities that constitute contemporary multicultural America come from diverse cultural, religious, linguistic, racial, historical, and geographical backgrounds. This book has introduced you to some of their experiences. Since the current racial and ethnic minority groups in the United States are collectively projected to become the majority by 2050, America will change in fundamental ways. Undoubtedly, this transformation will usher in tremendous changes in power and social relations and it will augment a new self-perception about what it means to be an American.

The Significance of Barack Obama

Perhaps no other recent phenemonon captures the essense of this change more than Barack Obama's candidacy as the Democratic Party's nominee for the U.S. presidency. The likelihood of a biracial man, whose black father is from Kenya and whose white mother is from Kansas and who spent a part of his childhood in Indonesia, becoming the next president of the United States was inconceivable even a decade ago.

The outcome of the 2008 presidential contest is a transformational event. Whether it represents a cosmic shift in the political landscape is not yet clear; but the fact that Obama first won the Iowa caucuses in January 2008, where 97% of the registered voters are white, and continued on to win the Democratic nomination and ultimately the popular vote for president, where the majority of the national electorate is also white, signifies an important positive development in America's race relations.

Obama's broadbased popularity suggests a desire on the part of a substantial sector of the American public to transcend the issues of race and ethnicity. Seen in this light, given the historical legacy of racism, the presidency of

Obama, a multiracial and multiethnic man leading primarily a white nation, marks a major turning point in American history. His far-reaching public appeal and his inspirational message of change and healing has turned a page in the history of minority majority relations in America. The country is at the crossroads of change, attempting to redefine itself and reconfigure the place of race, ethnicity, and power. To borrow a phrase from Abraham Lincoln, the success of Barack Obama represents a "summoning [of] the better angels of our nature."

Contradiction in American Attitudes and Behaviors

Nonetheless, America remains a paradox. In the same country where Barack Obama is now the president-elect, a substantial amount of race-based, ethnicity-based, religion-based, and sexual orientation—based prejudice and discrimination still persists. According to a recent FBI report, victims of hate crimes are most likely to be African American but between 2005 and 2006 attacks against Muslims increased by 22%, attacks against gays and lesbians increased by 18%, and attacks against Hispanics escalated by 10%.[3] A report by the Southern Poverty Law Center (SPLC) suggests the level of hate crimes against Latinos will continue to climb due to rising tensions and conflict over immigration policy, especially the issue of illegal immigrants.[4] Experts find hate crimes against Latinos are usually carried out by people who think they are attacking immigrants. During the past three years, approximately 300 new anti-immigrant groups were formed; and the SPLC 2008 annual report classifies about half of these groups as "nativist extremists," representing a significant threat to the safety of Latinos and anyone who is perceived as a noncitizen.[5]

Further evidence of the inconsistency or paradox in American attitudes and behaviors is found in the results of widely respected public opinion polls. A series of national polls conducted by the New York Times and CBS News reveal that more than two-thirds of Americans feel that the country is ready to elect a black president.[6] Growing numbers of the poll respondents also feel that real progress has been made in getting rid of racial discrimination, including a growing percentage of black respondents. However, a plurality of those same respondents (48%) think most people feel uncomfortable talking about race, while 68% of the black respondents and 52% of the Hispanic respondents can recall a specific incident when they were personally discriminated against because of their race compared to only 26% of the white respondents.[7]

The Persistance of Inequality and Discrimination

One of the lessons repeated throughout the chapters of this book is that the ideal of racial equality and nondiscrimination has yet to be realized in America. To be sure, as we discussed in the introductory chapter, we have come a long way in improving minority—majority relations but not far enough. Aware of the fact that the creation of a better future requires a critical examination of the status quo, the contributers to this volume have attempted to debunk the pervasive stereotypes and misperceptions, chronicle examples of inequality and discrimination, and analyze their underlying causes in the hope that this will elevate public consciousness and sensitivity on these issues and, thus, render America a more tolerant and inclusive society for all. Only then can "the strangers to these shores" and those generations of Americans who constitute a part of the ethnic and racial mosaic that is multicultural America fully pursue and achieve their American Dream with all the rights that the U.S. Constitution and the covenant of citizenship grants them.

Appendix

Racial-Ethnic Characteristics of the United States, 2005–2006

	July 1, 2006 Population	July 1, 2005 Population	Numeric Change July 1, 2005, to July 1, 2006	Percent Change July 1, 2005, to July 1, 2006	Percent of Total Population	Total July 1, 2006 Population
White, alone or in combination	243,825,488	241,837,199	1,988,289	0.82	81.44	299,398,484
Black, alone or in combination	40,240,898	39,718,528	522,370	1.32	13.44	299,398,484
AIAN, alone or in combination	4,497,895	4,453,026	44,869	1.01	1.50	299,398,484
Asian, alone or in combination	14,907,198	14,447,663	459,535	3.18	4.98	299,398,484
NHPI, alone or in combination	1,007,644	991,067	16,577	1.67	0.34	299,398,484
Non-Hispanic	255,077,446	253,634,970	1,442,476	0.57	85.20	299,398,484
Hispanic	44,321,038	42,872,091	1,448,947	3.38	14.80	299,398,484
Non-Hispanic, white alone	198,744,494	198,235,448	509,046	0.26	66.38	299,398,484

Source: US Department of Commerce, US Census Bureau News, May 17, 2007, downloaded on March 7 2008 from http://www.census.gov/Press-Release/www/releases/archives/population/010048.html

Notes

Chapter 1

1. Arman Batheja, *Fort Worth Star Telegram*, March 1, 2008, p. 1.
2. Alan Fram, "Democratic Voters More Diverse This Year," AP News, March 1, 2008, http://www.mlive.com/elections/index.ssf/2008/03/democratic_voters_more_diverse.html (accessed October 16, 2008).
3. It may be more accurate to characterize Obama as biracial because his mother was white and his father was black; however, racial identification is primarily a social construction, and Obama is generally perceived by others as black and self-identifies as such. See Barack Obama, *Dreams from My Father: A Story of Race and Inheritance* (New York: Three Rivers Press, 2004).
4. Joel Lieske, "Race and Democracy," *PS* 32, no.2 (June 1999): 217–224.
5. Ibid.; Gary Orfield and John Yun, *Resegregation in American Schools* (Cambridge, MA: Civil Rights Project, Harvard University, 1999), http://www.civilrightsproject.ucla.edu/research/deseg/reseg_schools99.php#fullreport (accessed June 1, 2000); and Gary Orfield and Chungmei Lee, *Brown at 50: King's Dream or Plessy's Nightmare?* (Cambridge, MA: Civil Rights Project, Harvard University, 2004).
6. Melvin L. Oliver and Thomas M. Shapiro, *Black Wealth/White Wealth: A New Perspective on Racial Inequality,* 2nd ed. (Oxford: Taylor & Francis, 2006).
7. Vincent N. Parrillo, *Strangers to These Shores,* 8th ed. (Boston: Pearson/Prentice Hall, 2006); Lieske, "Race and Democracy."
8. U.S. Department of Commerce, *U.S. Bureau of the Census News,* May 17, 2007, http://www.census.gov/Press-Release/www/releases/archives/population/010048.html (accessed March 7, 2008).
9. Ibid.

10. For more detailed information, Table 1 in the Appendix shows the total numbers for each Census Bureau–identified minority group in 2006 and 2005, their numeric and percentage changes between 2005 and 2006, and their percentage of the total population. It also includes the statistics for whites alone or in combination with other and non-Hispanic whites for comparison purposes.

11. Department of Commerce, *U.S. Bureau of the Census News*, March 18, 2004, http://www.census.gov/Press-Release/www/releases/archives/population/001720. html; Jeffery S. Passel and D'Vera Cohn, "US Population Projections: 2005–2050," Pew Research Center Report, http://pewhispanic.org/files/reports/85.pdf (accessed February 11, 2008).

12. All of the reported statistics on religious identity and affiliation in the United States are from Pew Forum on Religion and Public Life, "The US Religious Landscape Survey" (Washington DC: Pew Research Center, 2008), http://religions. pewforum.org/reports.

13. Ibid.

14. Rick Lyman, "Census Shows Growth of Immigrants," *New York Times*, March 15, 2006, http://www.nytimes.com/2006/08/15/us/15census.html?_ r=1&oref=slogin.

15. See Michi Weglyn, *Years of Infamy: The Untold Story of America's Concentration Camps* (New York: Morrow, 1976).

16. James J. Zogby, "Arab Pendulum Swings on Civil Rights," http/www.aaiusa.org/ watch/112403.htm (accessed November 23, 2003).

17. Claire Bergeron and Jeanne Batalova, "Spotlight on Naturalization Trends in Advance of the 2008 Elections," in *Migration Information Source* (Washington DC: Migration Policy Institute, January 2008).

18. Michael C. LeMay *The Perennial Struggle: Race, Ethnicity and Minority Group Relations in the United States*, 2nd ed. (Upper Saddle River, NJ: Pearson/Prentice Hall, 2005), 6.

19. In the United States, the dominant group is usually identified as white Anglo-Saxon Protestant (WASP). However, some scholars argue that whites from other European areas, who were once themselves the target of WASP oppression, have adapted and/or muscled their way into the dominant group. See Parrillo, *Strangers to These Shores*, especially chapter 14.

20. See Pew Research Center, "Blacks See Growing Gaps between Poor and Middle-Class: Optimism about Black Progress Declines, Racial Attitudes in America Survey," in *Social and Demographic Trends* (Washington DC: Pew Research Center, November 13, 2007); National Conference for Community and Justice, *Taking America's Pulse III: Survey of Inter-Group Relations in America* (Brooklyn, NY: NCCJ, July 18, 2006).

21. Multiple scientific tests prove that currently there are no pure, mutually exclusive races, if they ever existed. "Race," therefore, is a socially constructed concept rather than a biological absolute. See Eugena Shanklin, *Anthropology and Race* (Belmont, CA: Wadsworth, 1994); and Richard T. Schaefer, *Race and Ethnicity in the United States*, 4th ed. (Upper Saddle River, NJ: Pearson/Prentice Hall, 2007), 7.

22. See Parrillo, *Strangers to These Shores.*
23. See LeMay, *The Perennial Struggle,* chapters 1, 3–8.
24. Charles Wagley and Marvin Harris, *Minorities in the New World* (New York: Columbia University Press, 1958) as discussed in Schaefer, *Race and Ethnicity,* 7; Parrillo, *Strangers to These Shores,* 16.

Chapter 2

1. Christian D. Berg, "Syrians in Valley Cast Votes for President." *Morning Call,* Allentown, PA (July 10, 2000), p. B01.
2. Ana Mendieta, "Venezuelans Here to Vote in Election," *Chicago Sun Times,* July 6, 2000, 12.
3. Peter Katel, "Don't Stop Thinking About Manana," *Time,* June 11, 2001; Howard LaFranchi, "Where Mexico's Voters Are: Here," *Christian Science Monitor,* June 19, 2000, 1, 10.
4. Theresa Puente, "8 Million Votes too Alluring: Mexico Considers Expatriate Rights," *Chicago Tribune,* July 13, 2001.
5. Taylor E. Dark, "Americans Abroad: The Challenge of a Globalized Electorate." *PS Online* (October 2003): 733–740, www.apsanet.org; Sheila Croucher, "'They Love Us Here:' American Migrants in Mexico." *Dissent* (Winter 2007): 69–74.
6. Roland Robertson, "Globalization and Societal Modernization," *Sociological Analysis* 47 (March 1987): 38.
7. James Mittelman, ed., *Globalization: Critical Reflections* (Boulder, CO: Lynne Rienner, 1996), 2.
8. United Nations Conference on Trade and Development, *World Investment Report 2001* (Geneva: United Nations, 2001).
9. United Nations Development Program, *Human Development Report* (New York: Oxford University Press, 2002), 10.
10. Anthony Giddens, "The New Context of Politics," *Democratic Dialogue* 1 (1995): 10.
11. United Nations Development Program, *Human Development Report* (New York: Oxford University Press, 1999), 28.
12. Computer Industry Almanac, *Worldwide Internet Users Top 1 Billion in 2005,* January 4, 2006, http://www.c-i-a.com/pr0106.htm (accessed October 12, 2008).
13. United Nations Population Division, World Migrant Stock: The 2005 Revision, Population Database, 2005, http://esa.un.org/migration/p2k0data.asp [accessed October 12, 2008].
14. Sheila Croucher, *Globalization and Belonging: The Politics of Identity in a Changing World* (Lanham, MD: Rowman and Littlefield, 2004), 13.
15. Hugh Seton-Watson, *Nations and States: An Enquiry into the Origins of Nations and Nationalism* (Boulder, CO: Westview Press, 1977).
16. Valery Tishkov, "Forget the 'Nation:' Post-Nationalist Understanding of Nationalism," *Ethnic and Racial Studies* 23, no. 4 (2000): 627.

17. Walker Connor, "A Nation Is a Nation, Is a State, Is an Ethnic Group...," *Ethnic and Racial Studies* 1, no 4 (1978): 379.

18. Max Weber, *Essays in Sociology*, trans. H. H. Gerth and C. Wright Mills (London: Routledge, 1948), 171–172.

19. Connor, "A Nation Is a Nation," 396 (citing Rupert Emerson).

20. Arjun Appadurai, *Modernity at Large: Cultural Dimensions of Globalization* (Minneapolis: University of Minnesota Press, 1996).

21. Benedict Anderson, *Imagined Communities* (London: Verso, 1991); Sheila Croucher "Perpetual Imagining: Nationhood in a Global Era," *International Studies Review* 5 no. 1 (2003): 1–24.

21a. John Quincy Adams, Niles Weekly Register (April 19, 1820) pp. 157–58 as quoted in Moses Rischin (ed) Immigration and the American Tradistion 1976 Indianapolis: Bobbs-Merrill, p. 47.

22. Craig Whitney, "Europeans Redefine What Makes a Citizen," *New York Times*, January 7, 1996, 6.

23. Eric Hobsbawm, *Nation and Nationalism Since 1780* (Cambridge: Cambridge University Press, 1990), 182.

24. Appadurai, *Modernity at Large*, 168.

25. Cited in Alejandro Portes, "Conclusion: Towards a New World—The Origins and Effects of Transnational Activities," *Ethnic and Racial Studies* 22, no. 2 (1999): 466.

26. Nina Glick-Schiller, Linda Basch, and Christina Szanton Blanc, eds., *Towards a Transnational Perspective on Migration: Race, Class, Ethnicity, and Nationalism Reconsidered* (New York: New York Academy of Sciences, 1992): 1–2.

27. Glick-Schiller, Basch, and Szanton Blanc, *Towards a Transnational Perspective*, 1–2.

28. United Nations Development Program, 2004 World Population Prospects, the 2004 Revision Population Database, http://esa.un.org/unpp/p2k0data.asp (accessed October 12, 2008).

29. Migration Policy Institute, Migration Information Source, 2006, www.migrationinformation.org (accessed December 11, 2006).

30. Portes, "Conclusion," 217.

31. Moni Basu, "Citizens of Two Worlds," *Atlanta Journal-Constitution*, July 3, 2002.

32. Michael Jones-Correa, "Under Two Flags: Dual Nationality and Its Consequences for the United States" (working paper on Latin America 99/00–3, David Rockefeller Center for Latin American Studies, New York, 2000), 18.

33. Anthony Gribbin, "Dual Citizenship Explodes in U.S.," *Washington Times*, November 14, 1999, 3; Jones-Correa, "Under Two Flags," 19).

34. Basu, "Citizens of Two Worlds."

35. Alison Mountz and Richard Wright, "Daily Life in the Transnational Migrant Community of San Agustin, Oaxaca and Poughkeepsie, New York," *Diaspora* 6, no. 3 (1996): 403–428.

36. Celia Dugger, "Return Passage to India: Emigres Pay Back," *New York Times*, February 29, 2000, A1.

37. Ginger Thompson, "A Surge in Money Sent Home by Mexicans," *New York Times*, October 28, 2003.

38. Monica Campbell, "Remittances Help Keep Kids in School—and in Mexico," *Christian Science Monitor*, May 15, 2006, 1, 10.

39. Jason Felch, "Still Rooting for Home Team from Abroad," *Los Angeles Times*, July 10, 2006, 3.

40. CNN.Com, "Judge: Woman Can't Cover Face on Driver's License," June 10, 2003, http://www.cnn.com/2003/LAW/06/06/florida.license.veil/ (accessed December 11, 2006).

41. Celia Dugger, "New Law Bans Genital Cutting in the United States," *New York Times*, October 12, 1996, 1, 6; Linda Burstyn, "Female Circumcision Comes to America," *Atlantic Monthly* 276, no. 4 (1995): 28–35.

42. "Court Convicts Man of Genital Mutilation," 2006. Yahoo News, http://news.yahoo.com/s/nm/20061102/us_nm/crime_usa_mutilation (accessed November 30, 2006).

43. Ian Wilhem, "Did September 11 Produce a Generation of Volunteers?" *Chronicle of Philanthropy*, August 31, 2006, http://www.cityyear.org/sites/clipp.cfm?Site=skc&CatID=2&Clipp=083106 (accessed December 10, 2006).

44. Sheila Croucher, "North America," in *Encyclopedia of Nationalism*, vol. 1 (New York: Academic Press, 2001), 559; Michael Lind, *The Next American Nation: The New Nationalism and the Fourth American Revolution* (New York: Free Press, 1995), 48.

45. Lind, *The Next American Nation*, 29.

46. Patrick Buchanan, *The Death of the West: How Dying Populations and Immigrant Invasions Imperil Our Country and Civilization* (New York: St. Martin's Press, 2002), 3, 12.

47. Patrick Buchanan, "U.S. Pays the High Price for Empire," Op-Ed, *Los Angeles Times*, September 18, 2001, B9.

48. Dana Milbank, "Attacks Shelve GOP Efforts to Woo Hispanics," Washington Post, December 20, 2001, A4.

49. Mark Krikorian, "Tight Focus Would Weed Out Radicals," Cincinnati Enquirer December 1, 2002, F1.

50. "Polling the Nation," http://www.poll.orspub.com. As cited in Deborah Schildkrut, "The More Things Change...American Identity and Mass/Elite Responses to 9/11." *Political Psychology* 23 (3) (September 2002): 511–535, p. 525.

51. Human Right Watch "We Are Not the Enemy: Hate Crimes Against Arabs and Muslims after September 11," (Vol 14, no. 6, November 2002) http://www.hrw.org/reports/2002/usahate/ [accessed October 12, 2008].

52. Charisse Jones, "States Try to Block Illegal Workers," USA *Today*, July 10, 2006, http://www.usatoday.com/news/nation/2006-07-09-states-illegal-workers_x.htm.

53. Patrick Jonsson, "Backlash Emerges Against Latino Culture," *Christian Science Monitor*, July 19, 2006, 3.

54. Benjamin Barber, "Constitutional Faith," in *For Love of Country: Debating the Limits of Patriotism*, ed. Martha Nussbaum (Boston: Beacon Press, 1996) 1996, 30, 32.

55. Rudolph Giuliani, Leadership, (New York: Miramax 2002), xi.

55a. David Van Biema. "As American As…" Time Magazine (Sept 23, 2001) http://www.time.com/time/magazine/article/0,9171,175969-1,00.html [accessed Oct 12, 2008].

56. Christian Joppke and Ewa Morawska, eds., *Towards Assimilation and Citizenship: Immigrants in Liberal Nation-States* (New York: Palgrave, 2003).

57. Joppke and Morawska, *Towards Assimilation*.

58. Robert Jervis, "An Interim Assessment of September 11: What Has Changed and What Has Not?" *Political Science Quarterly* 117, no. 1: 37–55" 2002.

59. Patrick Johnson, "Noncitizen Soldiers: The Quandaries of Foreign-Born Troops," *Christian Science Monitor*, July 5, 2005, 1, 10.

60. Jean-Marie Colombani, "Nous Sommes Tous Americains" ["We Are All Americans Now"], *Le Monde*, September 12, 2001.

61. Charles Taylor, "Why Democracy Needs Patriotism," in *For Love of Country: Debating the Limits of Patriotism*, ed. Martha Nussbaum (Boston: Beacon Press, 1996), 121.

62. Hilary Putnam, "Must We Choose Between Patriotism and Universal Reason?" in *For Love of Country* (see note 61), 97.

63. Alexandra Marks, "Radical Islam Finds US to Be 'sterile ground.'" *Christian Science Monitor*, October 23, 2006, 1.

64. Joppke and Morawska, *Towards Assimilation*.

Chapter 3

1. Guillermina Gina Núñez, "In Search of the Next Harvest," in *Homelands: Women's Journeys Across Race, Place, and Time*, ed. Patricia Justine Tumang and Jenesha de Rivera (Emeryville, CA: Seal Press, 2006).

2. Hazel Markus, Marie Crane, Stan Bernstein, and Michael Siladi, "Self-Schemas and Gender," *Journal of Personality and Social Psychology* 42, no. 1 (1982): 38–50.

3. Fredrik Barth, *Ethnic Groups and Boundaries: The Social Organization of Culture Difference* (Boston: Little, Brown and Company, 1969); Anthony Paul Cohen, *The Symbolic Construction of Community* (London: Ellis Horwood/Tavistock, 1985).

4. For specific issues facing immigrants who come to the United States as technical workers, particularly Asian immigrants, see Edward J. W. Park and John S. W. Park, *Probationary Americans: Contemporary Immigration Policies and the Shaping of Asian American Communities* (New York: Routledge, 2005). In some cases even well-educated immigrants will not have the social networks necessary to acquire well-paid jobs in their areas of training, see Alejandro Portes and Rubén G. Rumbaut, *Legacies: The Story of the Immigrant Second Generation* (New York: Russell Sage Foundation, 2001), 70–72.

5. Núñez, "In Search of the Next Harvest," 18.

6. Ibid., 19.

7. Ibid.

8. See Eric Schlosser, *Fast Food Nation: The Dark Side of the All American Meal* (New York: Harper Perennial, 2001), 160–165; Pierrette Hondagneu-Sotelo,

Doméstica: Immigrant Workers Cleaning and Caring in the Shadows of Affluence (Berkeley: University of California Press, 2001); and Esabel Valle, *Fields of Toil: A Migrant Family's Journey* (Pullman, WA: Washington State University Press, 1994).

9. David E. Hayes-Bautista, *La Nueva California: Latinos in the Golden State* (Berkeley: University of California Press, 2004), 97; see also Sarah J. Mahler, *American Dreaming: Immigrant Life on the Margins* (Princeton: Princeton University Press, 1995).

10. Hayes-Bautista, *La Nueva California*, 98.

11. Ibid., 99.

12. Núñez, "In Search of the Next Harvest," 19.

13. Juan Gonzalez, *Harvest of Empire: A History of Latinos in America* (New York: Penguin Books, 2000).

14. Jeffrey G. Reitz. *Warmth of the Welcome: The Social Causes of Economic Success for Immigrants in Different Nations and Cities* (Boulder, CO: Westview Press, 1998).

15. Jeffrey Passel, *Unauthorized Migrants: Numbers and Characteristics* (Washington DC: Pew Hispanic Center, 2005).

16. Francisco Balderrama and Raymon Rodriquez, *Decade of Betrayal: Mexican Repatriation in the 1930s* (Albuquerque: University of New Mexico Press, 1995).

17. Núñez, "In Search of the Next Harvest," 23.

18. See Kenneth Hyltenstam and Niclas Abrahamsson, "Maturation Constraints in SLA," in *The Handbook of Second Language Acquisition*, ed. Catherine J. Doughty and Michael Long (Malden, MA: Blackwell, 2003), 539–588, esp. 545.

19. For an articulation of classic assimilationism, see Milton Gordon, *Assimilation in American Life* (New York: Oxford University Press, 1964); on the failure of assimilation to account for enduring ethnic identities, see Nathan Glazer and Daniel Moynihan, *Beyond the Melting Pot: The Negroes, Puerto Ricans, Jews, Italians, and Irish of New York City*, 2nd ed. (Cambridge, MA: MIT Press, 1970).

20. Portes and Rumbaut, *Legacies*; Richard Alba and Victor Nee, *Remaking the American Mainstream: Assimilation and Contemporary Immigration* (Cambridge, MA: Harvard University Press, 2003).

21. Portes and Rumbaut, *Legacies*, 274.

22. Gloria Anzaldúa, *Borderlands/La Frontera: The New Mestiza* (San Francisco: Spinster/Aunt Lute Books, 1987); W. E. B. Du Bois, *The Souls of Black Folks* (New York: Signet Classic, 1995); Jayne O. Ifekwunigwe, *Scattered Belongings: Cultural Paradoxes of "Race," Nation and Gender* (New York: Routledge, 1999).

23. Ifekwunigwe, *Scattered Belongings*, 34.

24. Ibid., 35.

25. Edwina Barvosa, "Mestiza Autonomy as Relational Autonomy: Ambivalence and the Social Character of Free Will," *Journal of Political Philosophy* 15, no. 1 (March 2007): 1–21; Edwina Barvosa, *Wealth of Selves: Multiple Identities, Mestiza Consciousness, and the Subject of Politics* (College Station: Texas A & M University Press, 2008, forthcoming).

26. Núñez, "In Search of the Next Harvest," 20.

27. Núñez., 20–21.

28. For an account of how racial hierarchies continue to be socially constructed in various aspects of American primary school education, see Amanda Lewis, *Race in the Schoolyard: Negotiating the Color Lone in Classrooms and Communities* (New Brunswick, NJ: Rutgers University Press, 2003).

29. For a discussion with reference to political views and remittances of Dominican transmigrants, see Peggy Levitt, *The Transnational Villagers* (Berkeley: University of California Press, 2001), 155–158.

30. Portes and Rumbaut, *Legacies.*

30a. Mia Tuan, *Forever Foreigners or Honorary Whites?: The Asian Ethnic Experience Today.* (New Brunswick, N.J. : Rutgers University Press, c1998).

31. Ifekwunigwe, *Scattered Belongings,* 37.

32. Ibid., 36.

33. Portes and Rumbaut, *Legacies,* 44–69.

34. Ifekwunigwe, *Scattered Belongings,* 150.

35. Ibid.

36. Ibid.

37. Ibid., 40.

37a. Núñez, "In Search of the Next Harvest," 24.

38. Ibid., 24.

Chapter 4

1. The identity of the immigrant has been changed at his request.

2. *U.S. soil* is defined as the continental United States, any commonwealth of the United States, or land held by the United States, such as an embassy or military base.

3. Loopholes exist in these, as with all laws. Special cases exist in the areas of international adoptions, participation in the U.S. armed forces, asylum, and Temporary Protected Status cases.

4. Margaret Gray, "Rights for Residency" (presented at the meeting of the Latin American Studies Association, Washington DC, September 6–8, 2001).

5. Kelly Jefferys, "Refugees and Asylees: 2005," Annual Flow Report, U.S. Citizenship and Immigration Service (USCIS), May 2006. http://www.dhs.gov/xlibrary/assets/statistics/publications/Refugee_Asylee_5.pdf.

6. According to the USCIS, 27,491 total applications were submitted and 7,446 were granted. See http://www.uscis.gov/graphics/shared/aboutus/statistics/msraug06/ASYLUM.HTM for more information.

7. Deborah Meyers and Jennifer Yau, "US Immigration Statistics in 2003," Migration Policy Institute, November 1, 2004. http://www.migrationinformation.org/USfocus/display.cfm?id=263.

8. Mary Beth Sheridan, "Immigrants' Protected Status Extended," *Washington Post,* November 2, 2004, A03.

9. Ibid.

10. American Immigration Law Foundation, "Realities of Immigration Emerge in 2000 Census," AILF Policy Report, March 2002.

11. It is important to note that Mexicans have historically resided in what is now considered the American Southwest as it was one time part of the Mexican nation-state. For more on this, see Jason Porterfield, The Treaty of Guadalupe Hidalgo, 1848: A Primary Source Examination Of The Treaty That Ended The Mexican-American War. NY: The Rosen Publishing Group 2006.

12. Michael E. Fix and Jeffrey S. Passel, "Building a Wall Will End Illegal Entrance of Migrants," May 1, 1994, http://www.urban.org/url.cfm?ID=305184.

13. American Immigration Law Foundation, "Realities of Immigration."

14. Department of Homeland Security, http://uscis.gov/graphics/shared/statistics/index.htm.

15. Jeffrey S. Passel, Unauthorized Migrants: Numbers and Characteristics (Washington DC: Pew Hispanic Center, 2005), http://pewhispanic.org/files/reports/46.pdf.

16. Immigration and Naturalization, http://www.ncjrs.org/ondcppubs/publications/enforce/border/ins_3.html.

17. Kate Campbell, "Rotting Pears Crops Illustrate Farmers' Plight," California Farm Bureau Federation, September 13, 2006, http://www.cfbf.com/agalert/AgAlertStory.cfm?ID=668&ck=192FC044E74DFFEA144F9AC5DC9F3395.

18. Ibid.

19. Jeffrey S. Passel, Randy Capps, and Michael Fix, Undocumented Immigrants: Facts and Figures (Washington DC: Urban Institute, 2004).

20. Daniel T. Griswold, "Individual Liberty, Free Markets, and Peace," Cato Institute, February 18, 2002, http://www.cato.org/research/articles/griswold-020218.html.[2]

21. Eduardo Porter, "Illegal Immigrants Are Bolstering Social Security with Billions," New York Times, April 5, 2005.

22. James Brown. "Ten Myths and Facts about Undocumented Workers." Farmworkers Self-Help, Inc., April 10, 2008. http://fshflorida.org/node/16.

23. Michael Fix, Wendy Zimmermann, and Jeffrey S. Passel. The Integration of Immigrant Families in the United States (Washington DC: Urban Institute, 2001).

24. Susan Donaldson James. 2006. "Primer: Immigration" Journalism Center on Children and Families. http://www.journalismcenter.org/jcommunity/articles/JamesPrimer_9.18.06.htm#benefits.

25. Kaiser Family Foundation, Center on Budget and Policy Priorities, Covering New Americans: A Review of Federal and State Policies Related to Immigrants' Eligibility and Access to Publicly Funded Health Insurance, November 2004. http://www.kff.org/medicaid/7214.cfm.

26. Passel, Capps, and Fix. Undocumented Immigrants.

27. Randy Capps, Michael Fix, Jeffrey S. Passel, Jason Ost, and Dan Perez-Lopez. A Profile of the Low-Wage Immigrant Workforce (Washington DC: Urban Institute, 2003).

28. Friends Committee on National Legislation, Questioning Immigration Policy— Can We Afford to Open Our Arms? Document G-606-DOM, January 25, 1996.

29. Jeffrey S. Passel, *Immigrants and Taxes: A Reappraisal of Huddle's "The Cost of Immigration"* (Washington DC: Urban Institute, 1994), 51.

30. Daniel T. Griswold, "Individual Liberty, Free Markets, and Peace," Cato Institute, February 18, 2002, http://www.cato.org/research/articles/griswold-020218.html.

31. Richard Vedder, Lowell Gallaway, and Stephen Moore, *Immigration and Unemployment: New Evidence* (Arlington, VA: Alexis de Tocqueville Institution, 1994), 13.

32. U.S. Department of Commerce, Economics and Statistics Administration. 2001. "Hispanic-Owned Businesses: 1997." http://www.census.gov/prod/2001pubs/cenbr01-4.pdf. U.S. Census Bureau.

33. Ed Stoddard, "Illegal Immigrants $18 Billion Boost to Texas: Report." Reuters, December 8, 2006. http://www.reuters.com/article/idUSN0836112120061208.

34. Alan Greenspan, testimony before the Special Committee on Aging, U.S. Senate, February 27, 2003.

35. Andrew Sum, Mykhaylo Trubskyy, Ishwar Khatiwada, et al., *Immigrant Workers in the New England Labor Market: Implications for Workforce Development Policy*, Center for Labor Market Studies, Northeastern University, Boston (prepared for the New England Regional Office, Employment and Training Administration, and U.S. Department of Labor, Boston), October 2002, http://www.nupr.neu.edu/11–02/immigration.PDF.

36. Vedder, Gallaway, and Moore, *Immigration and Unemployment*, 13.

37. John Pucher, "Renaissance of Public Transportation in the United States?" *Transportation Quarterly* 56, no. 1 (Winter 2002): 33–46.

38. Marie E. Enchautegui, *The Effect of Immigration on the Wages and Employment of Black Males* (Washington DC: Urban Institute, May 1993), 17.

39. James P. Smith and Barry Edmonston, eds. (for the National Research Council), *The New Americans: Economic, Demographic, and Fiscal Effects of Immigration* (Washington DC: National Academy Press, 1997), S-5.

40. Passel, Capps, and Fix, *Undocumented Immigrants*.

41. Greenspan, testimony before the Special Committee on Aging.

42. Ronald D Lee, testimony before the Senate Immigration Subcommittee Economic and Fiscal Impact of Immigration, September 9, 1997.

43. State-level tax payments approximate natives. Immigrants in New York State pay over $18 billion a year in taxes, over 15% of the total, and roughly proportional to three times their size in the state's population, according to a study by the Urban Institute. Average annual tax payments by immigrants are approximately the same as those of natives—$6,300 for immigrants vs. $6,500 for natives. See http://www.urban.org/url.cfm?ID=900094 for more information.

44. Julian L. Simon, *Immigration: The Demographic and Economic Facts* (Washington DC: Cato Institute and National Immigration Forum, 1995).

45. Ibid.

46. Roger Lowenstein, "The Immigration Equation," *New York Times*, July 9, 2006.

47. Ibid.

48. Daniel T. Griswold, "Immigrants Have Enriched American Culture and Enhanced Our Influence in the World," *Insight on the News* (Feb. 18, 2002). http://www.freetrade.org/node/329.

48a. James p. Smith, Chair. 1997. "The New Americans: Economic, Demographic, and Fiscal Effects of Immigration." National Academy of Science. Supra note 6.

49. U.S. Census Bureau, http://www.census.gov/prod/2002pubs/censr-4.pdf.

50. Ibid.

51. See American Immigration Lawyers Association, "Myths & Facts in the Immigration Debate," August 14, 2003, http://www.aila.org/contentViewer.aspx?bc= 17,142#section4; and Simon Romero and Janet Elder, "Hispanics in the US Report Optimism," *New York Times*, August 6, 2003.

51a. Ibid.

52. See Stuart Anderson and Stephan Moore. "Cato Handbook for Congress" 105th Congress. Cato Institute, http://www.cato.org/pubs/handbook/hb105–29.html.

53. Simon Romero and Janet Elder.

54. Cato Institute.

55. Elizabeth Grieco, *English Abilities of the U.S. Foreign-Born Population* (Washington DC: Migration Policy Institute, 2003).

56. Cato Institute.

57. Ibid.

58. Stuart Anderson, "Muddled Masses," *Reason* (February 2000).

59. National Science Board, *Science and Engineering Indicators – 2002*. Arlington, VA:National Science Foundation, 2002 (NSB-02-1). Chapter 3.

60. For more, see Association of International Educators, 2004. "The Economic Benefits of International Education to the United States of America: A Statistical Analysis, 2003-2004" http://www.nafsa.org/_/File/_/usa.pdf (Enrollment figures from the Institute of International Education's *Open Doors 2004* report, found at: http://www.opendoors.iienetwork.org.) /.

61. Rima Merriman, "Impact of US Security Measures on Foreign Students," *Jordan Times*, January 27, 2004.

62. American Immigration Law Foundation, "U.S. Soldiers from Around the World: Immigrants Fight for an Adopted Homeland," AILF Policy Report, updated March 2003.

63. A total of 716 of the 3,406 Medal of Honor recipients have been immigrants, just over 21%.

64. American Immigration Law Foundation, "U.S. Soldiers from Around the World."

65. Ibid.

66. Associated Press/Dow Jones,Newswires "US Senate Subcommittee Hears Immigration Testimony," October 17, 2001; as reported in Daniel Griswold, "Don't Blame Immigrants for Terrorism," Cato Institute, http://www.cato.org/dailys/10–23–01.html.

67. Tamar Jacoby, "Immigration Nation," *Foreign Affairs* (November/December 2006), http://www.foreignaffairs.org/20061101faessay85606/tamar-jacoby/immigration-nation.html%3Fmode%3Dprint.

68. Ibid.

69. For more, see *Ines Ferre, Lydia Garlikov, Keith Oppenheim, Scott Spoerry, Kristi Keck and Harris Whitbeck* "Hundreds of Thousands March for Immigrant Rights:

Schools, Businesses Feel Impact as Students, Workers Walk Out," May 3, 2006. http://www.cnn.com/2006/US/05/02/immigrant.day/index.html.

70. Specifically, they would extend (1) from ten miles west of the Tecate, California, port of entry to ten miles east of the Tecate, California, port of entry; (2) from ten miles west of the Calexico, California, port of entry to five miles east of the Douglas, Arizona, port of entry (requiring installation of an interlocking surveillance camera system by May 30, 2007, and fence completion by May 30, 2008); (3) from five miles west of the Columbus, New Mexico, port of entry to ten miles east of El Paso, Texas; (4) from five miles northwest of the Del Rio, Texas, port of entry to five miles southeast of the Eagle Pass, Texas, port of entry; and (5) from 15 miles northwest of the Laredo, Texas, port of entry to the Brownsville, Texas, port of entry (requiring fence completion from 15 miles northwest of the Laredo, Texas, port of entry to 15 southeast of the Laredo, Texas, port of entry by December 31, 2008).

Chapter 5

1. Information for this story came from "Somali Immigrants Rile Maine Mayor, Hundreds March in Solidarity with Somalis over Maine Mayor's Letter," Associated Press/CBS News, October 14, 2002, http://www.cbsnews.com/stories/2002/10/14/national/main525534.shtml - 83k - Cached ; Jonathan Tilove, "Somali Migration Transforms Lewiston," *Kennebec Journal/Morning Sentinel*, September 8, 2002; Judith Gaines, "Changes Afoot in a Hipper L/A," *Boston Globe*, June 25, 2006; *The Letter: An American Town and the "Somali Invasion,"* DVD, directed by Ziad H. Hamzeh (Hamzeh Mystique Films, 2003); William Finnegan, "New in Town: Letter from Maine," *New Yorker*, (December 11, 2006): 46–58; personal interviews with Deena and Jack Weinstein and Lesli and Neal Weiner (December 20, 2006) and authors' firsthand knowledge of the events.

2. The unique problem of being both black and Muslim immigrants in the United States was highlighted by both Abdirizak A. Mahboub, a Somali elder, and Ismael Ahmed, a Somali community activist, in *The Letter* (see note 1).

3. The religious and racial agenda of this group was hard to overlook. Brother David Stearns, a member of the World Church, made clear the impetus behind his desire to see the Somali Muslims leave the town of Lewiston: "Before any diversity or equal opportunity, these were Christian white men that ran this country... 'All men created equal' was meant for if you were white and you were Christian." From *The Letter* (see note 1).

4. One attendee, Jack Weinstein, explained that he felt a moral imperative to support the Somali immigrants, likening it to supporting Jewish immigration during World War II. Personal interview (see note 1).

5. As Abdirizak A. Mahboub, a Somali elder, said, "[The rally] is behind us, so it's just like the work has begun now, the real work has begun, and we have been given a mandate, which is to build this community as one." From *The Letter* (see note 1).

6. The Quran that Ellison used was originally owned by Thomas Jefferson, who was born in the Virginia district that Goode now represents.

7. P. D. Numrich, "How the Swans Came to Lake Michigan: The Social Organization of Buddhist Chicago," *Journal for the Scientific Study of Religion* 39 (2000): 189–203; D. E. Sherkat, "Tracking the 'Other': Dynamics and Composition of 'Other' Religion in the General Social Survey, 1973–1996," *Journal for the Scientific Study of Religion* 38 (1999): 551–560; D. E. Sherkat, "Tracking the Restructuring of American Religion: Religious Affiliation and Patterns of Religious Mobility, 1973–1998," *Social Forces* 79 (June 2001): 1459–1493; Tom W. Smith, *Counting Flocks and Lost Sheep: Trends in Religious Preference Since World War II.* GSS Social Change Report 26 (Chicago: National Opinion Research Center, 1991); R. S. Warner, "Approaching Religious Diversity: Barriers, Byways, and Beginnings," *Sociology of Religion* 59 (1998): 193–215; R. S. Warner, "Religion and Migration in the United States," *Social Compass* 45 (1998): 123–134.

8. Diana L. Eck, *A New Religious America: How a "Christian Country" has Now Become the World's Most Religiously Diverse Nation* (San Francisco: HarperCollins, 2001), 1.

9. Susan Levine, "A Place for Those Who Pray: Along Montgomery's 'Highway to Heaven,' Diverse Acts of Faith," *Washington Post*, August 3, 1997, B1.

10. Michael Ruane, "A Church with Four Faces," *Washington Post*, February 21, 1999, A1.

11. Kenneth D. Wald, "The Public Role of Private Religion in the United States" (paper presented at Religious Cultures/Communities of Belief, a conference organized by the Bavarian American Academy in cooperation with the Goethe-Institut, Munich, Germany, June 17–19, 2004).

12. Eck, *A New Religious America*; Wald, "The Public Role of Private Religion."

13. Wald, "The Public Role of Private Religion."

14. Roger Finke and Rodney Stark. *The Churching of America, 1776–1990: Winners and Losers in Our Religious Economy* (New Brunswick, NJ: Rutgers University Press, 1992).

15. Eck, *A New Religious America*; Wald, "The Public Role of Private Religion."

16. Joseph R. Gusfield, *Symbolic Crusade: Status Politics and the American Temperance Movement* (Urbana: University of Illinois Press, 1963).

17. James Guth, John Green, Corwin Smidt, Lyman Kellstedt, and Margaret Poloma, *The Bully Pulpit: The Politics of Protestant Clergy* (Lawrence: University Press of Kansas, 1997); Corwin Smidt, "Evangelical and Mainline Protestants at the Turn of the Millennium: Taking Stock and Looking Forward," in *American Religion and Political Mobilization*, ed. Matthew Wilson (Washington DC: Georgetown University Press, 2007).

18. Eck, *A New Religious America*; Frank Lambert, *The Founding Fathers and the Place of Religion in America* (Princeton, NJ: Princeton University Press, 2003); Seymour Martin Lipset, *The First New Nation* (Garden City, NY: Doubleday-Anchor, 1967); New Immigrant Survey, http://nis.princeton.edu; Wald, "The Public Role of Private Religion."

19. A. James Reichley, *Religion in American Public Life* (Washington DC: Brookings Institution, 1985).

20. Ibid., 52.

21. Alan Wolfe, *The Transformation of American Religion: How We Actually Live Our Faith* (New York: Free Press, 2003); Robert Wuthnow, *America and the Challenges of Religious Diversity* (Princeton: Princeton University Press, 2005).

22. Eck, *A New Religious America*, 5.

23. Council on American–Islamic Relations, "Muslims Win Accommodation in Public Schools," 2001, http://www.cair-net.org.

24. Samuel S. Huntington, "Paradigms of American Politics: Beyond the One, the Two, and the Many," *Political Science Quarterly* 89 (1974): 1–26; Ted G. Jelen and Clyde Wilcox, "Religion and Politics in an Open Market: Religious Mobilization in the United States," in *Religion and Politics in Comparative Perspective: The One, the Few, and the Many*, ed. Ted G. Jelen and Clyde Wilcox (New York: Cambridge University Press, 2002).

25. Alexis de Tocqueville, *Democracy in America*, trans. George Lawrence, ed. J. P. Mayer (New York: HarperCollins, 1945 [1835, 1840]), 314–315.

26. Eck, *A New Religious America*.

27. Kenneth D. Wald and Allison Calhoun-Brown, *Religion and Politics in the United States*, 5th ed. (Lanham, MD: Rowman & Littlefield, 2007).

28. Ibid., 20.

29. Guth et al., *The Bully Pulpit*; Smidt, "Evangelical and Mainline Protestants."

30. Robert Wuthnow, "The Moral Minority," *American Prospect* 11, no. 13 (May 22, 2000): 31–33.

31. Lawrence Bobo and Franklin D. Gilliam, Jr., "Race, Sociopolitical Participation, and Black Empowerment," *American Political Science Review* 84, no. 2 (1990): 377–393; Allison Calhoun-Brown, "African American Churches and Political Mobilization: The Psychological Impact of Organizational Resources," *Journal of Politics* 58 (1996): 935–953; Allison Calhoun-Brown, "While Marching to Zion: Otherworldliness and Racial Empowerment in the Black Community," *Journal for the Scientific Study of Religion* 37 (1998): 427–439; Fredrick C. Harris, "Something Within: Religion as a Mobilizer of African-American Political Activism," *Journal of Politics* 56 (1994): 42–68; Fredrick C. Harris, *Something Within: Religion in African-American Political Activism* (New York: Oxford University Press, 1999); Katherine Tate, *From Protest to Politics: The New Black Voters in American Elections* (Cambridge, MA: Harvard University Press, 1993).

32. Iva E. Carruthers, Frederick D. Haynes III, and Jeremiah A. Wright, Jr., eds. *Blow the Trumpet in Zion!: Global Vision and Action for the 21st Century Black Church* (Minneapolis, MN: Augsburg Fortress, 2005); C. Eric Lincoln and Lawrence H. Mamiya, *The Black Church in the African-American Experience* (Durham, NC: Duke University Press, 1990); R. Drew Smith and Fredrick C. Harris, eds., *Black Churches and Local Politics: Clergy Influence, Organizational Partnerships, and Civic Empowerment* (Lanham, MD: Rowman

& Littlefield, 2005); Clyde Wilcox and Leopoldo Gomez, "Religion, Group Identification and Politics Among American Blacks," *Sociological Analysis* 51 (1990): 271–285.

33. Pew Research Center, "Religion and the 2006 Elections," 2006, http://pewforum.org/docs/index.php?DocID=174.

34. Wald and Calhoun-Brown, *Religion and Politics in the United States.*

35. Clyde Wilcox and Carin Robinson, "Prayers, Parties, and Preachers: The Evolving Nature of Political and Religious Mobilization," in *American Religion and Political Mobilization* (see note 17).

36. Eck, *A New Religious America*; Wald and Calhoun-Brown, *Religion and Politics in the United States.*

37. Smidt, "Evangelical and Mainline Protestants."

38. Ted G. Jelen, *The Political Mobilization of Religious Beliefs* (New York: Praeger, 1991).

39. Clyde Wilcox, Mark J. Rozell, and Roland Gunn, "Religious Coalitions in the New Christian Right," *Social Science Quarterly* 77 (1996): 543–559.

40. Robert Wuthnow, *The Restructuring of American Religion* (Princeton: Princeton University Press, 1988).

41. Mark Carl Rom, "Introduction: The Politics of Same-Sex Marriage," in *The Politics of Same-Sex Marriage*, ed. Craig A. Rimmerman and Clyde Wilcox (Chicago: University of Chicago Press, 2007).

42. Elliot N. Dorff, Daniel S. Nevins, and Avram I. Reisner. "Homosexuality, Human Dignity, and Halakhah: A Combined Responsum for the Committee on Jewish Law and Standards," 2006, http://www.rabbinicalassembly.org/docs/Dorff_Nevins_Reisner_Final.pdf; Leonard Levy, "Same-Sex Attraction and Halakhah," 2006, http://www.rabbinicalassembly.org/docs/Levy_Final.pdf; Joel Roth, "Homosexuality Revisited," 2006, http://www.rabbinicalassembly.org/docs/Roth_Final.pdf.

43. Zahid Bukhari, "Demography, Identity, Space: Defining American Muslims," in *Muslims in the United States: Demography, Beliefs, Institutions*, ed. Philippa Strum and Danielle Tarantolo (Washington DC: Woodrow Wilson International Center for Scholars, 2003), 7–20; Project Muslims in the American Public Square (MAPS), 2001, 2004, http://www.projectmaps.com.

44. League of Women Voters of Fairfax Area Educational Fund, "Diversity: Muslims in Fairfax," 2001, http://www.lwv-fairfax.org/pdf_study_folder/lwvfa_muslim.pdf.

45. Pluralism Project, "Statistics by Tradition," http://www.pluralism.org/resources/statistics/tradition.php.

46. Eck, *A New Religious America*; Warner, "Approaching Religious Diversity."

47. Wuthnow, *America and the Challenges of Religious Diversity.*

48. Bukhari, "Demography, Identity, Space"; Tom W. Smith, "The Polls—Review. The Muslim Population of the United States: The Methodology of Estimates," *Public Opinion Quarterly* 66, no. 3 (2002): 404–417; Tom W. Smith, "Religious Diversity in America: The Emergence of Muslims, Buddhists, Hindus, and Others," *Journal for the Scientific Study of Religion* 41, no. 3 (2002): 577–585.

49. Pluralism Project, "Statistics by Tradition."

50. Wuthnow, *America and the Challenges of Religious Diversity*.

51. New Immigrant Survey, http://nis.princeton.edu.

52. Interestingly, support for the display of the menorah was relatively low among Jews.

53. Ted G. Jelen and Clyde Wilcox, *Public Attitudes Toward Church and State* (Armonk, NY: M. E. Sharpe, 1995).

54. Ibid.

55. See Wuthnow, *America and the Challenges of Religious Diversity*, for the key results of the survey.

56. These are not, of course, strictly contradictory ideas. A respondent may believe that new traditions could pose a threat in the future but that so far the net results have been positive.

57. See Jelen and Wilcox, *Public Attitudes Toward Church and State*, for a discussion.

58. Thomas F. Pettigrew, "Generalized Intergroup Contacts Effects on Prejudice," *Personality and Social Psychology Bulletin* 23 (1998): 173–185.

59. We employ ordinary least squares multiple regression techniques in this data analysis, using the Religion and Diversity Survey, 2002–2003, http://www.thearda.com/Archive/Files/Descriptions/DIVERSTY.asp. For our code, numerical regression results, and other data queries, please contact the authors.

60. For these responses, we focused on two sets of questions. The first set of questions asked, "Please tell me if you favor or oppose the U.S. government doing each of the following: making it illegal for [Muslim, Hindu, Buddhist] groups to meet in the United States," with responses of "Favor" and "Oppose." The second set of questions asked, "In the next few years, would you welcome or not welcome each of the following groups becoming a stronger presence in the United States: [Muslims, Hindus, Buddhists]," with responses of "Welcome," "Indifferent," and "Not welcome." We created two dependent variables (a "welcoming" variable and a "making illegal" variable) that are scales of the mean values of all three questions in each set.

61. Robert D. Putnam, *Making Democracy Work: Civic Traditions in Modern Italy* (Princeton: Princeton University Press, 1993); Robert D. Putnam, *Bowling Alone: The Collapse and Revival of American Community* (New York: Simon and Schuster, 2000).

62. Doris Buss and Didi Herman, *Globalizing Family Values: The Christian Right in International Politics* (Minneapolis: University of Minnesota Press, 2003); Carin Robinson, "Doctrine, Discussion and Disagreement: Evangelicals and Catholics Together in the Christian Right" (PhD dissertation, Georgetown University, 2008).

63. David C. Leege, Kenneth D. Wald, Brian S. Krueger, and Paul D. Mueller, *The Political Mobilization of Cultural Differences: Social Change and Voter Mobilization Strategies in the Post-New Deal Period* (Princeton: Princeton University Press, 2002).

64. Geoffrey Layman, *The Great Divide: Religious and Cultural Conflict in American Party Politics*. (New York: Columbia University Press, 2001).

65. Clyde Wilcox and Carin Larson, *Onward Christian Soldiers? The Religious Right in American Politics*, 3rd ed. (Boulder, CO: Westview Press, 2006).

66. Paul A. Djupe and John C. Green, "The Politics of American Muslims," in *American Religion and Political Mobilization* (see note 17); Project Muslims in the American Public Square (MAPS), 2004.

67. Clifford Brown, Jr., Lynda Powell, and Clyde Wilcox, *Serious Money: Contributing and Fundraising in Presidential Nomination Campaigns* (New York: Cambridge University Press, 1995).

67a. Ralph Reed, *Politically Incorrect: The Emerging Faith Factor in American Politics.* (Dallas:Word Publishers, 1994).

68. Wilcox and Robinson, "Prayers, Parties, and Preachers."

68a. Alan Cooperman, "War on Christmas is Alleged," *Washington Post*, March29, 2006, A12.

69. Eck, *A New Religious America*, 57–58.

70. *Gentleman's Agreement*, DVD, directed by Elia Kazan (1947; 20th Century Fox, 2003).

71. Smidt, "Evangelical and Mainline Protestants."

72. Pew Forum Analysis "Prospects for Inter-Religious Understanding: Will Views Toward Muslims and Islam Follow Historical Trends?" 2006, http://pewforum. org/publications/surveys/Inter-Religious-Understanding.pdf, 3.

73. Brian Steensland, Jerry Z. Park, Mark D. Regnerus, L. D. Robinson, W. B. Wilcox, and R. D. Woodberry, "The Measure of American Religion: Toward Improving the State of the Art," *Social Forces* 79 (2000): 291–318.

74. G. Jasso, D. Massey, M. Rosenzweig, and J. Smith, "Exploring the Religious Preferences of Recent Immigrants to the United States: Evidence from the New Immigrant Survey Pilot," in *Religion and Immigration: Christian, Jewish, and Muslim Experiences in the United States*, ed. Yvonne Yazbeck Haddad, Jane I. Smith, and John L. Esposito (Walnut Creek, CA: AltaMira Press, 2003), 217–253.

Chapter 6

1. Redwing Cloud, "Lummi to Host Historic Meeting of the Nations," *Indian County Today*, July 12, 2007.

2. Author has copy of this unpublished document.

3. Ibid.

4. Michael Janofsky, "Senate Opens Hearings on Lobbyists for Tribes," *New York Times*, September 30, 2004.

5. *Indian Naturalization Act of 1924*, 43, U.S. *Statutes at Large* 253 (1924).

6. Vine Deloria, Jr., "American Indians," in *Multiculturalism in the United States: A Comparative Guide to Acculturation and Ethnicity*, ed. John D. Buenker and Lorman A. Ratner (New York: Greenwood Press, 1992), 31.

7. *1934 Indian Reorganization Act*, 48, U.S. *Statutes at Large* 984 (1934).

8. See Duane Champagne, *Social Order and Political Change: Constitutional Governments Among the Cherokee, the Choctaw, the Chickasaw, and the Creek* (Stanford, CA: Stanford University Press, 1992), for a good treatment of these nations' constitutional efforts in the 1800s.

9. Duane Champagne, "Remaking Tribal Constitutions: Meeting the Challenges of Tradition, Colonialism, and Globalization," in *American Indian Constitutional Reform and the Rebuilding of Native Nations*, ed. Eric D. LeMont (Austin: University of Texas Press, 2006), 13.

10. Russel L. Barsh, "The Nature and Spirit of North American Political Systems," *American Indian Quarterly* 3 (Summer 1986): 184.

11. Taiaiake Alfred, *Peace, Power, and Righteousness: An Indigenous Manifesto* (Ontario: Oxford University Press, 1999), 25.

12. Vine Deloria, Jr., and Clifford M. Lytle, *American Indians, American Justice* (Austin: University of Texas Press, 1984), 82.

13. Ella Deloria, *Speaking of Indians* (1944; reprint Lincoln, NE: University of Nebraska Press, 1998), 24, 32.

14. Vine Deloria, Jr., and David E. Wilkins, *Tribes, Treaties, and Constitutional Tribulations* (Austin: University of Texas Press, 1999), 12.

15. David E. Wilkins and K. Tsianina Lomawaima, *Uneven Ground: American Indian Sovereignty and Federal Law* (Norman: University of Oklahoma Press, 2001), see especially chapter 3, which addresses the plenary power doctrine.

16. Lindsay G. Robertson, *Conquest by Law: How the Discovery of America Dispossessed Indigenous Peoples of Their Lands* (New York: Oxford University Press, 2005).

17. Wilkins and Lomawaima, *Uneven Ground*, 64–97.

18. *Northwest Ordinance*, 1, U.S. *Statutes at Large* 50 (1789).

19. *Native American Church v. Navajo Tribal Council*, 272 F.2d 131 (10th Cir. 1959), 134.

20. 118 U.S. 375, 384 (1886).

21. 31 U.S. 515, 557 (1832).

22. 104 U.S. 621 (1881).

23. 492 U.S. 408 (1989).

24. See *South Dakota v. Bourland*, 508 U.S. 679 (1993); *Strate v. A-1 Contractors*, 520 U.S. 438 (1997); *Nevada v. Hicks*, 533 U.S. 353 (2001); and *City of Sherill v. Oneida Indian Nation*, 544 U.S. 197 (2005). These are cases in which the Supreme Court has elevated local and state governmental authority over Native governmental authority.

25. Frank Pommersheim, *Braid of Feathers: American Indian Law and Contemporary Tribal Life* (Berkeley: University of California Press, 1995), see especially chapter 5, "Tribal–State Relations: Hope for the Future?".

26. Glenn A. Phelps, "Mr. Gerry Goes to Arizona: Electoral Geography and Voting Rights in Navajo Country," *American Indian Culture and Research Journal* 15 (1991): 70.

27. Previously, some American Indians had gained U.S. citizenship via specific treaty provisions and a handful of federal laws that applied to specific categories of individuals; in 1919 Congress enacted a law that extended the franchise to honorably discharged American Indians who had fought in World War I.

28. 112 U.S. 94 (1884).

29. Ibid., 99.

30. See Daniel McCool, Susan M. Olson, and Jennifer L. Robinson's excellent study *Native Vote: American Indians, the Voting Rights Act, and the Right to Vote* (New York: Cambridge University Press, 2007), for a detailed analysis of the history of Indian voting in the United States, with emphasis on the contemporary efforts of Native individuals who have filed lawsuits under the Voting Rights Act.

31. See Nathan R. Margold, "Suffrage-Discrimination Against Indians," in *Opinions of the Solicitors of the Department of the Interior Relating to Indian Affairs, 1917–1974* (August 12, 1937; Washington DC: Government Printing Office, 1974), 778.

32. *Allen v. Merrell*, 6 Utah 2nd 32, 39 (1956).

33. "Bad New Days for Voting Rights," *New York Times*, April 18, 2004. http://query. nytimes.com/gst/fullpage.html?res=9C0CE4D9133BF93BA25757C0A9629 C8B63.

34. Kevin Gover, "The American Indian Vote Comes of Age," *Indian Country Today*, November 15, 2002.

35. McCool, Olson, and Robinson, *Native Vote*, ix–x.

36. Jerry D. Stubben, *Native Americans and Political Participation: A Reference Handbook* (Santa Clara, CA: ABC-CLIO, 2006), 131, table 4.1.

37. David E. Wilkins, *American Indian Politics and the American Political System*, 2nd ed. (Lanham, MD: Rowman & Littlefield, 2007), 204–206.

38. Harvard Project on American Indian Economic Development, *The State of the Native Nations: Conditions Under U.S. Policies of Self-Determination* (New York: Oxford University Press, 2008), 61.

Chapter 7

1. CNN.com, "Katrina Timeline," http://www.cnn.com/SPECIALS/2005/katrina/ interactive/timeline.katrina.large/frameset.exclude.html (accessed March 11, 2007).

2. David Carr, "More Horrible than Truth," *New York Times*, September 19, 2005, C1.

3. Maureen Dowd, "United States of Shame," *New York Times*, September 3, 2005, A21.

4. Wil Haygood, "To Me, It Just Seems like Black People Are Marked," *Washington Post*, September 2, 2005, A1, final edition.

5. Ibid.

6. Video Recording, "National Black Summit 2007," http://www.tavistalks.com Accessed March 11, 2007).

7. Barack Obama's standing as a serious contender was enhanced further when candidates announced their first-quarter 2007 political contributions and it was revealed that Obama's campaign had raised an unexpected $25 million, putting him only a million dollars behind the Democratic frontrunner Hillary Clinton for the year. See Jeff Zeleny and Patrick Healy, "Obama Shows His Strength in a Fund-Raising Feat on Par with Clinton," *New York Times*, April 5, 2007, A15.

8. Howard Schuman, Charlotte Steeh, Lawrence Bobo, and Maria Krysan, *Racial Attitudes in America* (Cambridge, MA: Harvard University Press, 1997).

9. Jon Hurwitz and Mark Peffley, "Explaining the Great Racial Divide: Perceptions of Fairness in the U.S. Criminal Justice System," *Journal of Politics* 67 (2005): 762–783.

10. Gregory B. Lewis, "Black–White Differences in Attitudes Toward Homosexuality and Gay Rights," *Public Opinion Quarterly* 67 (2003): 59–78.

11. Miroslav Nincic and Donna J. Nincic, "Race, Gender, and War," *Journal of Peace Research* 39 (2002): 547–568.

12. Robert S. Erikson and Kent L. Tedin, *American Public Opinion*, updated 7th ed. (New York: Pearson Longman, 2007).

13. Donald R. Kinder and Lynn M. Sanders, *Divided by Color: Racial Politics and Democratic Ideals* (Chicago: University of Chicago Press, 1996).

13a. The Pew Research Center for the People and the Press, "Huge Racial Divide Over Katrina and Its Consequences: Two-in-Three Critical of Bush's Relief Efforts," September 8, 2005, http://people-press.org/report/255/two-in-three-critical-of-bushs-relief-efforts.

14. In fact, an ABC/*Wall Street Journal* poll put President Bush's approval rating among blacks at a remarkable 2%. Michael Fletcher and Richard Morin, "Bush's Approval Rating Drops to New Low in Wake of Storm; He Says Race Didn't Affect Efforts; Blacks in Poll Disagree," *Washington Post*, September 13, 2005, A8.

15. Pew Research Center for the People and the Press.

16. See Michael C. Dawson, *Behind the Mule: Race and Class in African American Politics* (Princeton: Princeton University Press, 1994); Patricia Gurin, Shirley Hatchett, and James S. Jackson, *Hope and Independence: Blacks' Response to Electoral and Party Politics* (New York: Russell Sage Foundation, 1989); Katherine Tate, *From Protest to Politics* (Cambridge, MA: Harvard University Press, 1993).

17. William J. Wilson, *When Work Disappears: The World of the New Urban Poor* (New York: Knopf, 1996).

18. While the black middle class has managed to put some residential distance between itself and poorer blacks, it is important not to minimize the continued role of residential segregation in the lives of the black middle class. As Massey and Denton point out, blacks at every income level experience higher rates of segregation than the rest of the population. Douglas S. Massey and Nancy A. Denton, *American Apartheid: Segregation and the Making of the Underclass* (Cambridge, MA: Harvard University Press, 1993).

19. A quick Internet search in March 2007 revealed over 31,000 hits for the term "Obama black enough."

20. Cathy Cohen, *Boundaries of Blackness: AIDS and the Breakdown of Black Politics* (Chicago: University of Chicago Press, 1999).

21. Michele T. Berger, *Workable Sisterhood: The Political Journey of Stigmatized Women with HIV/AIDS* (Princeton: Princeton University Press, 2004).

22. Melanye Price, "Warring Souls, Reconciling Beliefs: Unearthing the Contours of African American Ideology" (PhD dissertation, Ohio State University, 2003).

23. Paul M. Sniderman and Thomas Piazza, *The Scar of Race* (Cambridge, MA: Harvard University Press, 1993).

24. Paul M. Sniderman and Edward G. Carmines, *Reaching Beyond Race* (Cambridge, MA: Harvard University Press, 1997).

25. Carol Swain actually argues that there is a dangerous new white nationalist movement on the rise in the United States and that the continued emphasis on affirmative action programs to advance blacks is making whites who oppose such programs vulnerable to being recruited. Carol M. Swain, *The New White Nationalism in America: Its Challenge to Integration* (New York: Cambridge University Press, 2002).

26. Ira Katznelson, *When Affirmative Action Was White: An Untold History of Racial Inequality in Twentieth-Century America* (New York: Norton, 2005); Linda F. Williams, *The Constraint of Race: Legacies of White Skin Privilege* (University Park: Pennsylvania State University Press, 2003).

27. The series of setbacks and partial victories on the affirmative action front is exemplified by recent events. Supporters won an important victory in 2003 when the U.S. Supreme Court in *Grutter v. Bollinger* affirmed the constitutionality of affirmative action. However, the precariousness of this 5–4 majority was brought home in 2005 when President George Bush made two conservative appointments to the Supreme Court.

28. In the late 1960s, the country's prison population stood at about 200,000. By 2000 that number had grown by a factor of 10 to over 2 million. While blacks make up only 12.3% of the U.S. population, they make up an alarming 43.9% of the American prison population. For more on racial inequities in the criminal justice system, see Human Rights Watch at http://www.hrw.org and the Sentencing Project at http://www.sentencingproject.org.

29. Matthew A. Crenson and Benjamin Ginsberg, *Downsizing Democracy: How America Sidelined Its Citizens and Privatized Its Public* (Baltimore: Johns Hopkins University Press, 2002); Adolph Reed, Jr., 1986. *The Jesse Jackson Phenomenon: The Crisis of Purpose in Afro-American Politics* (New Haven, CT: Yale University Press, 1986).

30. Hannah F. Pitkin, *The Concept of* Representation (Berkeley: University of California Press, 1967). This formalistic view of representation may clash with the advantages available to incumbents. For various reasons, most members of Congress who seek reelection will return to Congress. For example, as Davidson and Oleszek show, in the 1990s over 90% of members of Congress who ran were reelected. Roger H. Davidson and Walter J. Oleszek, *Congress and Its Members*, 8th ed. (Washington DC: Congressional Quarterly Press, 2002). For African Americans, that statistic is even higher as they are more likely to represent safe districts. For more, see Carol M. Swain, *Black Faces, Black Interests: The Representation of African Americans in Congress* (Cambridge, MA: Harvard University Press, 1993).

31. Katherine Tate, *Black Faces in the Mirror* (Princeton: Princeton University Press, 2003), 98.

32. Ibid.

33. This act was reauthorized in 1970, 1975, 1982, 1992, and 2006. Each time the act has been reauthorized it has also been expanded to cover other racial minorities and language minorities and to cover more jurisdictions. The VRA now covers seven entire states (e.g., Alabama, Alaska, Texas, and Arizona) and partial jurisdiction of seven other states (e.g., California, North Carolina, New York, Michigan, and South Dakota). For more on the VRA and covered districts, see http://www.usdoj.gov/crt/voting/.

34. Bernard Grofman, Lisa Handley, and Richard Niemi, *Minority Representation and the Quest for Voting Equality* (New York: Cambridge University Press, 1992).

35. The Joint Center for Political and Economic Studies has tracked the number of black elected officials since 1970. In that year they report 1,469 black elected officials. The Center's 2001 report, authored by David A. Bositis, counts 9,101 or the largest number of black elected officials ever. More information about black elected officials and other policy questions relevant to African Americans can be found at the Joint Center's website at http://www.jointcenter.org.

36. Swain, *Black Faces, Black Interests*. Relatively few African American candidates have been successful at winning office in majority white settings. However, the 2006 elections ushered in Deval Patrick, the new black governor of Massachusetts, and Representative Keith Ellison of Minnesota, both of whom won election in majority white settings.

37. Jane Mansbridge, "Should Blacks Represent Blacks and Women Represent Women? A Contingent 'Yes.'" *Journal of Politics* 61 (1999): 628–657.

38. Mansbridge also cautions that the association between these two kinds of representations can lead to "essentialism—that is, the assumption that members of certain groups have an essential identity that all members of that group share and of which no others can partake." Ibid., 637.

39. Ibid.

40. See Tate, *Black Faces in the Mirror*, and Janet M. Box-Steffensmeier, David C. Kimball, Scott R. Meinke, and Katherine Tate, "The Effects of Political Representation on the Electoral Advantages of House Incumbents," *Political Research Quarterly* 56 (September 2003): 259–270. This finding is also true for whites. Box-Steffensmeier et al. demonstrate that in the 1994 House race voters expressed more support for their representatives when they shared their race or gender.

41. Lawrence Bobo and Franklin Gilliam, "Race, Socioeconomic Status, and Black Empowerment," *American Political Science Review* 84 (1990): 377–394.

42. In the last five presidential elections, Democrats have received 80%–95% of the black vote. Gurin, Hatchet, and Jackson, *Hope and Independence*; Katherine Tate, "Black Political Participation in the 1984 and 1988 Presidential Elections," *American Political Science Review* 85 (1991): 1159–1176;

43. For more on this shift in the voting patterns of white southerners, see Earl Black and Merle Black, *The Rise of Southern Republicans* (Cambridge, MA: Harvard University Press, 2002).

44. The last Democratic presidential candidate to win a majority of white votes was Lyndon Johnson in 1964.

45. Robert C. Smith, *We Have No Leaders: African Americans in the Post–Civil Rights Era* (Albany: State University of New York Press, 1996).

46. Ibid.

47. Paul Frymer, *Uneasy Alliances: Race and Party Competition in America* (Princeton: Princeton University Press, 1999).

48. More information can be found for the 2000 presidential election at www.cnn.com/ELECTION/2000 and for the 2004 presidential election at www.cnn.com/ELECTION/2004.

49. These and other political ads can be viewed in their entirety at http://www.livingroomcandidate.org (accessed March 18, 2007). For more on racial appeals to white voters, see Nancy Benac, "AP Poll: GOP Outreach to Blacks Seems Likely to Be Spurned Again," found at www.USAToday.com, November 1, 2006; Tali Mendelberg, *The Race Card: Campaign Strategy, Implicit Messages, and the Norm of Equality* (Princeton: Princeton University Press, 2001).

50. Georgia A. Persons, "Black Mayoralties and the New Black Politics: From Insurgency to Racial Reconciliation," in *Dilemmas of Black Politics: Issues of Leadership and Strategies*, ed. Georgia A. Persons (New York: HarperCollins, 1993), 38.

51. Joseph P. McCormick and Charles E. Jones, "The Conceptualization of Deracialization: Thinking Through the Dilemma," in *Dilemmas of Black Politics* (see note 50).

52. Byron D'Andra Orey and Boris E. Ricks, "A Systematic Analysis of the Deracialization Concept," *National Political Science Review* 11 (2007): 330.

53. Aldon D. Morris, *The Origins of the Civil Rights Movement: Black Communities Organizing for Change* (New York: Free Press, 1984); Doug McAdam, *Political Process and the Development of Black Insurgency, 1930–1970* (Chicago: University of Chicago Press, 1982).

54. Ronald W. Walters, *Black Presidential Politics in America: A Strategic Approach* (New York: State University of New York Press, 1988); Reed, *The Jesse Jackson Phenomenon*.

54a. Tate, "Black Political Participation."

55. On the Democratic side, civil rights activist Al Sharpton and former Illinois senator Carol Moseley Braun have tested the waters in Democratic primaries, and Alan Keyes has run for the Republican nomination. Prior to the 2000 election, Colin Powell's name was being floated by political operatives in both parties, but he ultimately chose not to run.

56. The fascination with the Vietnam War era status of presidential candidates began in 1992 with characterizations of Bill Clinton as a "draft dodger" and continued in 2000 and 2004 with accusations about George W. Bush's National Guard service and the legitimacy of medals earned by John Kerry as well as controversy surrounding his activities as a Vietnam War veteran who protested the war upon his return.

57. Lynette Clemetson, "The Racial Politics of Speaking Well," *New York Times*, February 4, 2007, sec. 4, p. 1.
58. Ronald W. Walters, "Obama Should Not Get a Free Pass From Black America," January 25,2007, http://newpittsburghcourieronline.com/articlelive/articles/36959/1/Commentary-Obama-should-not-get-a free-pass-from-Black-America/Page1.html.
59. As one possible alternative, Walters pointed to John Edwards who was running a campaign emphasizing poverty and had launched his candidacy from the Ninth Ward, the black center of devastated New Orleans.
60. Walters, "Obama Should Not Get a Free Pass."
61. If blacks are able to use their seniority and the leadership positions that result to push a black agenda, this will be true historical reversal. During the Jim Crow era, white southern Democrats used the seniority they gained as a result of being virtually invincible in the one-party South to preempt most attempts to legislate on behalf of African Americans.
62. W.E.B. DuBois. *The Souls of Black Folk* (Millwood, NY: Kraus-Thomson Organization Ltd, 1973).

Chapter 8

1. A previous version of this chapter was presented at the Annual Meeting of the Western Political Science Association, Las Vegas, NV, March 8–10, 2007. Our thanks to Gabriel Sánchez, Valerie Martínez-Ebers, Rodolfo Rosales, and other audience members for their helpful comments.
2. Jessica Lavariega Monforti, "Rhetoric or Meaningful Identifiers? Latina/os and Panethnicity?" *Latino/a Research Review* 6, no. 1–2 (2007). pp. 7–32.
3. The treaty was signed on February 2, 1848, in the village of Guadalupe Hidalgo, just outside Mexico City. It confirmed U.S. claims to Texas and set its boundary at the Rio Grande. Mexico also agreed to cede to the United States California and New Mexico (which included present-day California, Nevada, and Utah and parts of Arizona, New Mexico, Colorado, and Wyoming) in exchange for $15 million and assumption by the United States of claims against Mexico by U.S. citizens. The treaty was ratified by the U.S. Senate on March 10, 1848, and by the Mexican Congress on May 25.
4. Louis DeSipio, *Counting on the Hispanic Vote: Hispanics as a New Electorate*. (Charlottesville: University of Virginia Press, 1996); Ronald Schmidt, Sr., Edwina Barvosa-Carter, and Rodolfo D. Torres, "Latino/a Identities: Social Diversity and U.S. Politics," *PS: Political Science and Politics* Vol. 33, No. 3 (Sep., 2000), pp. 520–527.
4a. Puerto Rico Democracy Act of 2007, 110TH CONGRESS 1ST SESSION H. R. 900, http://www.govtrack.us/congress/billtext.xpd?bill=h110-900.
5. Roberto R. Ramirez and G. Patricia de la Cruz, "The Hispanic Population in the United States: March 2002," U.S. Census Bureau, June 2003, http://www.census.gov/prod/2003pubs/p20–545.pdf.

6. The complexity of the conflict is a result of the multiplicity of interests and actors involved, including the government's official forces, left-wing guerrillas—the Revolutionary Armed Forces of Colombia (FARC) and the much smaller National Liberation Army (ELN)—and extreme right paramilitary groups.

6a. "Miami Temporary Residency Advocated." March 26, 2007. Miami Herald. 2b, Metro and State.

7. "Other Hispanics" was broken down further in 2000. Central Americans comprised 4.8%, Dominicans comprised 2.2%, South Americans comprised 3.8%, Spaniards comprised 0.3%, and all other Hispanics comprised 17.3%. U.S. Census Bureau, Census 2000 Summary File 1. http://www.census.gov/prod/2001pubs/c2kbr01-3.pdf.

8. Hispanics are concentrated in the following states: Florida, New York, New Jersey, Texas, California, New Mexico, Arizona, Illinois, and Colorado.

9. Liliana Martinez, 2000, U.S. Latino and Latina World War II Oral History Project, http://www.lib.utexas.edu/ww2latinos/template-stories-indiv.html?work_urn= urn%3Autlol%3Awwlatin.055&work_title=Idar%2C+Ed.

10. R. Michael Alvarez and Lisa García-Bedolla, "The Foundations of Hispanic Voter Partisanship: Evidence from the 2000 Election," *Journal of Politics* 65, no. 1. (February 2003): 31–49; DeSipio, *Counting on the Hispanic Vote*; Rodolfo O. de la Garza, F. Chris García, and Louis DeSipio, *Hispanic Voices: Mexican, Puerto Rican, and Cuban Perspectives on American Politics* (Boulder, CO: Westview Press, 1992); F. Chris García and Rodolfo O. de la Garza, *The Chicano Political Experience: Three Perspectives* (North Scituate, MA: Duxbury Press, 1977); Jorge Ramos, *The Hispanic Wave: How Hispanics Are Transforming Politics in America* (New York: Harper, 2005).

11. Robert Suro, Richard Frye, and Jeffrey Passel, "Hispanics and the 2004 Election: Population, Electorate, and Voters" (Washington DC: Pew Hispanic Center, 2005). http://pewhispanic.org/reports/report.php?ReportID=48.

12. Donald Philip Green and Bradley Palmquist, "Of Artifacts and Partisan Instability," *American Journal of Political Science* 34, no. 3 (1990): 872–902; Warren E. Miller, "Party Identification, Realignment and Party Voting: Back to the Basics," *American Political Science Review* 85, no. 2 (1991): 557–568; Paul R. Abramson and Charles W. Ostrom, "Macropartisanship: An Empirical Reassessment," *American Political Science Review* 85, no. 1 (1991): 181–192.

13. David Knoke, "A Causal Model for the Political Party Preferences of American Men," *American Sociological Review* 37 (1972): 679–689; David Knoke and Michael Hout, "Social and Demographic Factors in American Party Affiliations, 1952–1972," *American Sociological Review* (1974) vol 39: 700–713; Paul R. Abramson, *Political Attitudes in America* (San Francisco: Freeman, 1983); Warren E. Miller and J. Merrill Shanks, *The New American Voter* (Cambridge, MA: Harvard University Press, 1996).

14. Jessica Lavariega Monforti, "A Candle in the Wind? Latinos and the 2004 Elections in Texas." in De la Garza, Rodolfo O., Louis DeSipio, and David L. Leal (eds.). *Beyond the Barrio: Latinos in the 2004 Elections*. South Bend, IN: University of Notre Dame Press. Forthcoming 2009.

15. Alvarez and García Bedolla, "The Foundations of Hispanic Voter Partisanship."
16. The term "Anglo" is used to describe the non-Hispanic white population in the United States.
17. Leighley, Jan E. and Arnold Vedlitz. "Race, Ethnicity, and Political Participation: Competing Models and Contrasting Explanations." *The Journal of Politics*, Vol. 61, No.4 (Nov., 1999), 1092–1114.
17a. Armando Navarro. *Mexicano Political Experience in Occupied Aztlán: Struggles and Change*. (Walnut Creek: Rowman Altamira, 2005). pp. 276.
17b. Dexter Filkins and Dana Canedy. "Counting the Vote: Mimai–Dade County; Protest Influenced Miami-Dade's Decision to Stop Recount." *New York Times* (November 24, 2000) http://query.nytimes.com/gst/fullpage.html?res=9907E3D D103AF937A15752C1A9669C8B63&sec=&spon=&pagewanted=all#.
18. Alvarez, R. Michael and Lisa García-Bedolla. "The Foundations of Latino Voter Partisanship: Evidence from the 2000 Election." *The Journal of Politics*, Vol. 65, No. 1. (Feb., 2003), pp. 31–49.
19. Julie Leininger Pycior, *LBJ and Mexican Americans The Paradox of Power*. Austin, TX:University of Texas Press 1997.
20. Dario Moreno, "Cuban Americans in Miami Politics: Understanding the Cuban Model," in *The Politics of Minority Coalitions: Race, Ethnicity, and Shared Uncertainties*, ed. Wilbur Rich (Westport, CT: Praeger, 1996), 145–162.
21. Karen M. Kaufman and John R. Petrocik, "The Changing Politics of American Men: Understanding the Sources of the Gender Gap," *American Journal of Political Science* 43, no. 3 (1999): 864–887.
22. Lisa García Bedolla, *Fluid Borders: Hispanic Power, Identity, and Politics in Los Angeles* (Berkeley: University of California Press, 2005).

Chapter 9

1. I thank Janet Wong for her patience and support, without which this manuscript would not have been completed.
2. William Petersen, "Success Story, Japanese-American Style," *New York Times Magazine*, January 9, 1966; "Success Story of One Minority Group in the U.S.," *U.S. News and World Report*, December 26, 1966.
3. Timothy P. Fong, *The Contemporary Asian American Experience: Beyond the Model Minority* (Upper Saddle River, NJ: Prentice Hall, 2002); Timothy P. Fong and Larry H. Shinagawa, *Asian Americans: Experiences and Perspectives* (Upper Saddle River, NJ: Prentice Hall, 2000).
4. Charles Hirschman and Morrison G. Wong, "The Extraordinary Educational Attainment of Asian-Americans: A Search for Historical Evidence and Explanations," *Social Forces* 54, no. 1 (1986): 1–27; Charles Hirschman and Morrison G. Wong, "Socioeconomic Gains of Asian Americans, Blacks, and Hispanics: 1960–1976," *American Journal of Sociology* 90, no. 3 (1984): 574–607; Charles Hirschman and Morrison G. Wong, "Trends in Socioeconomic Achievement Among Immigrant

and Native-Born Asian-Americans, 1960–1976," *Sociological Quarterly* 22 (1981): 495–513; Morrison G. Wong, "The Education of White, Chinese, Filipino and Japanese Students: A Look at 'High School and Beyond,'" *Sociological Perspectives* 33 (1990): 335–374; Morrison G. Wong, "Model Students? Teachers' Perceptions and Expectations of Their Asian and White Students," *Sociology of Education* 53 (1980): 236–246.

5. U.S. Bureau of the Census, *1990 Census of the Population, Social and Economic Characteristics, Metropolitan Areas* (Washington DC: Government Printing Office, 1994), CP-2–1B, tables 6 and 9.

6. Paul Ong and Suzanne J. Hee, "Work Issues Facing Asian Pacific Americans: Labor Policy," in *The State of Asian Pacific Americans: Policy Issues to the Year 2020* (Los Angeles: LEAP Asian Pacific American Public Policy Institute and UCLA Asian American Studies Center, 1993), 11–23.

7. U.S. Census 2000, Summary File 4 (SF4), Sample Data, Detailed Tables, www.census.gov/summary.

8. Ibid.

9. Ibid.

10. Sucheng Chan, *Asian Americans: An Interpretive History* (Boston: Twayne Publishers, 1991), 170.

11. U.S. Census 2000, Summary File 4.

12. Pyong Gap Min, "Korean Americans," in *Asian Americans: Contemporary Trends and Issues,* ed. Pyong Gap Min (Thousand Oaks, CA: Pine Forge Press, 2006), 230–260.

13. U.S. Census 2000, Summary File 4.

14. Chan, *Asian Americans,* 170.

15. Pei-te Lien, *The Making of Asian America Through Political Participation* (Philadelphia: Temple University Press, 2001), 127.

16. Ronald Takaki, *Strangers from a Different Shore: A History of Asian Americans* (New York: Penguin Books, 1989); Mia Tuan, *Forever Foreigner or Honorary Whites: The Asian Ethnic Experience Today* (New Brunswick, NJ: Rutgers University Press, 1998).

17. Sam Chu Lin, "Radio Tirade," *Asian Week,* April 5, 1996.

18. Taeku Lee, "Asian Americans and the Electorate," The American Political Science Association, http:/www.apsanet.org/content_5154.cfm (accessed February 8, 2007).

19. Ibid.

20. Daniel Kikuo Ichinose and Dennis Kao, *Asian Americans at the Ballot Box: The 2004 General Election: Growing Voter Participation in Southern California* (Los Angeles: Asian Pacific American Legal Center of Southern California, 2004); Nancy W. Yu, , *The Asian American Vote 2004: A Report on the Multilingual Exit Poll in the 2004 Presidential Election* (New York: Asian American Legal Defense and Education Fund, 2005).

21. Christian Collet, "Bloc Voting, Polarization, and the Panethnic Hypothesis: The Case of Little Saigon," *Journal of Politics* 67, no. 3 (2005): 907–933.

22. Wendy K. Tam Cho, "Tapping Motives and Dynamics Behind Campaign Contributions: Insights from the Asian American Case," *American Politics Research* 30 (2002): 347–383.

23. Lien, *The Making of Asian America*, 162.

24. S. Kwoh and M. Hui, "Empowering Our Communities: Political Policy," in *The State of Asian Pacific Americans* (see note 6), 189–198; Lien, *The Making of Asian America*; Pei-te Lien, Christian Collet, Janelle Wong, and K. Ramakrishnan, "Asian Pacific American Politics Symposium: Public Opinion and Political Participation," *PS: Political Science and Politics* 34 (2001): 625–630; Don T. Nakanishi, "Beyond Electoral Politics: Renewing a Search for a Paradigm of Asian Pacific American Politics," in *Asian Americans and Politics: Perspectives, Experiences, and Prospects*, ed. G. Change (Palo Alto, CA: Stanford University Press, 2001); Janelle S. Wong, Pei-Te Lien, and M. Margaret Conway, "Group Based Resources and Political Participation Among Asian Americans," *American Politics Research* 33(2005):554.

25. Jun Xu, "The Political Behavior of Asian Americans: A Theoretical Approach," *Journal of Political and Military Sociology* 30, no. 1 (2002): 71–89.

26. Nancy W. Yu, *The Asian American Vote 2004*.

27. Ichinose and Kao, *Asian Americans at the Ballot Box*.

28. Phillip A. Olaya, Glenn D. Magpantay, Nancy W. Yu, and Margaret Fung, *Asian Americans and the Voting Rights Act: The Case for Reauthorization* (New York: Asian American Legal Defense and Education Fund, 2006), 37.

29. Ibid., 19–21; Glenn D. Magpantay, "The Voting Rights Act: Asian Americans and Access to the Vote, Circa 2006," *Democracy Dispatches* (May 16, 2006): 1–6 http://www,demos.org/democracydispatches/articlee.cfm?type=2&id=3EFCBFE9–3fff-2257–C5518BC826FDDB65. (accessed March 19, 2007).

30. Magpantay, "The Voting Rights Act," 2.

31. Ibid.

32. Ibid., 3.

33. Ibid.

34. Ibid.

35. Olaya et al., *Asian Americans and the Voting Rights Act*, 20.

36. Ibid., 19, 21.

37. Nancy W. Yu, *The Asian American Vote 2004*.

38. Pei-te Lien, *The Political Participation of Asian Americans: Voting Behavior in Southern California*; (New York: Garland, 1997); Jan Lin, *Restructuring Chinatown* (Minneapolis: University of Minnesota Press, 1998); Don T. Nakanishi, "Political Trends and Electoral Issues of the Asian Pacific American Population," in *American Becoming: Racial Trends and Their Consequences*, vol. 1, ed. Neil J. Smelser, William Julius Wilson, and Faith Mitchell (Washington DC: National Academy Press, 2001).

39. Alejandro Portes and Ruben G. Rumbaut, *Immigrant America* (Berkeley: University of California Press, 1990).

40. Xu, "The Political Behavior of Asian Americans," 83.

41. Paul Ong and Tania Azores, *Reapportionment and Redistricting in a Nutshell* (Los Angeles: LEAP Asian Pacific American Public Policy Institute, 1991).

42. Lien, *The Making of Asian America*, 113.

43. Asian American Legal Defense and Education Fund, *Asian Americans and the Voting Rights Act*, 21–22; Karen K. Narasaki, A Bill to Reauthorize and Amend the Voting Rights Act of 1965: Part II'" Legislative Hearing Act on H.R. 9. May 4, 2006. http://www.advancingequality.org/files/VRA_Senate_Hearing_Statement_706.pdf.

44. Narasaki,:"A Bill to Reauthorize and Amend the Voting Rights Act of 1965," p.

45. Ibid., 5.

46. Ibid., 5.

47. Ibid., 5.

48. Olaya et al,, *Asian Americans and the Voting Rights Act*, 19–20.

49. Ibid., 21.

50. Ibid.

51. Ibid., 22.

52. Ibid.

53. Ibid., 32.

54. Narasaki, "A Bill to Reauthorize and Amend the Voting Rights Act of 1965: Part II."

55. Petersen, "Success Story, Japanese-American Style"; Harry H. L. Kitano, *Japanese Americans: The Evolution of a Subculture* (Englewood Cliffs, NJ: Prentice Hall, 1969); Thomas Sowell, *"The Economics and Politics of Race* (New York: Quill, 1983); Moon H. Jo, "The Putative Political Complacency of Asian Americans," *Political Psychology* 5 (1984): 583–685; David Bell, "The Triumph of Asian Americans," *New Republic* 193 (July 15–22, 1985): 24–31; Moon H. Jo and Daniel Mast, "Changing Images of Asian Americans," *International Journal of Politics, Culture and Society* 6 (1993): 417–441.

56. Lien, *The Making of Asian America*, 83.

57. Asian American Action Fund, *Trends Show Dramatic Increase in Asian American Political Participation This Election Year* http://www.aaa-fund.org/downloads/2006-05-31_AAAFund_Report.pdf. Accessed March 19, 2007.

58. Cho, "Tapping Motives and Dynamics Behind Campaign Contributions."

59. William Wei, *The Asian American Movement* (Philadelphia: Temple University Press, 1993); Lien, *The Political Participation of Asian Americans*; Nakanishi, "Beyond Electoral Politics."

60. Cho, "Tapping Motives and Dynamics Behind Campaign Contributions."

61. Andrew Aoki, "The Political Incorporation of Asian Pacific Americans," in *The New Face of Asian Pacific America: Numbers, Diversity & Change in the 21st Century* (San Francisco/Los Angeles: AsianWeek/UCLA Asian American Studies Center Press, 2003).

62. Asian American Action Fund, *Trends Show Dramatic Increase*.

63. Lien, *The Making of Asian America*, 96–104.

64. James S. Lai, Wendy K. Tam Cho, Thomas P. Kim, and Okiyoshi Takeda, "Asian Pacific-American Campaigns, Elections, and Elected Officials," *PS: Political*

Science and Politics 34, no. 3 (2001): 611–617; Okiyoshi Takeda, "The Representation of Asian Americans in the U.S. Political System," in *Representation of Minority Groups in the U.S.: Implications for the Twenty-First Century*, ed. Charles E. Menifield (Lanham, MD: University Press of America, 2001), 77–109.

65. Andrew L. Aoki and Don T. Nakanishi, "Asian Pacific Americans and the New Minority Politics," *PS: Political Science and Politics* 34, no. 3 (2001): 605–610; Al Kamen, "DOE Trips on Security Blanket," *Washington Post*, May 25, 2001.

66. Morrison G. Wong, "Post-1965 Immigrants: Demographic and Socioeconomic Profile," *Urban Affairs Annual Review* 487 (1985): 51–71; Morrison G. Wong, "Post-1965 Asian Immigrants: Where do They Come From, Where Are They Now, and Where Are They Going?" *Annals of the American Academy of Political and Social Science* 487 (1986): 150–168; Morrison G. Wong and Charles Hirschman, "The New Asian Immigrants," in *Culture, Ethnicity, and Identity: Current Issues in Research*, ed. William C. McCready (New York: Academic Press, 1981), 381–405.

67. Wen Ho Lee and Helen Zia, *My Country Versus Me: The First-Hand Account by the Los Alamos Scientist Who Was Falsely Accused of Being a Spy* (New York: Hyperion, 2002).

Chapter 10

1. Sander L. Gilman, "The Jewish Nose: Are Jews White? Or, the History of the Nose Job," in *The Other in Jewish Thought and History: Constructions of Jewish Culture and Identity*, ed. Laurence J. Silberstein and Robert L. Cohn (New York: New York University Press, 1994), 385–386. Also see Sander L. Gilman, *The Jewish Body* (London: Routledge, 1991), chap. 7.

2. Scholars debate whether the term "anti-Semitism" should be spelled with or without a hyphen. To highlight the ideological character of the struggle against the Jews as an alien Semitic tribe, I prefer the hyphenated form. The definition of "anti-Semitism" is subject to even greater debate. In January 2005, an international definition was adopted for the first time since the term was coined in the nineteenth century (see note 6). The definition was the result of the collaborative effort of a center in Vienna, Austria, established by the European Union to monitor racism and xenophobia, and a center in Warsaw, Poland, founded by the Organization for Security and Cooperation in Europe to strengthen the institutions of democracy and human rights among its 55 member states. The definition formulated jointly by these institutions reads, "Anti-Semitism is a certain perception of Jews, which may be expressed as hatred toward Jews. Rhetorical and physical manifestations of anti-Semitism are directed toward the Jewish community institutions and religious facilities" (reported by Dina Porat, "What Makes an Anti-Semite," *Ha-Aretz*, January 28, 2007, 1). A somewhat more nuanced definition is "Antisemitism [*sic*] is hatred toward Jews and is directed toward the Jewish religion, Jews as a people, or,

more recently, the Jewish state. Antisemitism frequently charges Jews with conspiring to harm non-Jews and is often given as an explanation why things go wrong. It is expressed in speech, writing, visual forms, and action, and regularly employs stereotypes" (Kenneth S. Stern, *Antisemites Today. How It Is the Same, How It Is Different, and How to Fight It* [New York: American Jewish Committee, 2006], 8).

3. Karl Eugen Duehring, "The Question of the Jew Is a Question of Race" (1881), translated in The Jew in the Modern World: A Documentary History, 2nd rev. ed., ed. P. Mendes-Flohr and Judah Reinharz (New York: Oxford University Press, 1995), 333.

4. A conversation with an anonymous anti-Semite reported by Jacob Wasserman, *My Life as German and Jew* (London: Allen & Unwin, 1933), 72.

5. Johann Gottlieb Fichte, "Beitrag zur Berichtung der Urteile des Publicums über die Französische Revolution" (1793), translated in Mendes-Flohr and Reinharz, eds., *The Jew in the Modern World* (see note 3), 309.

6. Wilhelm Marr, *Der Sieg des Judenthums ueber das Germanenthum von nicht confessionelle Standpunkt ausberactet* (1879), translated in Mendes-Flohr and Reinharz, eds., *The Jew in the Modern World* (see note 3), 331–332.

7. See Leo P. Ribuffo, "Henry Ford and the International Jew," in *The American Jewish Experience*, ed. Jonathan D. Sarna (New York: Holmes and Meier, 1986), 175–190.

8. R. A. Goldwin, *Why Blacks, Women and Jews Are not Mentioned in the Constitution and Other Unorthodox Views* (Washington DC: AEI Press, 1990).

9. On the origins and significance of the term "Jewish question," see Jacob Toury, "'The Jewish Question.' A Semantic Approach," *Leo Baeck Institute Year Book* XI (1966): 85–106.

10. Lewis Abraham, "Correspondence Between George Washington and Jewish Citizens," *Proceedings of the American Jewish Historical Society* 3 (1895): 90–91.

11. George Washington, "A Reply to the Hebrew Congregation of Newport (August 1790)," *Proceedings of the American Jewish Historical Society* 3 (1895): 91–92.

12. Wilbur J. Carr, Consular Service, Department of State, to Albert Johnson, Chairman of the Committee on Immigration, House of Representatives, December 4, 1920, in *Temporary Suspension of Immigration*, 66th Cong., 3rd sess., House of Representatives, Report 1109, December 6, 1920, Appendix A.

13. Cited in David de Sola Poll, *Portraits Etched in Stone: Early Jewish Settlers, 1682–1831* (New York: Columbia University Press, 1952).

14. Stanley Mckenna, "Reviving a Prejudice: Jewish Patronage Not Welcome at Manhattan Beach," *New York Herald*, July 22, 1879, reprinted in Mendes-Flohr and Reinharz, eds., *The Jew in the Modern World* (see note 3), 465–467.

15. Anti-Defamation League, *Anti-Semitism in America 2006*, http://www.adl.org/PresRele/ASUS_12/4993–12.htm.

16. *Seattle Post-Intelligencer*, July 29, 2006.

17. Ibid.

18. Anti-Defamation League, *Anti-Semitism in America 2006*.

Chapter 11

1. "Young U. S. Muslims: A Threat?"*Christian Science Monitor*, May 31, 2007. 8.
2. Ibid.
3. Alexander Mark, "Arabic school in N.Y.C. creates stir"*Christian Science Monitor*, June 1, 2007. 3.
4. Ibid.
5. Arthur Goldschmidt, Jr., *A Concise History of the Middle East* (Boulder, CO: Westview Press, 2002).
6. Albert Hourani, *Islam in European Thought* (New York: Cambridge University Press, 1991), 7–8.
7. Fawaz A. Gerges, *America and Political Islam: The Clash of Cultures or the Clash of Interests?* (New York: Cambridge University Press, 1999), 9.
8. Edward Said, *Covering Islam: How the Media and the Experts Determine How We See the Rest of the World* (New York: Pantheon Books, 1981).
9. Edward Said, *Orientalism* (New York: Vintage Books, 1978).
10. Akbar S. Ahmed, *Postmodernism and Islam: Predicament and Promise* (London: Routledge, 1992), 39.
11. Susan M. Akram and Kevin R. Johnson, "Race and Civil Rights Pre-September 11, 2001: The Targeting of Arabs and Muslims," in *Civil Rights in Peril:The Targeting of Arabs and Muslims*, ed. Elaine C. Hagopian (Chicago: Haymarket Books, 2004), 18.
12. Gerges, *America and Political Islam*, 125.
13. Ibid., 7.
14. Ibid., 125.
15. Ibid.
16. Ibid., 69–70.
17. Ibid., 7.
18. Ibid., 47–48.
19. Ibid., 48.
20. James Brooke, "Attacks on U.S. Muslims Surge Even as Their Faith Takes Hold" *New York Times*, August 28, 1995. 1.
21. Shibley Telhami, "Arab and Muslim America: A Snapshot," in *Perspectives on Terrorism: How 9/11 Changed U.S. Politics*, ed. Allen J. Cigler (New York: Houghton Mifflin, 2002), 14.
22. Robert Morlino, "Our Enemies Among US!: The portrayal of Arab and Muslim Americans in Post-9/11 American Media," in *Civil Rights in Peril* (see note 11), 71. This type of Islamophobia and anti-Muslim sentiment is no longer confined to a "lunatic fringe." Indeed, it has become mainstream. For example, the executive director of the Missouri Baptist convention, Rev. David Clippard, told the 1,200 participants in the group's annual convention in 2006 that "Islam is the greatest threat facing America. Today Islam has a strategic plan to defeat and occupy

America. Islamic strategy for taking over America was to wait until there was a Muslim majority here and then eradicate those who do not conform to their religion." See 'Islam is threat to U.S., Baptist group is told" *Star-Telegram*, November 2, 2006. 1.

23. Ibid., 72.

24. Ibid.

25. M. Cherif Bassiiouni, "Don't Tread on Me: Is the War on Terror Really a War on Rights?" in *Civil Rights in Peril* (see note 11), 2.

26. Nancy Murray, "Profiled: Arabs, Muslims, and the Post 9/11 Hunt for the 'Enemy Within,'" in *Civil Rights in Peril* (see note 11), 28.

27. Akram and Johnson, "Race and Civil Rights Pre-September 11, 2001," 10.

28. Ibid.

29. Ibid., 11.

30. Jack G. Shaheen, *Reel Bad Arabs: How Hollywood Vilifies a People* (New York: Olive Branch, 2001).

31. Jack G. Shaheen, *The TV Arab* (Bowling Green, OH: Bowling Green State University Popular Press, 1984). See also Suha J. Sabbagh, *Sex, Lies, Stereotypes: The Image of Arabs in Popular American Fiction* (Washington DC: ADC Research Institute, 1990).

32. Hamid Naficy, "Mediating the Other: American Pop Culture Representation of Postrevolutionary Iran," in *The US Media and the Middle East: Image and Perception*, ed. Yahya M. Kamalipour (Westport, CT: Praeger, 1995), 84.

33. Ibid.; Shaheen, *Reel Bad Arabs*; Shaheen, *The TV Arab*.

34. Shaheen, *Reel Bad Arabs*, 11.

35. Some of the movies released in 2007 such as *In the Valley of Elah* and *Rendition* are refreshingly different from the pervasive Hollywood mainstream negative depiction of Muslims and Arabs.

36. Jane Lapman, "New Congressman to Sear on Koran: Outrage Ensues"*Christian Science Monitor*, December 7, 2006. 1.

37. Dafna Linzer and Joby Warrick, "US Finds Iran Halted Nuclear Arms Bid in 2003," *Washington Post* (December 4, 2007) http://www.washingtonpost.com/wp-dyn/content/story/2007/12/03/ST2007120300896.html.

38. Transcript, "The Republicans' First Presidential Candidates Debate", *New York Time* (May 3, 2007) *http://www.nytimes.com/2007/05/03/us/politics/04transcript. html?_r=2&pagewanted=1&oref=slogin.*

39. Fareed Zakaria, "Stalin, Mao And…Ahmadinejad?" *Newsweek*, October 29, 2007. 1. Accessed on October 17, 2008 at: http://www.newsweek.com/id/57346/output/print

40. John L. Esposito, *Unholy War: Terror in the Name of Islam* (New York: Oxford University Press, 2002), 155.

41. Paul Kennedy, "As Others See Us," *Wall Street Journal*, October 5, 2001 (as cited by Esposito, *Unholy War*).

Chapter 12

1. James Thurlow Adams, *The Epic of America* (Phoenix, AZ: Simon Publications, 2003, 1934); Jim Cullen, *The American Dream: A Short History of an Idea that Shaped a Nation* (New York: Oxford University Press, 2003).

2. Jennifer Hochschild, *Facing Up to the American Dream: Race Class and the Soul of the Nation* (Princeton: Princeton University Press, 1995).

3. Marisol Bello, "FBI: Hate Crimes Escolate 8% in 2006," *USA Today*, November 19, 2007.

4. Brentin Mock, "Immigrant Backlash: Violence Engulfs Latinos," Southern Poverty Law Center, November 27, 2007, http://www.splcenter.org/intel/news/item.jsp?site_area=1&&aid=292 (Accessed on July 5, 2008).

5. John Holthouse and Mark Potok, "The Year in Hate: Active U.S. Hate Groups Rise to 888 in 2007," Intelligence Report, Southern Poverty Law Center, no.129, Spring 2008, http://www.splcenter.org/intel/intelreport/article.jsp?aid=886.

6. *New York Times*/CBS News Poll, July 7–14, 2008, p 27, http://graphics8.nytimes.com/packages/pdf/politics/20080716_POLL.pdf.

7. Ibid., 22, 24.

Index